Controlling the Dragon ————————————————

Controlling the Dragon

Confucian Engineers and the Yellow River in Late Imperial China

RANDALL A. DODGEN

University of Hawai'i Press

Honolulu

Library of Congress Cataloging-in-Publication Data

Dodgen, Randall A.
    Controlling the dragon : Confucian engineers and the Yellow River in late
imperial China / Randall A. Dodgen.
        p. cm.
    Includes bibliographical references and index.
    ISBN 0–8248–2191–2 (alk. paper)—ISBN 0–8248–2366–4 (pbk. : alk. paper)
    1. Yellow River (China)   I. Title.
DS793.Y45 D63   2001
951'.1—dc21   00-059940

University of Hawai'i Press books are printed on acid-free paper and meet the
guidelines for permanence and durability of the Council on Library Resources.

Designed by Nighthawk Design

Printed by The Maple-Vail Book Manufacturing Group

For Rose and Grace

Contents

Acknowledgments

THIS WORK HAS BENEFITED from the suggestions and insights of many people, none of whom bears any responsibility for its shortcomings. Jonathan Spence, Conrad Totman, and Beatrice Bartlett all devoted a great deal of time and energy to directing the research and writing of the early versions of this work. Conversations with and comments from Bin Wong, Ken Pomeranz, David Kelley, Yu Ying-shih, Dan Markwyn, Valerie Hansen, Jane Kate Leonard, and the anonymous readers of the manuscript helped me refine the overall direction of the book. I owe a special note of thanks to Monica Yu for her help in extracting the dynamic reality of Qing river engineering from the abstruse language of bureaucratic documents. Naomi Igra did splendid work on the maps. Funding for research was provided by the Committee for Scholarly Communication with the People's Republic of China, the American Council of Learned Societies, and the Council on East Asian Studies at Yale University. Additional funding came from the China Times Cultural Foundation. I am deeply indebted to the staff of the Palace Museum Archives, particularly Ms. Wang Ching-hung and Mr. Chang Pi-te, and the staff of the No. One Historical Archives, especially Mr. Zhu Deyuan. I would also like to thank Professor Wei Qingyuan and Ms. Yang Xueping for their support during my stay at People's University.

Introduction

SINCE EARLIEST TIMES, the Yellow River has twisted and woven its perilous unpredictability into the fabric of China's cultural and political development. The river's countless floods enriched and renewed the soil of the great alluvial fan that is the North China Plain, but they also threatened political stability by causing widespread suffering and social turmoil. A government that failed to respond quickly to the people's suffering would face mass migration, banditry, and perhaps dynastic challengers. Even a strong state could not lightly dismiss the agricultural disruption, reduced tax income, and high cost of dike repair and disaster relief that followed in the wake of a flood.

The link between state power and the Yellow River found early mythic expression in the legend of the Great Yu. Yu established his fitness to rule by bringing flooding under control when others had failed. He went on to found China's first dynasty, the Xia. The political significance of river control was given further weight by the doctrine of the Mandate of Heaven, which held that a virtuous ruler occupied the throne with Heaven's consent. If the ruler lost virtue and began to rule badly, Heaven would withdraw its support and manifest its displeasure in "droughts, floods, or earthquakes."[1] It is too simple to say that dynastic legitimacy was called into question every time the Yellow River breached its dikes; the river flooded many times without significant political consequences. But any flood was a blemish on imperial prestige. Imperial edicts often reveal the deep sense of uneasiness felt by emperors faced with a Yellow River flood.

Through much of China's early history, rulers sought to protect fields and population centers from the Yellow River by building dikes and diversion channels. That defensive approach changed dramatically after the Yuan dynasty (1279–1368) constructed the Grand Canal to link the North China Plain and the capital at Beijing with the Yangzi valley. Where the canal crossed (and incorporated a part of) the Yellow River, simply relying

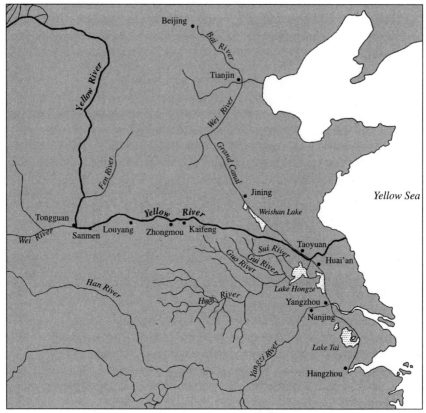

Map 1   The Yellow River and its tributaries in the early nineteenth century.

on defensive measures was no longer sufficient. An expanded repertoire of hydraulic systems was required to keep the river confined to its bed and channel it in ways helpful to canal transport. The decision of the third emperor of the Ming dynasty (1368–1644) to relocate the Ming capital from Nanjing on the Yangzi River to Beijing in the north amplified the importance of the Grand Canal to the maintenance of state power. The canal became the strategic artery carrying annual shipments of tribute grain to feed the bureaucracy in Beijing and the military defending the sensitive northern borders. Where the canal and the river intersected, engineers created a complex hydraulic system to control the river's peripatetic tendencies and facilitate canal transport. By binding their strategic well-being to Grand Canal transport and Yellow River control, the rulers of the Ming and Qing dynasties (1644–1911) linked the symbolic and the pragmatic to an unprecedented degree. Inevitably, managing the Yellow River became one of the central tasks of imperial administration. The Yellow River control system that reached its maturity in the Qing dynasty was larger and more complex than any previous system. It linked the river to the Grand Canal, Lake Hongze, and the Huai River through a network of spillways, locks, and dams. The river itself was hemmed in by dikes that stretched eight hundred kilometers, from the foothills of western Henan Province to the river's delta in the Yellow Sea. As a technological achievement, that hydraulic system easily rivals the Great Wall. As an expression of dynastic ambition, it reveals an imperial state confident of its ability to subordinate the forces of nature on a massive scale.

Modern perceptions of the relationship between the Yellow River and dynastic power have been strongly influenced by Chinese historical writing. Throughout China's history, as successive dynasties penned the records of their predecessors, each justified its own possession of the mandate by pointing to the decline of the former dynasty. One oft-cited symptom of decline was the inability to control the Yellow River. Modern historians, both Chinese and Western, have rejected the role of Heaven in awarding the mandate and have translated the dynastic cycle model into the language of contemporary social science, but their analysis has retained both the implicit moral critique inherent in the dynastic cycle model and the traditional view that the efficacy of Yellow River management can be used to measure dynastic vitality.

The obvious importance of hydraulics in shaping state power in China led Karl Wittfogel to describe dynastic rule as "oriental despotism," a form of government emerging from the need to mediate between scarce water resources and the demands of regional agriculture. Wittfogel argued that such mediation led to the rise of "colossal political and social structures" that dominated the society that produced them.[2] Influenced by Wittfogel, Hu Ch'ang-tu depicted the "Yellow River conservancy" of the late Qing as a swollen bureaucratic monolith dedicated only to its own perpetuation. Reiterating the link between Yellow River control and dynastic power, Hu charged that the river conservancy was but a microcosm of Qing administration in general.[3]

Even historians who have given careful consideration to the problems created by population growth, fiscal difficulties, and, in the case of the

Yellow River, hydrologic factors, have not entirely broken free of the moralistic view implicit in the concept of a dynastic cycle.[4] Most studies of the Qing state in the nineteenth century depict a dynasty of bloated bureaucracies packed by patronage with incompetent, corrupt, careerist officials: an environment where the honest and upright are marginalized and the innovative ignored. That atmosphere of decay spread under the unfocused gaze of emperors who were either well-meaning but ineffectual or who lacked the courage or imagination to confront the failings of the system.

Viewing the state's ability to control the Yellow River as a marker of dynastic vitality overlooks two related and important points. First, pretending that the primary variable in successful Yellow River control was the absence of corruption in an administration assumes that the technical problems of Yellow River control changed little. But the Yellow River–Grand Canal hydraulic system underwent a technological and hydrological evolution that made the problems of hydraulic management in the nineteenth century far more complex than those faced in the Yuan, or even in the early Qing. By 1800 the system was more extensive, technologically sophisticated, fiscally demanding, and administratively challenging than it had been at any earlier time. Effective administration, though important, was only one layer in a many-tiered and mutually influential set of factors that determined the state's ability to manage the river.

Second, since the evolution of the Yellow River–Grand Canal hydraulic system was transdynastic, its abandonment in the nineteenth century does not necessarily reflect the failings of any one dynasty. The intervention by imperial administrations in the natural cycles of the river created technical problems that in turn altered the administrative and fiscal structures of dynasties. That interaction between state and river was a contest of resources and technology against the relentless powers of nature. If the abandonment of the Yellow River–Grand Canal complex in the middle of the nineteenth century points to failings, they are failings not only of the Qing but also of the late imperial state in general.

To many, the terrible floods of the Jiaqing reign (1796–1821) seem compelling evidence of the connection between Yellow River control and dynastic decline. Most historians locate the turning point of Qing fortunes in the last decades of the eighteenth and the first decades of the nineteenth century. In the twenty-five years of Jiaqing's rule, the Yellow

River broke its banks fourteen times, a number almost equal to the total for the entire sixty years of the preceding Qianlong reign (1736–1796). The Jiaqing floods also can be linked to the pernicious influence of the powerful Manchu official Heshen, whose patronage network supposedly included the Yellow River conservancy.[5] The subsequent Daoguang reign is often viewed as a continuation of an inexorable process of decay exacerbated by weak imperial leadership. The collapse of the Yellow River–Grand Canal hydraulic system in the 1850s is the inevitable end product.

If the Jiaqing floods are taken as symptomatic of dynastic decline, what do we make of the record of the subsequent Daoguang reign (1821–1850)? The thirty years of Daoguang's rule was the most successful period of Yellow River control in a century and one of the most successful in post-Yuan dynastic history. The first two decades of the Daoguang reign saw only one serious flood in the Yellow River control system. Not until the 1840s did the river again begin to display the destructive pattern of the early years of the century.

The prevailing image of Daoguang's reign as a time of administrative weakness and imperial ineptitude has been challenged by Jane Leonard. In her study of the 1824 break of the Gaoyan Dike, Leonard depicts imperial rule as rational and effective. The eventual collapse of the hydraulic system was not a product of decline but of forces—geologic, demographic, fiscal—beyond the control of emperors and their officials. Rather than to condemn Daoguang and his advisers for their failures, Leonard examines the limits within which both the emperor and his officials were forced to operate in dealing with an intractable problem.[6] Although Leonard's revision of the "decline" thesis is intended to affirm the rationality and competence of Daoguang's administration, her case study raises a larger question: had the imperial system (not just the Qing version of it) reached the limits of its capacity to respond to China's natural and social problems?

Those problems were many. The fiscal crisis of the early nineteenth century was of particular consequence to the river conservancy because it coincided with the emergence of serious hydraulic problems within the Yellow River control system. Sedimentation of the riverbed increased meander activity, which required an ever more extensive network of dikes, defensive revetments (sao), locks, spillways, and drainage canals to keep the river in check. Those were expensive to build and to maintain. Two hundred years after the decision had been made to confine the Yellow River to its course, the hydraulic system was bedeviled by a myriad of interlocking problems and had developed a seemingly insatiable appetite for state resources. River control projects demanded specialized technical skills, a huge labor force, and substantial infusions of money.[7] The costs could be colossal. In the case of the Yellow River in the first half of the nineteenth century, annual expenditures may have exceeded 10 percent of the state revenues.

In the early nineteenth century, rising costs in the river conservancy clashed with the state's attempts to regain fiscal balance. The surplus of seventy million taels in the Qing treasury in 1786 was gone by the turn of the century, depleted by military campaigns in Xinjiang, in Sichuan, and against the White Lotus rebels in North China. The late imperial state was, in the words of Madeline Zelin, a "political system that worshipped the balance of expenditure against income and considered central government reserves essential lest man be unprepared for the ravages nature could bring."[8] As river conservancy costs rose and resources shrank, the state responded by imposing on hydraulic officials more rigorous cost controls, tighter regulations, and harsher sanctions.

As the pressure to practice fiscal restraint increased, corruption became an important issue in the hydraulic bureaucracy. The attractions of wealth increased as the money economy of the late imperial period created more opportunities to get rich. Government bureaucrats were also aware of and perhaps attracted by the conspicuous consumption of the commercially successful. The emphasis in Chinese society on particularistic ties also encouraged some degree of nepotism and favoritism.[9]

In spite of those temptations, there is little objective evidence of widespread corruption in the hydraulic bureaucracy in the Daoguang period. For one thing, regulations prescribing harsh punishments for officials judged responsible for a flood held both high officials and loyal subordinates in check. No doubt there was peculation in the form of phantom construction and inflated budgets, and it is clear that friends, family members, and secretaries of hydraulic officials were sometimes enriched by being allowed to "take charge" of small construction projects. But such practices were unlikely to have undermined major construction. Moreover, the emperors seemed willing to accept petty peculation as long as important work was not compromised. In 1802 the Jiaqing emperor stated that "if the river officials, in undertaking a river project, were generally correct in their estimates on labor and materials, and if the work were reasonably strong when completed, then graft and self-enrichment would be considered excusable."[10]

Where the issue of corruption became influential was in shaping the relationship between the emperor and his hydraulic officials. The Yongzheng emperor (1721–1736), notably fond of strict rules, expanded the regulations dealing with hydraulic administration. During his reign accounting guidelines were tightened and punishments and fines for officials held responsible for a disaster were codified and made harsher, a trend followed in subsequent reigns. As fiscal problems mounted, so did fear of corruption. Imperial concern over corruption made it a handy issue for those who wanted to impugn the opposition or make a case for their own integrity. The river and canal administrations, with their rising costs, were easy targets for innuendo and outright condemnation. As a result, the fear of corruption came to exert undue influence over crucial administrative and technological decisions.

At the center of those bureaucratic storms stood the Confucian engineers. Specialists in a system that admired generalists, technologists in a system that prized knowledge of Confucian ethics, they served in demanding posts where the whim of nature could undermine years of successful administration.[11] Like all in the bureaucratic elite, they were trained in the ethical and literary skills instilled by a Confucian—or Neo-Confucian, to be more accurate—education. What they knew about hydraulic engineering they learned on the job from subordinates or from the writings of their predecessors.

The job of a Confucian engineer in the late imperial period was not much sought. Even those who showed talent as engineers feared that a reputation for technical skill would stunt their careers. Promising men of broad talent seldom remained in a hydraulic post for long. Rather than gamble with the uncertainties of the river, they chose to pursue careers in less technical posts.

For those who were technically inclined, the hydraulic bureaucracy offered an opportunity to shine, but any failure of luck or skill could end a career in an instant. Though often talented and sometimes brilliant, hydraulic officials remained stigmatized by their specialist reputation and rarely engendered the respect and influence that would have allowed them to play a significant role in deciding the national policies whose consequences were so deeply felt in the river conservancy.

Nevertheless, the contributions of Confucian engineers were recognized and lauded. Right up to the end of the Daoguang reign, successful technical innovation continued to be rewarded.[12] The imperial state's commitment to large-scale hydraulic projects encouraged the publication of books on engineering. Those who wrote knowledgeably were lionized, and their works became the canons of later generations of hydraulic officials. By the middle years of the Qing dynasty, an official assigned to a post along the Yellow River or the Grand Canal would have at his disposal a substantial corpus of writing on river work *(hegong)* and river defense *(hefang)* to help him prepare for the job.

Technically capable as the Confucian engineers often were, they could do little to counter the inherent contradictions between the late imperial state's commitment to a minimal bureaucracy of generalists and its aspiration to continue the large-scale engineering of nature. Without a tax structure capable of funding the system or a cadre of engineering specialists with sufficient prestige to establish long-term engineering solutions, emperors responded to the fiscal demands of hydraulic management with a grudging mixture of increased funding and growing doubt about the reliability of administrative technologists. Eventually, suspicion from above and criticism of and dissension within the hydraulic bureaucracy shifted the focus away from engineering and toward administrative integrity.

From the perspective of hydraulic officials, the problems they faced in the first decades of the nineteenth century were similar to those of their counterparts in the provincial bureaucracy: in particular, a desperate shortage of funds and "an inability to keep up with expanding responsibilities." Challenged to maintain a complex and proliferating hydraulic system, officials turned to a variety of solutions: some made dangerous cost-cutting compromises in construction, and others used technical and administrative innovation to compensate for a shortage of resources and personnel. It has been argued that already in the early Qing, emperors and officials knew that maintaining the Yellow River–Grand Canal complex eventually was doomed to fall victim to the river's geologic imperatives.[13] If that pessimistic view was widely held, one sees no evidence of it in the lives and careers of the men who took charge of the system in the Daoguang reign. They were realists, not fatalists; their careers in managing the Yellow River give every evidence that they continued to believe nature could be constrained by human ingenuity and subordinated to the needs of man.

This book examines Yellow River engineering from two perspectives: the first section (chapters 1–3) looks at long-term efforts to manage the river, starting from the early Ming dynasty, at the nature of the bureaucracy created to do the job, and finally at two of the Confucian engineers who served successfully in the decade before the system was abandoned.

The second section (chapters 4–6) presents two contrasting case studies of Yellow River floods and evaluates the state's capacity to manage crisis in the 1840s. If, as the prevailing wisdom suggests, there were fatal weaknesses in administration, if corruption was a fundamental problem, if ineffectual men were being chosen to run a decaying bureaucracy, those flaws should be evident in the debates over administrative reform and technical innovation that took place in the 1830s and in response to the floods of the 1840s. Chapter 6 assesses the impact of those floods on the state's commitment to the Yellow River–Grand Canal system.

As midcentury approached and the problems of the Qing compounded, it was left to the Confucian engineers to contain the powerful geologic energies of the Yellow River within parameters defined by the needs of human political and social institutions. This is an account of the world in which they operated and of their successes and failures.

I

The Evolution of the Yellow River Control System in Late Imperial China, 1495–1835

THE YELLOW RIVER IS A RESTLESS, unpredictable, and dangerous stream. It has changed course many times since records were first kept, and its countless floods have wrought terrible destruction on the North China region. Yet for all its destructive power, it is not a large river. Its average discharge of 1,365 cubic meters per second (m^3/s) is a mere dribble compared to that of a behemoth like the Amazon (180,000 m^3/s) or even that of the Mississippi (17,545 m^3/s).[1] The Yellow River's history of destruction arises from two unfortunate characteristics: most famously, the river carries a huge quantity of silt; but equally important is the radical variation in the river's flow, from a trickle in the dry periods to a raging torrent during flood season.

The trouble starts when the river turns south at the top of the "great bend" and begins to drop, falling almost nine hundred meters as it travels across the loess plateau between Shaanxi and Shanxi Provinces. The plateau is an arid, almost lunar landscape where deposits of powdery loess soil hundreds of meters deep have been carved into stark, treeless arroyos that branch out from the river's main channel in an endless fan of tributaries. Every heavy rain that falls on the deforested, overgrazed hills sends streams of mud cascading into the river. Runoff from the loess plateau also feeds major tributaries like the Wei and Wuding Rivers, which in turn contribute to the Yellow River's silt burden. By the time the river turns east onto the North China Plain, it carries an unrivaled thirty-four kilograms of silt per cubic meter of coffee-colored water. It is estimated that the Yellow River produces 920 million cubic meters of sediment per year; only the Amazon at 1 billion cubic meters per year and the Mississippi at 980 million produce more.[2]

When that muddy torrent emerges from the mountains, it slows to a crawl. For the next eight hundred kilometers, from a point just west of modern Zhengzhou to its outlet (most commonly in the Bohai Gulf or the Yellow Sea), the turbid river drops only ninety-five meters. The velocity of a stream determines how much silt it can carry; as the river slows, the loess soil settles out. Before the river reaches the sea, it deposits an estimated 40 percent to 50 percent of its silt burden in its channel. As a result the bed in the downstream provinces rises steadily. Seasonal high water levels deposit sediment along the banks of the river, allowing the bed inside the banks to rise above the land outside. Eventually the river breaks through its banks to seek a lower course. Over the centuries, flooding and the resulting sedimentation have created a cone-shaped elevation along which the river flows until it encounters the Shandong massif, at which point it is deflected north or south.[3] The construction of dikes to prevent a change of course exacerbated the rise of the river's bed so that it stood well above the surrounding plain along much of its lower course.

As it slows, the river forms great loops known as meanders (zuowan) within its dikes. Those bends threaten the dikes in several ways. Their primary danger lies in the fact that the current on the outside of a meander moves much more quickly than the current on the inside, carving at the soft soil of the riverbank with great erosive power. Keeping those erosive forces away from the dikes was one of the fundamental goals of river control. Huge defensive structures several kilometers long were built to deflect the current back out toward the center of the riverbed. As the river rose during flood season, the huge loops could carve their way up and down the channel at alarming speed. In a span of hours, the river could move to threaten a section of dike that had been hundreds of meters from the water. In extreme cases the current might swerve ninety degrees and strike the dike almost perpendicular to it. Immediate action was required to prevent the current from tearing through the dikes.

The erratic rainfall patterns typical of the North China climate also complicated river control. For much of the year, the Yellow River is small stream; but when the rains come, the river quickly can swell to a massive torrent. In the tributary valleys that contribute the bulk of the Yellow

River's silt burden, 50 percent to 60 percent of the annual rainfall arrives in the June-to-August period and another 20 percent in the September-to-November period. Moreover, 35 percent of that rainfall comes as sudden downpours that run off quickly, carrying away large amounts of topsoil.[4] A downpour in a single tributary valley occurring at a time when the river was already swollen with seasonal rains could create flood conditions downstream.

The Yellow River is sometimes described as having had no tributaries along its lower course. That is not quite the case. Each time the river changed course, it moved to a lower bed, usually the channel of another river, and acquired new tributaries. The inexorable process of sedimentation would gradually raise the river higher and cut off those tributaries, which would then have to find new channels to the sea. After the Yellow River moved south and captured the lower course of the Huai River, the Huai and its tributaries became, for all practical purposes, tributaries of the Yellow River. Much of the complex hydraulic system constructed in the Ming and the Qing was designed to allow the Huai to continue to function as a tributary of the Yellow River and thus to facilitate grain transport along the Grand Canal.

Deforestation or defoliation brought on by population increase and changes in agriculture may have aggravated the problem of erosion in the loess region in recent centuries. In his travels through the area in 1923, the American forestry expert Walter Clay Lowdermilk observed that although virtually every part of the land in northern Shaanxi had once been under cultivation, much of it had since been abandoned to pasturage for sheep and goats and that the residents commonly burned off shrub cover to open the land to grass for grazing. Lowdermilk estimated that erosion gullies, some several hundred feet deep, covered 50 percent of the ground in the region. Migration and agricultural practices such as grazing have no doubt contributed to the problem, but the high silt content of the Yellow River was an ancient phenomenon and was noted in Chinese texts as early as 1 B.C.[5]

THE RECORD OF ATTEMPTS to control the Yellow River stretches back into China's earliest history. The Great Yu (traditional dates 2205–2197 B.C.), the legendary founder of the Xia dynasty (2205–1766 B.C.), is credited with the earliest success in subduing the river. More clearly documented than Yu's accomplishments are very early river control practices including levees for flood control, in use by the sixth century B.C., and canal construction, which appeared a short time later. As already noted, by 1 B.C. observers had remarked on the Yellow River's tendency to silt up drainage canals and raise its bed. Attempts to deal with that problem may have inspired one of the earliest statements of Chinese river engineering philosophy: "A good canal is scoured by its own water; a good embankment is consolidated by the sediment brought against it."[6]

Straightforward defensive measures such as the use of dikes and levees to protect land from flooding began very early, but active river control practices such as dredging developed more slowly. In the Song (960–1126), a growing awareness of the problem of silting led to wider use of mechanical methods of dredging. In the Yuan, the various methods of river conservancy used in earlier periods were systematized under three categories: dividing, dredging, and blocking.

Until the late Ming, the dominant method of Yellow River control was to divert excess waters into smaller streams or channels, a technique inspired (or rationalized) by the Great Yu's legendary practice of "separating the nine rivers" *(shu jiu he)*. The river's tendency to break out of its old bed and follow a divided channel was not always unwelcome; divisions were sometimes allowed or encouraged in an effort to split the river's flow. During the Yuan, the combination of the policy of dividing the flow and the river's inherent peripatetic tendencies resulted in a period of particular restlessness. From 1194 to 1288 the river flowed both north and south of the Shandong Peninsula. From 1288 to 1324 it turned south upstream of Kaifeng and flowed via the Huai River into Lake Hongze and then into the Yangzi River. After further floods and shifts, the river settled into two branches, with some flow in the northern channel and the main current following the lower course of the Huai southeast to the sea. In 1495 the northern channel was closed off. Although the Yellow River would continue to follow the southern route until 1855, it was not yet confined to a single course: its floodwater was regularly diverted into other streams branching off from its southern bank. The emphasis on diversion also dominated policy discussion, and disputes seldom strayed from the question of where and how the river waters should be diverted. Only in the last decades of the sixteenth century did engineers begin to confine the Yellow River to a single channel.[7]

The origins of the late imperial Yellow River control system can be traced to Mongol construction of the Grand Canal to bring food supplies to the North. As the Yuan dynasty lost its grip on power, the canal fell into disrepair. It was the Ming emperor Yongle (1403–1424) who made a series of strategic decisions that would turn Grand Canal transport and Yellow River management into key components of imperial power. The fourth son of the Ming founder, Yongle took the throne from his nephew by force to become the third (after eradicating any evidence of his nephew's reign) emperor of the Ming. Yongle's power base was the former Yuan capital city, Beijing. Although he moved to the Ming capital at Nanjing after his accession, concern about northern military security led him to relocate the capital in Beijing. That process began in the first year of his reign; after 1414 the emperor resided mainly in Beijing.[8]

Beijing was well located for frontier defense of the North and the West, but the surrounding region was poor with a weak economic base. In 1404 the emperor ordered the relocation of ten thousand households from Shanxi to Beijing to boost the city's population. That was followed over the next decade by massive construction projects and the relocation of hundreds of thousands of civilians, soldiers, and administrators and their families to the new capital, creating a large urban population that the northern provinces could not feed. Initially the Ming attempted to utilize both sea and overland shipment to supply the growing metropolitan population with grain from China's rich Yangzi provinces. That system was insecure and cumbersome, but it succeeded in moving huge quantities of grain. In 1414, the last year it operated, at least six hundred thousand metric tons of grain were shipped to Beijing.[9]

The joint land-sea transport of grain to the capital was abandoned in 1415 with the completion of work on the reconstruction of the Grand Canal, begun in 1411. The canal's north-south route included a portion of the lower course of the Yellow River, a fact that complicated both canal transport and river management. From that time forward, dynastic concern to maintain regular shipment of tribute grain to supply the metropolitan population and the northern military manifested itself in unprecedented efforts to regulate the Yellow River.

The relationship between the Grand Canal and the Yellow River has often been misunderstood. One misconception is that the canal caused floods by impeding the Yellow River's egress to the sea. Historians holding that view condemned the system and charged that "throughout the semi-feudal epoch in China, the government always considered the interest of grain transport above that of irrigation or flood control." Thus emperors impatient to enjoy the "fruit of rulership" ignored the unfortunate impact of the canal on river control and insisted on canal transport at the expense of the people who lived along the river.[10]

Neither the hydraulic facts nor the economic realities of the Grand Canal–Yellow River system support that assessment. Under the system developed in the late Ming, water from the Huai River flowed into Lake Hongze and was then used to float the grain-transport fleet onto the Yellow River. Since the lake stood above the Yellow River, the excess water was also beneficial in scouring silt from the river's lower course. Much later, as the Yellow River's bed rose above the surface of the lake, both river control and grain shipment were undermined. The fault lay not with the Grand Canal but with the steady accumulation of silt in the bed of the river and eventually in Lake Hongze. Efforts to fight the accumulation of silt may have slowed the process, but the steady rise of the river's bed ultimately impeded both the flow of water and transport on the canal.[11]

As important as the Grand Canal was to imperial strategic interests, it had other uses and became much more than a conduit for tribute grain. The canal continued to serve many of the flood control, irrigation, and military defense needs that had been the rationale for its earliest segments. More importantly, the canal became a vital trade artery, with private traffic increasing to the point where "governmental transport routes gradually became commercial routes." By the late Ming, the canal was a crucial trade link between Jiangnan and North China, and the region along its north-south axis had achieved a degree of economic integration unmatched elsewhere in China. The importance of the Grand Canal to private commerce was also recognized by contemporary observers.[12]

The canal's importance as a commercial artery was bolstered by the often-close relationship between government and private merchants in the region. That cooperative relationship was established early; measures introduced in the Yongle reign encouraged merchants to ship grain to northern border garrisons by awarding those who did so certificates to sell salt. In addition, some taxes were payable in silver, which was then shipped north and used to buy grain. Bureaucratic salaries also began to be paid in cash to reduce the amount of grain that had to be shipped. The widespread commercialization of state functions that emerged in the Qing extended to the grain transport system as well. By the mid-Qing, the commercialization of the region was so great that private trade networks could likely have ensured adequate food supplies for the Beijing metropolitan area. Ironically, the commercialization of the canal allowed less rather than more flexibility in dealing with the transport system. The system provided employment for thousands of transport and river workers and served as a source of income and a focus of political patronage for the merchants and officials, low and high, who controlled transport or engaged in subcontracting of repairs, hiring of labor, or provision of construction materials.[13] Those powerful groups were certain to oppose any attempt to reintroduce sea transport of tribute grain.

Sea transport and other alternatives to Grand Canal shipment of tribute grain were also opposed by those who recognized that reliance on the canal meant greater attention to flood defense along the Yellow River. One Ming official argued against the sea route by noting that it would not only impoverish the areas along the canal but would undermine both government and popular commitment to flood control.[14] That expressed what was usually an unstated fear of those who served or lived along the river: that without the need for Grand Canal transport, state commitment to Yellow River control would weaken. The decision made in the 1850s to abandon the canal and allow the river to change course was a confirmation of those fears.

Much of the engineering that followed the Ming reconstruction of the canal focused on the confluence of the Huai River–Lake Hongze–Grand Canal with the Yellow River at Qingkou. It was there that the heavily laden grain barges had to be moved onto the Yellow River and then upstream to Xuzhou, where they returned to the canal and continued north. The Qingkou intersection suffered its share of hydraulic problems, but the river threatened the canal in other ways. Floods along the northern bank west of Xuzhou destroyed the canal's levees and deposited tons of sediment in its channel. Breaches to the south were less likely to damage the canal, since the floodwaters could be channeled into the Huai and other rivers, but until the construction of the Central Transport Canal (Zhong Yunhe or Zhonghe) section of the Grand Canal in the Kangxi period (begun by Jin Fu in the 1680s and completed in 1703), any flood upstream drained the river of water and stopped transport. Attempts to control the situation led to the building of massive dikes, particularly along the north bank of the river.

In the second half of the sixteenth century, it was becoming obvious that a more comprehensive system of Yellow River control was required. Pan Jixun (1521–1595, *jinshi*, 1550), a native of Wucheng in Zhejiang Province, is credited with establishing the paradigm of hydraulic management that would dominate Yellow River engineering for the next three centuries. Beginning with his first appointment in 1565, Pan served four terms as river commissioner. In view of his profound influence on river engineering, his combined time in office was a surprisingly brief five years, with his longest sustained tour a two-year stint from 1578 to 1580. Pan's sporadic service reflected the political turmoil of the time.[15]

Pan, a southerner, had no prior experience with rivers like the Huai and the Yellow, which flowed across wide, flat plains. On arrival at his first post in the area, he studied the subject of river control and formed his own ideas about which methods and practices were most likely to be successful. According to his own account, he questioned experienced river workers and even peasants. It is evident that he also read widely in the available works on river control, adopting some ideas and rejecting others.[16]

Pan became convinced that Yellow River control should focus on the problem of silt rather than the problem of water. Drawing an explicit link between the speed of the current and its silt-carrying capacity, he proposed a system of dikes designed to restrict the lower course of the river to its narrow main channel even in periods of high water. Pan theorized that keeping the velocity of the stream high would not only reduce siltation but would also carve a deeper channel by cutting away earlier silt deposits. His approach came to be known by the phrase "restrict the current to attack the silt" *(shu shui gong sha)*. That method reduced reliance on reduction dikes and diversions in favor of an extensive and sturdy dike system.[17]

In 1578 Pan took charge of both grain transport and Yellow River conservancy and began to implement his solution. His proposals encountered wide opposition, some of which had little to do with river control but came from those who sought to attack Pan's mentor, Grand Secretary Zhang Juzheng (1525–1582). Among the alternative proposals to his river engineering plans were some that emphasized dredging, some that proposed cutting new channels to the sea, some that called for new diversion canals, and some that suggested the river be allowed to choose its own course. Pan rejected those approaches. He argued that the previous practice of dividing the flow of the Yellow River was self-defeating because the slowed current only increased the rate of sedimentation both in the main channel and in the diversion channels. Cutting new channels or dredging the old would provide only temporary relief—before the silt once more closed them up; allowing the river to choose its own course would expose those living along its banks to devastating floods and would do nothing to protect Grand Canal transport.[18]

Pan's plan called for the building of two pairs of dikes: one close-set, called "thread dikes" *(luti),* to keep the current in a confined channel in all but the worst flood conditions, and a second, outer set, known as "distant dikes" *(yaoti),* to contain the overflow during the highest flood stages. Ideally, when the river overflowed the inner dikes, silt deposited in the area between the two sets of dikes would gradually rise to become a natural barrier that would confine the river to its central channel. That system was to be constructed only in the downstream section of the river. Upstream in Henan only the large outer dikes would be built; they would create a massive retention basin during flood season. If it had operated as designed, Pan's system would have achieved the ideal, mentioned earlier, of a river that scours its own channel and builds its own banks.

Contemporary critics charged that Pan was abandoning tried and proven methods of river management in favor of a singular focus on narrowing the channel. In fact, Pan drew heavily upon the practices of the opposing schools of river conservancy in designing the system's emergency safeguards and maintenance program. Both mechanical means and human labor were to be used to dredge the river's channel, and when necessary the current was to be diverted into side channels by reduction dikes, weirs, and flash-lock gates built along the banks of the river to direct floodwaters north into Weishan Lake or south into Lake Hongze. Pan also strengthened dikes along the Huai River and Lake Hongze.[19] As Pan's system evolved, it resulted in an extensive system of gates and a complex network of dikes that paralleled the river from Zhengzhou in western Henan to Yuntiguan on the Zhejiang coast.

Under this system, the waters of the Huai River and its tributaries flowed into Lake Hongze and then into the lower course of the Yellow

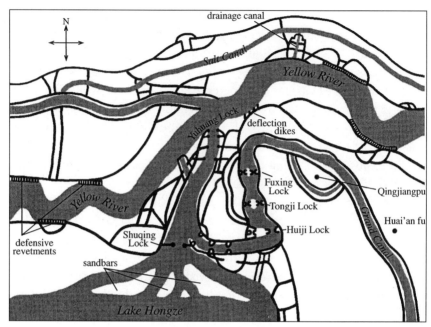

Map 2   The confluence at Qingkou, ca. 1840.

River. Although the total volume of silt carried in that part of the river was increased thereby, the current moved more swiftly, and since the lake waters carried much less silt than the Yellow River, the amount of silt per unit of water was reduced. As noted already, Pan believed that the accelerated flow would not only reduce sedimentation but also scour old silt deposits from the lower channel.

In his four terms as head of Grand Canal and Yellow River conservancy, Pan was unable to complete all the elements of his system, but the impact of his ideas on subsequent Chinese river conservancy thinkers was singular. The strength of his analysis was partly a result of his ability to consolidate earlier river conservancy achievements into a systematic engineering vision and partly the result of his own imaginative solution to a perennial problem. Speaking of Pan's *Hefang Yilan*, the *Si Ku Quan Shu Zongmu Tiyao* comments that "although changes in methods were afterwards necessary to fit changing circumstances, yet experts in river control always take this book as a standard guide." By identifying silt rather than water as the primary problem of Yellow River control, Pan's theories also led to the permanent eclipse of the "divide-the-streams" approach.[20]

Some of the flaws in Pan's engineering vision were already evident in the early Qing. Jin Fu noted that scouring slowed but did not stop the process of silt accumulation in the lower course. Others faulted Pan's failure to attend to the downstream section of the river and the problem of blockage near the outlet to the sea.[21] In spite of the criticisms leveled at his policies, Pan's name—later linked with that of Jin Fu in the compound Pan-Jin—came to be used as a metonym for the imperial vision of hydraulic engineering on the Yellow River.

The apotheosis of Pan Jixun, both in the dynastic period and by modern historians who emphasize the uniquely modern quality of his engineering vision, has obscured his place in a longer process of hydraulic development driven by the imperial state's decision to intervene to an unprecedented degree in the Yellow River's natural processes for the sake of administrative and military needs. Eighty years before Pan Jixun served, in 1493, Liu Daxia was dispatched to deal with the flooding of the Yellow River along its northern branch. After educating himself in the work of earlier river experts and recruiting the best of contemporary talent, Liu decided that the northern branch should be abandoned and the river confined to the southern course. It took two years of effort and a huge expenditure of labor, but that task was completed in 1495.[22] The work of Pan at the end of the sixteenth century was only the next step in the imperial state's determined effort to subordinate nature to human purpose.

The hydraulic system that emerged from those efforts incorporated far more than the Yellow River and the Grand Canal; the Huai River, Lake Hongze, and dozens of other lakes and streams were part of the structure. With those components linked to the operation of the system, dividing the flow of the Yellow River during flood season no longer was a viable solution; diverting the overflow into other channels only led them by circuitous routes back to the confluence at Qingkou or into the canal. If the Yellow River was to be managed in such a way that its seasonal floods did not disrupt the schedule of tribute grain shipment, some method had to be found to keep it within its channel.

Pan's attempt to craft a system in which the force of the river was harnessed to do the work of man may seem modern in its assumption of the capacity of technology to manipulate nature, but it points to a contradiction at the heart of the late imperial system. As the state arrogated to itself more and more complex technical tasks, it failed to anticipate the fiscal or bureaucratic consequences. A weak tax system and an ad hoc approach to technical training proved inadequate to the job of financing, managing, and maintaining the Yellow River–Grand Canal system.

Those flaws were already evident during Pan Jixun's career. Pan took up the mantle of hydraulic engineer in the context of a crisis provoked when the Ming dynasty's minimalist bureaucracy and its generalist bureaucrats showed themselves incapable of meeting the state's administrative and technical challenges. Zhang Juzheng's many reforms delayed collapse but could not survive him because they were incompatible with an administrative system "too stylized and too shallow" to carry them out.[23] Pan had detractors and informed critics. In many cases his ideas turned out to be flawed. Pan's canonization in later decades was not a consequence of the specific policies he proposed but of his commitment to a technical approach that promised success with existing fiscal and bureaucratic machinery. For over 250 years, the engineering vision identified so closely with Pan Jixun managed to keep the river in its course, but not without severely testing both the fiscal and the administrative resources of the state.

The ambitious model of river management that emerged in the late Ming inevitably led to changes in hydraulic administration. The old ad hoc method of dealing with river crises was replaced by structure, routine, and regulation. Those changes appeared first in the management of the Grand Canal. In 1430 the official Zhou Chen (1381–1452) was given the appellation *zongdu* and ordered to take charge of tribute grain collection and shipment from the Yangzi valley. The title *zongdu* originally implied someone in a supervisory position that involved either a combination of civilian and military responsibilities or duties that required a transjurisdictional authority. In 1471, recognizing the need for a single official to oversee both the canal and its crucial junction with the Yellow River, the Ming appointed a *hedao zongdu*, or governor-general of the Yellow River and the Grand Canal, to take charge of both. That can probably be considered the beginning of the Ming-Qing Yellow River hydraulic bureaucracy. Local maintenance and dike repair continued to be undertaken by provincial officials, however, while major river control projects were managed by the Board of Works or were undertaken by officials appointed on an ad hoc basis. Much of the routine river work continued to be carried out by lower-level civil officials and funded mainly by local districts; counties and prefectures along the Yellow River in Henan were required to pay an additional tax for "river work" *(hegong)*. A river treasury did exist, but it was used only to pay officials dispatched for specific river projects.[24]

The Qing adopted the basic outlines of the Ming system. The Board of Works was in charge of river conservancy, staffed by board presidents, vice presidents, department directors, and secretaries as before. The main change was the appointment of one Manchu and one Han official to the post of board president and two Manchu and two Han officials as vice presidents.

Further growth came slowly, and much of the responsibility for the collection and transport of tribute grain was in the hands of provincial officials. Originally stationed at Jining, the *zongdu* moved to Qingjianpu in 1677. Growth at the highest levels of the conservancy began in earnest in 1724, when the post of vice governor *(fu zonghe)* was created to oversee river duties in Henan's Wuzhi and Zhongmou Counties. Five years later that post was upgraded to governor-general, dividing the hydraulic bureaucracy into two units, one in Jiangsu and the other in charge of Shandong and Henan. The following year (1730) saw the creation of a third governor-general of river affairs in Zhili, a position filled concurrently by the governor-general of Zhili.[25]

As the upper and middle levels of the Yellow River conservancy expanded, the lower bureaucracy followed suit. Initially the Qing system called for three circuit intendants *(daotai)* below the governor-general, one in charge of Zhili's Hebei circuit, one in charge of Henan's Kai-Gui-Chen-Xu circuit, and one in charge of the Yunho-Yanxi-Caoji circuit in Shandong. By the nineteenth century, a treasurer and four circuit intendants staffed the Jiangsu conservancy, with around 140 local officials doing at least some river conservancy work. The Henan conservancy had three circuit intendants and used the services of around 125 local officials.[26]

In addition to their duties in canal transport and river control, those officials also had some responsibility for military affairs in their areas and commanded a sizable force of specialized river soldiers *(hebing)*. In the first decade of the nineteenth century, the governor-general of the Jiangsu conservancy commanded 15,666 river soldiers, and another 4,241 were stationed in the Henan conservancy.[27]

That accounting does not include those managerial and clerical staff persons who helped in contracting laborers, gathering matériel, distributing relief, and supervising construction and dredging work. This group included not only private secretaries and other legitimate personnel in the service of a river official but also such hangers-on as unemployed literati, friends, family members, and household servants of river officials. Bottom feeders in the river conservancy, those men were blamed—like their counterparts in county and provincial government—for the growth of corruption and negligence. But they performed a valuable range of services, and their numbers increased because officials needed them to meet the demands of a growing workload.

As early as the late eighteenth century, the priorities of the system were becoming reversed; the river bureaucracy that had been established as an adjunct of Grand Canal transport had grown so large, its fiscal appetite so enormous, that the tail was now wagging the dog. Officials whose duties had once focused on the canal now found themselves inspecting hundreds of kilometers of dikes that paralleled the river along both banks from the foothills west of Zhengzhou to the Yellow Sea.

In the early Qing, the men who headed the river conservancy were drawn from the top ranks of the bureaucracy. But as informality gave way to routine and regulation, the top posts were more often filled from within the hydraulic bureaucracy. That was partly a product of necessity and perhaps partly one of self-selection: top officials recognized the risks of the job and sought to avoid it or escape it as soon as possible.

The result was the emergence of a new category of specialist bureaucrat, the Confucian engineer. Like their predecessors and contemporaries, those men were literati administrators, products of the examination system and schooled in Neo-Confucian ethics. What set them apart was not their preparation but their aptitude. Although most showed competence in general administration, they rose to high positions in the river conservancy because of their skill in hydraulic engineering. They differ from earlier hydraulic engineering notables such as Liu Daxia, Jia Lu, or even Jin Fu in that few enjoyed great influence or prestige outside their specialized arena. The appointment of those experts to high positions for extended tours of duty shows that even emperors dubious of such specialist skills recognized that officials with little experience in river works and no aptitude for engineering could not manage the Yellow River–Grand Canal hydraulic system.

The search for bureaucrats with technical leanings and proven hands-on ability to operate the system led to the lower ranks of the river and canal bureaucracy. Officials who excelled as river circuit intendants or as magistrates in counties along the river, where their duties included river engineering, were most often those recruited to fill the higher posts. The results of that practice were mixed. Promoting officials from within provided proven competence, but it also could lead to charges of cronyism. Opponents of Grand Canal transport often pointed to patronage as a source of corruption and a reason the system needed to be abandoned.

Beginning in the second half of the eighteenth century, the emergence among some Chinese intellectuals and bureaucrats of an interest in "practical statecraft" (jingshi) gave a new level of respectability to officials who commanded technical skills. Statecraft advocates believed administration could be improved in part by greater attention to the pragmatic aspects of the job, including the know-how required for river control and other hydraulic engineering tasks. Although the statecraft movement remained diffuse and unstructured, it gave encouragement to specialist officials.

The Yellow River's change of course in the early years of the Xianfeng reign (1851–1862) continues to be seen as a milestone in Qing dynastic history. Coinciding as it did with the beginning of the Taiping Rebellion (1850–1864), the river's shift seems an obvious corollary of the Qing loss of social control. Some lay the blame for the collapse on administrative decline and imperial ineptitude, others on fiscal shortages and geologic inevitability. There is some truth in all of those assertions, but as with most problems, the closer one looks, the more difficult it is to resort to simple schemata and existing labels. From the perspective of the officials who served in the river conservancy on the cusp of this great change, the job was a challenge, a duty, a great risk as well as an opportunity. Those men differed radically in their training and background, in their approach to the job, and in their fates. Some ended their careers in disgrace, some in quiet despair; some died as martyrs to the Taiping while others became gods. Although in many ways they were forerunners of the pragmatic officials who participated in the "self-strengthening" effort of the second half of the century, their achievements have been overshadowed by the fact that they served on the eve of China's transition from the glories of the high Qing to the great midcentury cataclysms.

2

Rising Waters

TWO INELUCTABLE REALITIES underlay the engineering crisis of the Yellow River control system in the early nineteenth century: the river's rising bed and the imperial state's fiscal difficulties. The conflict between the geologic and the fiscal was mediated, however, by administration and technology. That core conflict was therefore articulated in terms of administrative discipline, fiscal restraint, and technological competence. The oft-cited problems of corruption, mismanagement, and incompetence were less fundamental causes of the crisis than they were the coin of political discourse about how the state could safeguard and best use its resources. As the crisis deepened, those issues influenced both perception of the crisis and the state's response.

As the bed of the Yellow River rose above the surrounding countryside, the engineering system keeping it in its course grew more extensive, convoluted, and complex. Fiscal support for river control and canal maintenance grew, but it did not keep pace with the expansion of the system. Similarly, although the state paid intermittent heed to the fact that those developments demanded river officials with both technical and administrative skills, no sustained and systematic effort was made to guarantee that sufficient numbers of technically trained river officials would be available to meet the needs of hydraulic administration. The result was a bureaucracy in which technically skilled administrators remained in short supply. Hard-pressed hydraulic officials were forced to resort to a range of creative and sometimes risky fiscal, technical, and administrative strategies in order to perform effectively in spite of those limitations. In the long run, those gambles undermined administrative cohesion and imperial confidence.

Fiscal Shoals

The economic difficulties of the Qing in the early nineteenth century are well known. The draining of the treasury by the scandalous corruption surrounding the suppression of the White Lotus sect in the last decade of the eighteenth century, the depletion of the Yunnan silver mines, and the outflow of silver resulting from the growing trade in opium all contributed to economic instability. The instability caused price fluctuations and long-term inflation, which increased the cost of construction materials, wage labor, and the salaries of private secretaries and clerks. All of those had a direct impact on the expense of river control.[1]

One consequence of the economic changes was the growing tension that gradually emerged between the emperor, who insisted on fiscal restraint, and river officials unable to hold down costs. Caught between rising costs and the emphasis on fiscal rigor, river officials circumvented and manipulated accounting procedures designed to limit spending and expanded accounts established as temporary expedients into major sources of funding.

The informal method of funding Yellow River conservancy that prevailed in the Kangxi period gave way in the Yongzheng reign to clearer accounting methods, but funding continued to be drawn from an eclectic combination of land, customs, and salt taxes. An edict of 1730 listed these annual sources of income for the river conservancy treasury:

Source	Amount (in taels)
Jiangsu Province (land tax)	112,237
Anhui Province (land tax)	23,453
Zhejiang Province (land tax)	10,525
Huai customs	26,824
Kuayi customs	7,666
Liang Huai salt administration	300,000
Liang Huai salt controller	50,000
Guangdong salt controller	10,000
Liang-Zhe salt controller	10,000
Changlu salt controller	10,000
Shandong salt controller	7,000
Fujian salt controller	3,000
Suzhou financial commissioner	99,828[2]

Later, land and labor taxes *(diding)* from the provinces through which the river flowed accounted for the bulk of the funding for annual maintenance and repair. Those funds were supplemented by irregular sources such as the sale of degrees, titles, and posts *(juanna);* exactions from the Consoo fund; and personal "gifts" by wealthy commoners and officials. Small amounts also came from rent paid for restored lands that lay within the dikes or along lakes.[3] Repairs demanded by major floods like those at the end of the Jiaqing reign created an added tax burden that further slowed the recovery of afflicted areas. Aware of that, the state often turned instead to the salt intendants and the Cohong for additional funds.

The category of regular expenditures *(zhengxiang)* created during the late Kangxi and the Yongzheng reigns to fund river work included the cost of yearly maintenance and repairs *(suixiu),* emergency repairs *(qiangxiu),* and major works *(dagong)*—projects such as dike renewal or flood repair. Each year the river circuit intendants were expected to present an estimate *(tigu)* of the funds needed for yearly maintenance and repairs and for purchases of matériel to be stored along the dikes in case emergency repairs were required. When work was completed or the purchases were made, a final account *(tixiao)* was submitted.[4]

Imperial strategies for controlling expenditures emphasized direct involvement by high officials in the fiscal affairs of their subordinates, oversight of river conservancy accounts by provincial officials outside the river bureaucracy, and the on-site inspection of maintenance and repairs by top river officials. Succeeding reigns introduced strict deadlines for budgetary requests and increasingly specific rules concerning repair and maintenance projects. An edict of 1736 ordered any subprefect or circuit intendant who handled water conservancy repairs to make a full report of all expenditures, the materials used, and the labor required, accompanied by a map with written explanations of the work done. A Jiaqing regulation *(zhangcheng)* went further, requiring that expense reports for emergency repairs include the name of the site where the work was done; the height, length, thickness, and amount of material used in each section that had collapsed and had been repaired; and a section-by-section breakdown of costs.[5]

In spite of those requirements, the limits on spending for both annual repairs *(suixiu)* and emergency repairs *(qiangxiu)* had to be raised repeatedly. In Qianlong 13 (1748) the annual total for both types of expenditure in the Jiangsu conservancy was fixed at 400,000 taels. That amount was later increased to 500,000 taels per year, and then in Jiaqing 11 (1806) it was tripled to 1.5 million taels per year. The process in the Henan conservancy was similar. In Daoguang 2 (1822) an edict approved an additional 300,000 taels for repairs in Henan, but the emperor went on to complain that emergency repair funds had increased every year since Jiaqing 24.[6]

Inflation and the devaluation of copper cash can explain part of that increase. The Yellow River conservancy was particularly sensitive to the devaluation. Much of the copper cash minted by the Qing went directly to the Board of Works to pay for public works projects. When copper was devalued, suppliers of stalks and other construction materials were reluctant to accept it, and soldiers, including the river troops, balked at being paid in anything but silver.[7]

Not only did expenditures under the usual categories steadily increase, but ancillary accounts also sprang into being and, once established, exhibited a hardy persistence and a similar propensity for expansion.[8] The best examples of that process in the early nineteenth century are the categories of miscellaneous works *(ling'an)* and cost-assistance funds *(jintie)*. The use of the miscellaneous works category originated when funds set aside for yearly maintenance and emergency repairs proved inadequate for some construction projects. Once the miscellaneous works category was established, it became a handy mechanism used by river officials to bypass spending limits in the standard accounting categories. In 1806 the emperor attempted to bring spending back under control by tripling the budgets for yearly and emergency repairs and including miscellaneous works in them. Those measures failed to reduce the amount being spent on miscellaneous works.[9] In 1816, in an effort to pressure river officials to reduce the cost of miscellaneous works by highlighting them, the emperor ordered the governors-general of the Henan and Jiangsu conservancies to report all miscellaneous works expenditures at once and to compare the totals to those for the previous three years.

The hydraulic and fiscal nightmare of the Jiaqing reign did not dissipate when Daoguang took the throne in 1821. Repairs and relief efforts following a series of devastating floods in Henan were still under way.

Those expenses, combined with the loss of agricultural taxes from the region, constituted a major economic setback for the state. The cost of those floods remained unpaid in the late 1830s.[10]

The measures taken by Jiaqing in 1816 not only failed to reduce or eradicate miscellaneous works expenditures; his tactics could not even check their growth. The Daoguang emperor's understandable frustration with those costs is evident in the language of the regulatory edicts he sent down during his reign. In 1822, shocked by the expenditure in the Henan conservancy alone of over 1 million taels for miscellaneous works, Daoguang demanded to know why costs kept rising if construction and maintenance were being carried out as they should be. If there are years when costs rose, the emperor reasoned, should there not also be years when they fell? Again in 1828 Daoguang responded to a request from the Jiangsu conservancy for 1,290,000 taels for miscellaneous works by charging officials there with piling miscellaneous works one on top of another. Why, he asked, after 10 million taels had been spent on major projects such as the dredging of Qingkou and the addition of stone to the Gaoyan Dike, had expenditures in other areas not decreased? In spite of the imperial misgivings, spending in that category continued to rise. By 1832 miscellaneous works expenditures for the Jiangsu conservancy had reached a total of 3,382,000 taels, up approximately 1 million taels over the totals for the previous three years. The emperor was particularly upset because there had been no floods that year to justify an increase in spending.[11] The emperor's conflicted response to those costs reflects his own naive understanding of the nature of the hydraulic system. In spite of the clear evidence put forward by many officials in the river conservancy, Daoguang did not fully grasp the implications of the fact that the hydraulic system was not a fixed structure but a growing and expanding one that would inevitably demand more and more state resources. He repeatedly consented to greater expenditure, but he seemed to believe that the return would be lower costs at some time in the future. Not given to bold conceptual thinking, Daoguang remained, like most of the officials who served him, an ameliorative realist.

The process of expansion and eventual incorporation of ad hoc accounts as regular forms of spending was repeated with *jintie,* or cost assistance funds, which were originally created to meet rising matériel prices. When temporary shortages or an emergency forced officials to buy materials at prices higher than those approved by the state, cost assistance moneys were used and prices 20 percent to 50 percent above the statutory price (lijia) were paid, the extra costs to be repaid later out of taxes destined for the river conservancy treasuries. As early as 1784, the Qianlong emperor complained that along the Grand Canal in Shandong, cost assistance expenditures already equaled regular expenditures (zhengxiang). Qianlong, fearing that to insist on repayment of those funds would only encourage local officials to squeeze the people for more taxes, decided to forgive the entire amount.[12]

Facing little in the way of accountability, river officials had no incentive to reduce such expenditures. On the contrary, as inflation and demand drove up the cost of matériel, officials made even more extensive use of that type of account. In 1817 the Henan conservancy spent 182,350 taels on cost assistance, and the amount continued to rise in subsequent years. Eventually the state responded with the same measures used to control miscellaneous works expenditures, requiring cost assistance expenditures to be reported yearly and compared with those for the preceding three years.[13] Again, the goal was to track the costs as a means of pressuring officials to reduce them. The results were otherwise; tracking the funds legitimated them, and once again expenditures rose.

Rising costs helped undermine imperial faith in the integrity of river officials, an erosion that can be traced in the metamorphosis of guaranty (baogu) and restitution (peixiu) statutes. Those statutes held officials accountable for the work carried out under their aegis. From the founding of the dynasty in 1644, Qing statutes mandated loss of position and rank for river officials when construction work for which they were responsible failed. A new twist, introduced in 1694, required river officials or the officials in charge of construction to bear part of the financial burden of hydraulic failures.[14]

During the Yongzheng reign, the statutes on guaranty and restitution were made more explicit and inclusive. Officials were required to pay 40 percent of the cost of construction in cases of dike failure. Of that amount, circuit intendants and prefects would pay 20 percent, middle-level officials such as assistant prefects, subprefects, and captains were to pay 15 percent, and the lowest officials were held responsible for the final 5 percent. The state paid the remainder. Officials in charge of river defense at the time of a flood were to be deprived of rank but left in their posts. They could redeem themselves by successfully completing repairs.[15]

Restitution statutes were designed not only to broaden the scope of responsibility in the case of a hydraulic failure but also to encourage greater vigilance at all levels of administration. Eventually, fiscal responsibility included governors-general and provincial governors as well as subordinate river officials. An edict of 1774 divided the restitution burden into ten parts, assigning them in the following manner:

Governor-General	2.0 parts
Governor	1.0 part
Intendants	2.0 parts
Subprefects	1.0 part
Prefects	2.0 parts
Majors, Captains	1.5 parts
Lower officers	0.5 parts[16]

Although the state no doubt hoped restitution would ease the financial burden of hydraulic failures, those statutes originated as a means to encourage group responsibility—and mutual surveillance—among the river officials. That changed in the early nineteenth century, when the Qing's fiscal problems and the rising costs of river conservancy led the state to put greater effort into the collection of restitution. River officials responded by a steadfast refusal to pay. Their resistance to restitution is evident in many edicts dealing with the problem of arrears. Time limits were set for repayment of restitution, and official advancement could be delayed if payment was not made.[17]

The findings of an 1832 investigation by the Board of Works illustrate the ineffectiveness of restitution as a disciplinary tool. The board found that 417 officials had failed to pay restitution totaling 2,589,800 taels.[18] Nevertheless, the state continued to routinely demand payment of restitution and to assign 40 percent of the cost of flood repairs to be paid by the river and provincial officials responsible for the area where a flood occurred.

The fact that no official could ever hope to pay out of his salary the huge amounts required under the restitution statutes encouraged river officials to set aside part of the money marked for repairs and maintenance as insurance against the day when the river would prove uncontrollable.

An official fortunate enough not to need those funds could leave office with well-lined pockets.[19] The effect of the restitution statutes, like that of the state's attempts to control and reduce expenditures, was the opposite of what was intended. Not only did restitution encourage peculation, but the state's ineffectual efforts to enforce payment also robbed the statutes of any punitive force. Instead of greater control of expenditures, the state ended with less control.

As with restitution, regulations designed to discipline and punish river officials became stricter and more punitive, but actual punishments varied with the personality and goals of the emperor. One striking statistic indicates that in the Daoguang reign, imperial patience with top river officials was growing thin. In the years between 1644 and 1800, a total of six of the men who headed the Grand Canal–Yellow River conservancy left through demotion, dismissal, resignation, or suicide. Between 1800 and 1840, five were dismissed, resigned, or were demoted, four of them in the Daoguang reign alone. Such harshness may reflect only the personality of Daoguang, but when it is considered along with other regulatory developments, it seems more likely that Daoguang was applying to the top level of the hydraulic bureaucracy the same disciplinary standards applied in earlier reigns to the lower ranks.[20]

The hydraulic changes that took place in the Yellow River control system over the two and one-half centuries of its existence had implications beyond the mechanical aspects of river engineering. Hydraulic developments placed a greater administrative burden on river officials, which contributed to the creation of a larger but less tightly controlled bureaucracy. As fiscal problems moved to the forefront of the Qing government's agenda, the rising cost and limited success of Yellow River conservancy brought attempts to impose tighter controls on river expenditures, efforts that exacerbated the tension between the central government and river officials.

The Irregular Bureaucracy

One of the primary targets of critics of the hydraulic bureaucracy were the many supernumeraries employed by river and canal officials. The numbers of such helpers rose as hydraulic officials found themselves hard-pressed to meet their administrative responsibilities. As early as the turn of the nineteenth century, top provincial and hydraulic officials advocated administrative expansion to deal with the greater demands that changes in the system were putting on hydraulic officials. In 1802 Wu Jing, head of the Jiangsu conservancy, and Jiangsu governor Fei Chun presented a pair of memorials on the problem.[21] They pointed out that in addition to personally taking charge of material purchases, maintenance of stalk revetments, and defense during flood season, river officials had to maintain an increasing number of defensive sites: "Formerly, the number of stalk dikes bordering on the river was few . . . but since Qianlong 55 (1790), the river has meandered, requiring new stalk sections each year."[22]

In some parts of the Jiangsu conservancy, the number of stalk revetments had doubled since Qianlong 45 (1780). As a result river officials found themselves facing overwhelming workloads while managing a growing number of subordinates. Themselves experienced river officials, Wu and Fei saw only one solution: "For the last two years we have carefully examined regular and emergency engineering practices, and also flood defense duties from the simple to the complex. We have thoroughly discussed these matters with civil and military river officials. The reality is that the present [situation] is different from the past. There is no choice but to establish more administrative subunits."[23]

The creation of more subunits, though clearly necessary, was an inadequate response to the administrative problems faced by officials. The decision of some officials to expand their staff by hiring unemployed literati created new problems. As word spread of employment opportunities in the yamens of river and canal officials, degree-holders in droves arrived to offer their services. Precedent for hiring such men could be found in officially sanctioned programs that sent degree-holders still awaiting appointment to serve in the hydraulic bureaucracy in order to enhance their technical skills. But the jobless literati arriving in the early nineteenth century had no official sanction and counted on informal, particularistic ties to help them gain positions as secretaries and supervisors. The growing use of such literati supplicants and the employment of other specialist staff created a new stratum in the hydraulic administration—the "irregular bureaucracy." Operating beyond the reach of the disciplinary mechanisms to which regular literati bureaucrats were subject, that support staff represented a serious problem of administrative control. A request in 1837 that more officials awaiting appointment be sent to the

Henan conservancy was justified as necessary to counter the influx of un-employed literati seeking work as deputies *(weiguan)* or private secretaries *(muyou)* at river conservancy yamens. "When a major works project is reported," Governor-General Linqing wrote, "officials proffering their services follow closely after, obstructing every project."[24]

Another factor complicating administrative control grew out of the Qing state's more or less desperate measures to bring money into the state coffers through the sale of degrees, ranks, titles, and sometimes bureau-cratic posts. The buyers were wealthy men who wanted prestige or bureau-crats who sought more rapid advance within the bureaucracy. Many of the low-ranking positions in the Yellow River conservancy were staffed by officials who had purchased their degrees as well as some who had purchased their positions.[25]

The practice of selling ranks, degrees, and positions was an ancient one, and the Qing had made limited use of it since the Kangxi reign, mainly as a source of funds to meet emergency contingencies such as floods and famines. The dangers of the practice had been recognized. The Kangxi emperor had disapproved of the widespread sale of degrees, noting that most of those with the means to buy a degree were from the merchant class and might not have the best interests of the common people at heart.[26]

Necessity gradually undermined such doubts. Floods on the Yangzi, Yongding, and Yellow Rivers in the closing years of the Qianlong reign resulted in an increase in the sales of degrees and ranks. In the subsequent Jiaqing reign, a pattern began to emerge in which a round of selling fol-lowed each natural disaster. The pattern began in 1803, when a flood of the Yellow River at Hengjialou led to an increase in sales to fund repairs. River problems led to further sales in 1808, 1813, 1814, and 1819.[27]

An 1820 memorial by Senior Metropolitan Censor Wu Jie attested to the negative impact of that practice on the river conservancy. Wu charged that many subprefects along the Yellow River were men who had purchased their degrees and positions because they saw the job as a means of enriching themselves, their families, and their friends. Wu also asserted that many higher officials were themselves products of that sys-tem of advancement and so were reluctant to expose the widespread cor-ruption. The result was that those in low positions felt protected and encouraged in their crimes, while those in high positions looked upon the river conservancy as a market for commerce, played favorites with "local merchants" *(tuhuo)*, and recommended people without full knowledge of their abilities.[28]

In 1822, perhaps convinced by Wu Jie's critique, the newly enthroned Daoguang emperor forbade further expansion of the practice. His prohibition led to a steady decline in the overall numbers of degrees, ranks, and titles sold but did not end the practice. On the contrary, when the Gaoyan Dike broke in 1824, sales shot up again. Another rise paralleled the floods of the 1840s. Those sudden jumps support the conclusion that whatever Daoguang's attitude about the practice, the sale of ranks, degrees, and titles remained a mainstay of state emergency funding. Men with purchased degrees continued to find employment at the lowest levels of the river conservancy bureaucracy, particularly in such posts as assistant district magistrate *(xiancheng)* and first-class *(zhoutong)* and second-class *(zhoupan)* assistant district magistrates.[29]

In the same year that he called a halt to the sale of degrees, Daoguang sent an edict to the acting head of the Henan conservancy, Yan Lang, demanding to know whether the rumors of corruption, poor construction, and fraud in the Yellow River conservancy were true. Yan painstakingly explained that many of the stories were based on outmoded construction techniques that had not been used for decades and claimed that improved testing had eliminated most of the corrupt practices the emperor referred to. In the end, however, Yan was forced to admit that abuses did exist.[30]

Rumors of corruption also fed the gossipy "unofficial histories" *(yeshi)* of the day. In one account entitled "The Excesses of the Jiangsu Conservancy River Officials in the Daoguang Period," a hydraulic official throws a lavish party in order to attract secretaries and guests to his yamen. Featured dishes included live monkey brain, camel's-hump soup prepared in the hump of a *live* camel, and other exotic and wasteful delicacies, usually prepared with great cruelty toward the animals. The narrator insists that river officials engaged in an endless round of these dinner parties, interspersed with gambling and theatrical performances. The result of that lavish expenditure was that each river yamen had several hundred guests *(muke)*.[31]

Critics of the river conservancy also linked other forms of consumption with the problem of corruption. Bao Shichen (1775–1855), a proponent of sea transport of tribute grain and an ardent critic of the Grand

Canal and river bureaucracies, claimed that in the tiny town of Qing-jiangpu, over a million taels was spent annually on prostitution, the money pilfered from river conservancy funds. Besides stealing for themselves, river officials were supposedly subjected to a form of blackmail by needy friends and others who threatened to arouse "public opinion" against them. To prevent them from doing that, river officials readily passed out loans and jobs to acquaintances. The result was that hangers-on multiplied, many of them taking charge of repair jobs that the river officials were themselves reluctant to handle.[32] Thanks to such corruption, "hardly one tenth of the regular and extraordinary appropriations was spent for actual water conservancy."[33]

Obviously, such images of corruption are at odds with each other. River officials hardly had to throw banquets to attract followers if hangers-on were flooding in and blackmailing them for jobs. How can we assess the validity of the charges? It is important to keep in mind that critics of the Grand Canal and river conservancy—men like Wei Yuan, Bao Shichen, and Feng Guifen—were vocal opponents of Grand Canal transport of tribute grain and thus sought to depict the system as a waste of government funds. Corruption, banqueting, prostitution, nepotism, and employment of friends were commonplace in all areas of late imperial bureaucratic life, and such practices made easy targets, but were they so rampant, as critics claim, that they undermined river conservancy?

We can get some sense of the polemics involved by considering the charge, noted here and cited in many sources, that "hardly one tenth" of the budgeted funds were actually spent on river and canal work. Feng Guifen, a noted critic of the river conservancy and the Grand Canal, claimed that the yearly budget for the system totaled 5 million taels of silver. Xiao Yishan put the budget of the Jiangsu conservancy alone at 5 million to 6 million taels.[34] Working from either figure and accepting the 10 percent claim would lead to the unlikely conclusion that the vast hydraulic system of the early nineteenth century was being operated and maintained on a smaller real budget than the far less complex system of the early eighteenth century. Those critics, most of whom were tied to and voiced the complaints of the elite of the lower Yangzi region, over-stated the degree of waste to support their views. The abuses they depict certainly existed to some degree, but the heart of the hydraulic bureaucracy's problems lay elsewhere.

Actual cases of corruption reveal a different and in some ways more troubling portrait of the problems of the hydraulic bureaucracy than that drawn by critics. In one investigation in 1800, two river brigade commanders *(youji)* and several low-ranking river conservancy officials were indicted. According to investigators, a brigade commander named Zhuang Gang, in charge of the Huai-Xu brigade (Huaian-Xuzhou) in northern Jiangsu, parlayed the control of river duties into a fiefdom in which he was able to demand bribes from subordinates, siphon off money from purchase of matériel, and insist that county officials pay for his food and lodging and provide him with bearers for his sedan chair whenever he traveled to inspect construction. According to Zhuang's confession, extracted under torture, in the ten years of his tenure he had managed to pilfer over 2,000 taels from transactions involving the purchase of materials and another 3,000 to 4,000 taels in gifts and bribes. A second figure, a major named Liu Bu, who headed the Huai-Yang battalion, confessed to having peculated 1,700 to 1,800 taels from the purchase of matériel and another 3,000 taels from bribes, gifts, and unreported surpluses on construction jobs. Also involved was a subprefect named Mou Yun, who used money earmarked for a dredging job to set up a leather goods shop and other enterprises. Unfamiliar with dredging techniques, he handed over control of the actual work to others—simultaneously managing to justify 6,000 taels in surcharges for the job. Recipients paid him off either in cash from the funds appropriated for the dredging work or in gifts *(chouxie)*. He confessed to having set aside a total of 1,000 taels from those activities.[35]

The investigation also uncovered three county magistrates who had farmed out dredging jobs and pocketed some 400 taels, one second captain who managed to make 600 taels out of various dredging projects and material purchase transactions, and another second captain who took one hundred strings of cash from relief funds. Several lesser offenders, including private secretaries, were implicated as well. The total amount peculated by the dozen or so miscreants over a period of several years was around 15,000 taels. If investigators were expecting to find the offenders living like princes on the fruits of their corruption, they were disappointed by a search of the miscreants' homes and property, which found little in the way of rich furnishings. More telling was the discovery that the culprits had spent much of the stolen money to buy official posts in the Henan conservancy for their sons.[36]

The amounts stolen seem small in comparison to the huge amounts spent on river control, but the punishments meted out reflect the state's intense concern over the issue of corruption in the wake of Heshen's demise; Liu Bu and Zhuang Gang were sentenced to be executed for their crimes; others who had committed serious offenses were to be given one hundred strokes of the bamboo and sent into exile.[37]

Investigators concluded that one of the problems that led to those abuses was the breakdown in the division of labor between civilian and military river officials. By regulation and long-established precedent, civil officials were expected to handle decisions involving finance, whereas military officials were restricted to the management of the technical aspects of construction, including the supervision of laborers and river troops. By encroaching on the prerogatives of civil officials, military officials were able to indulge in various corrupt practices. Investigators suggested that further regulations be enacted to exclude the military from involvement in project planning and the purchase of materials and to increase the involvement of higher officials in both areas.[38] Those regulations, though well meant, had one serious drawback: they added to the already heavy administrative burden of civilian river officials and thus made it even less likely that they would be able to closely monitor the day-to-day activities of their subordinates.

Not all the corruption discovered in hydraulic projects and flood control were the result of petty peculation by low-ranking officials; high officials occasionally were found out in much larger crimes. In 1822 Henan governor Yang Zutong was accused of peculating 60,000 taels from a repair project at Yifeng. The arena in which Yang worked his scheme was not the lowly realm of stalk purchasing but the more lucrative one of converting silver to copper cash. All major works projects required large amounts of copper cash to pay laborers, so officials had to exchange silver for the needed cash. Yang had invented a regulation requiring that for each ounce of silver exchanged for copper cash, 80 *wen* were to be set aside under an accounting category known as "eight sons" *(bage zi)*. Those funds were then remitted to Yang. Yang was eventually undone when he carelessly allowed the account books to fall into the hands of the provincial treasurer. Several lower officials were implicated in the scheme, but most were cleared of complicity.[39] Although Yang was a provincial governor and not a river official, the case highlights the opportunities available to the enterprising and unscrupulous bureaucrat. Had Yang shown more composure and caution, he likely would have escaped detection; it is impossible to say how many officials more clever than Yang managed to squeeze funds out of the river conservancy without being caught.

It is likely that some of the defenders of the hydraulic status quo were motivated by self-interest and greed, but others had good reasons to resist abandoning the Grand Canal and the Yellow River control system. Provincial elites in Henan, northern Jiangsu, Shandong, and Zhili probably feared that abandoning the canal would mean the weakening of the state's commitment to Yellow River control. As we will see in chapter 3, local elites showed their strong support of capable river officials by backing them in their river conservancy efforts and by honoring them in local temples after their deaths. That elite support reflects an awareness of the consequences that counties along the river would face should the state abandon them to deal with the river on their own. Aware of the link between canal transport and funding for river control, few members of the northern elite suggested abandoning the canal. The Qing withdrawal from Yellow River conservancy in the years after the canal was abandoned in the 1850s shows that that concern was justified.

Although a direct cause-and-effect relationship is impossible to prove, heightened imperial attention to river conservancy in the Daoguang reign seems to have contributed to a reduction in the frequency of flooding. There were no floods along the Yellow River during the first two decades of Daoguang's reign and only one major flood in the entire Yellow River hydraulic system—the Gaoyan Dike break of 1824. Those statistics stand in stark contrast to the disastrous hydraulic record of the Jiaqing reign.[40] In spite of the success of Daoguang river officials, much of the emperor's attention continued to be focused on elimination or prevention of corruption and limiting expenditure. Caught between Daoguang's strident demands for fiscal restraint and the growing strain evident in the river control system, river officials sought to do more with less. It is against that background that Li Yumei's attempts at technical innovation in Henan and Linqing's effort at administrative revitalization in Jiangsu must be seen.

3

Confucian Engineers

WHEN THE DAOGUANG EMPEROR took the throne in 1821, he was determined that the incessant flooding of the Yellow River during Jianqing's reign would not be repeated while he was on the throne. Daoguang set out to restore the system, first allowing hydraulic officials of proven ability to take charge but later raising a new generation of technical experts to top posts. For the hydraulic officials placed in charge of Yellow River control in the 1830s, Li Yumei in Henan and Linqing in Jiangsu, the dilemmas of late imperial river control represented a promising but risky career opportunity. Technical mastery gave them access to a high rank that they could retain only if they succeeded in keeping the unpredictable Yellow River in check. The two men came to their positions by very different career paths, but both were innovators and both believed they could intervene to correct weaknesses in the hydraulic system. They differed in the solutions they proposed. Li Yumei fought for technical innovations that he believed would strengthen river construction and reduce costs. Linqing sought to improve administrative efficiency by raising the level of technical proficiency among hydraulic officials. The careers of the two also came to very different conclusions. Li died in office and later was acclaimed a god; Linqing saw his career cut short when a dike collapsed and spent his last years in reluctant retirement. What distinguished both was a missionary zeal for the task and an unflagging optimism about what could be achieved in the daunting struggle against the river.

The second decade of Daoguang's reign was a portentous one. The opium trade was flourishing, and alarm over domestic opium addiction was growing. Foreign traders and missionaries were increasingly restive at being confined to the southern port of Guangzhou. In 1830 Lin Zexu

(1785–1850) completed the three years of mourning for the death of his father and returned to continue a parabolic bureaucratic career that culminated in China's humiliating defeat in the Opium War (1839–1842). In 1836 a hopeful young Hakka scholar named Hong Xiuquan (1813–1864), while in Guangzhou for the *xiucai* exam, was given a set of Christian religious tracts that planted the seeds of the Taiping Rebellion (1850–1864). Yet few had any inkling of the cataclysms that awaited, and imperial attention remained firmly fixed on well-established priorities. One of the most important among those was the Grand Canal–Yellow River hydraulic system.

Li Yumei and Engineering Innovation in Henan

On the seventeenth day of the second month of the twentieth year of the Daoguang reign (March 20, 1840), governor-general of the Henan Conservancy Li Yumei was inspecting the Yellow River's southern dike near Hujia village when he became ill after eating a large lunch. His condition worsened in the afternoon and he died that same evening, at age sixty-two. Traditional biographies of Chinese notables often border on hagiography, but it is evident from the honors and popular approbation heaped posthumously upon him that Li Yumei's long career in Henan and Shandong earned him a reputation for competence and integrity.[1]

Li Yumei apprenticed for the post of governor-general of the Henan conservancy by serving in a wide range of bureaucratic positions in the Yellow River region. A *bagong* of 1801, his first appointment was as magistrate of Wuzhi County in Henan. The remainder of his career was spent almost entirely along the river in Henan and Shandong, a fact that gave Li familiarity with both the gentry and the geography of the region. Along the way he showed a predilection for hydraulic engineering, but he also demonstrated competence in fiscal administration, labor management, and disaster relief.[2]

Beginning with the magistracy at Wuzhi, many of Li Yumei's postings involved performing jobs related to river conservancy, from gathering matériel to construction of river works. Li had also seen firsthand the consequences of hydraulic failure. In 1815 he was charged with assessing the silt damage to fields caused by the Suizhou flood of 1813. Li requested tax relief for the region, organized the rebuilding of the Suizhou city wall, and arranged work relief *(yigong daizhen)* for displaced peasants. After the Maying breach of 1819, Li was again assigned to assess disaster conditions. He later worked as an assistant in the central office in charge of the repairs *(dagong zongju)*. In 1821 Yan Lang, governor-general of the Henan conservancy, praised Li for his river defense work.[3]

Li's experience with hydraulic engineering did not make him a "river official" by any means. He had considerable provincial-level experience outside the river conservancy, most importantly in posts that involved provincial finance. After serving as a judge in Kaifeng from 1825 to 1829, Li served briefly as Kai-Gui circuit intendant but was quickly transferred to a judgeship in Hubei, where he served for two years. In 1832 he returned to Kaifeng to serve as provincial treasurer, a post he retained until he became head of the Henan conservancy in 1835.

An incident that took place during Li's tenure as provincial treasurer gives a hint of the stubborn confidence in his own understanding of hydraulic matters that would later be the hallmark of his career at the head of the Henan conservancy. While visiting the river crossing at Heigang, Li heard of a threatened breach near Kaifeng (Xiangfu County). Hitching a ride with a load of repair material, Li arrived at the scene to discover that rising waters had created a branch stream that had forked off the main stream and was slicing through the silted bed in the direction of the southern dike. Ignoring the objections of the river officials on the scene, Li took over and ordered construction of a willow dam to lessen the impact of the current. Although some at the work site ignored him and even mocked him behind his back, he persevered and constructed a dike 120 meters long. Eventually the waters subsided and the branch stream was blocked off. Li was praised for taking timely action.[4]

It should come as no surprise that Li, confident to the point of arrogance, stirred up controversy during his tenure as head of the Henan conservancy. The roots of the controversy lay in a crisis that confronted Li when he arrived to take up his post in the fall of 1835. The northern dike in Yuanwu and Yangwu commanderies *(xun)* in western Henan was being threatened by erosion gullies *(goucao)* created by errant streams similar to the one Li had dealt with while serving as provincial treasurer. When the river rose, those could cause the main current to shift and strike a part of the main dike that was unprotected by revetments or deflection dikes.[5]

Not only were branching streams carving their way toward the dike; there was also a desperate shortage of construction material with which to mount a defense. Since there were no defensive revetments along that section of the river, no stores of stalks or stone were available to build deflection dikes or block off the marauding streams. Incessant rains had also reduced the land outside the dikes to a muddy plain and made the other important construction material—dry earth—unavailable.[6]

Li's solution was to substitute red brick, widely available along the river as a building material, for stalks and stone. Aware that brick was much lighter than stone and might be washed away in the heavy current, Li bound bricks into bundles weighing thirty to forty kilograms (jin) and threw them into the water to serve as a base for a deflection dike. As the base of the dike rose above the surface of the water, workers piled wet earth on top. Using that method, Li gradually extended the dike until it forced the branch current back toward the main course of the river. Earth dikes were then constructed to support the brick dike.[7]

Thus the immediate danger was averted, but problems continued to develop downstream. In the spring of 1836, Henan governor Guilang joined Li Yumei on an inspection of the problem area. To their alarm they discovered one branch stream over 370 meters in width flowing only 180 meters from the main dike. The accepted course of action in such situations was to construct new stalk revetments to defend the exposed section of dike. Instead, Li proposed the construction of a brick deflection dike that would push the wayward current away from the main dikes. Guilang concurred, and within the month construction was complete and the situation under control. The Daoguang emperor praised Li not only for the speed with which he responded to the crisis but also for finding the money to buy brick without resorting to requests for extraordinary funding.[8] Had Li been content to settle for that small success, no controversy would have arisen.

He soon made it clear, however, that he believed not only that brick should be part of every river official's tool kit but that brick might provide a way out of the fiscal dilemma of river control. Li lost no time in incorporating brick as a construction material. He ordered the lower officials in the river conservancy to purchase brick at the government-regulated price and began constructing brick deflection dikes along both banks of the Yellow River in Henan, building a total of seventy-five dikes between

September 1836 and April 1837. He also requested that brick—like rock, stalks, and earth—be included among the materials budgeted for purchase.[9]

Li Yumei's enthusiasm for brick stemmed partly from the expense and difficulty river officials faced in supplying construction material to the growing number of defensive sites up and down the dikes in Henan. The commitment to stalk revetments as the mainstay of defensive construction had many drawbacks; stalks were increasingly expensive and subject to price manipulation by merchants and producers, had a limited storage life, and rotted and required replacement every few years. Rock, widely used in the Jiangsu conservancy, posed problems of cost and supply in Henan. The only sources of rock suitable for river work were hundreds of kilometers away. Land transport was prohibitively expensive, and shipment by water was possible only for a few weeks in the spring and summer before the arrival of seasonal floods.[10] Li believed brick would solve many of those problems. Brick could replace the more expensive rock, and brick rubble facings could replace some stalk revetments on both the main dike and deflection dikes. On June 15, 1837, Li Yumei presented a memorial outlining his approach. In it he proposed including brick as a standard material for river construction.

Li's memorial also contained a companion proposal meant to counter the unpleasant realities of the market. In 1835, as Li's building programs increased the demand for bricks, suppliers had begun to hoard their stocks and refused to sell at the government-established price. Li had been forced to ask permission to pay the higher market price for bricks. That experience led Li to request that one hundred thousand taels be set aside to operate state-run kilns to supply bricks to the river conservancy on a one-year trial basis. Those bricks would be made to government specifications. The emperor, perhaps swayed by Li Yumei's recent success in western Henan, approved those measures without hesitation.[11]

Opposition was quick in coming. On July 1 the censor of the Shandong provincial circuit, Li Chun, presented a memorial that attacked both the use of brick in river conservancy and the establishment of state-run kilns. Li Chun opened his assault with the formalistic *ketou* to precedent, arguing that in river defense officials should emulate the successful methods of the ancients, not create new methods that might endanger the welfare of the people and the fiscal health of the nation. Citing such river conservancy classics as Jin Fu's *Zhi he fang lue* and Fu Zehong's

1725 compilation the *Xing shui jin jian,* he insisted that although river conservancy practices sometimes changed to meet new problems, the fundamental reliance on dikes to control the river and stalk revetments to protect the dikes had remained unaltered since ancient times.[12]

Brick threatened to unbalance that established system and introduce a plethora of technical, social, and economic risks. In terms of technical utility, brick was clearly inferior to stalks and stone, Li Chun noted. But its real danger was in the confusion it would bring to river engineering, where it would complicate river repairs and endanger existing structures. As proof that brick dikes were unreliable and difficult to repair, Li Chun detailed the failure of many of Li Yumei's brick dikes in the Henan conservancy during high-water periods in the fall of 1836 and the spring of 1837.[13] Also, because brick dikes were "scattered and formless," they reduced the holding capacity of the basin between the dikes.[14]

There were social dangers as well. Kilns built on sites close to the dikes would occupy scarce agricultural land. Furthermore, in times of hardship the poor would be tempted to dismantle their houses to sell the bricks, leaving themselves homeless.[15]

Striking a sarcastic note, Li Chun challenged the economy of brick, pointing out that bricks were made from the same soil used to build earth dikes. What savings could be expected, Li Chun asked, from using what was little more than expensive dirt.[16]

Li Chun dismissed Li Yumei's claim of a hydraulic crisis and call for drastic action, arguing: "Since your majesty ascended the throne, each place your kindness has touched has enjoyed the blessings of peace. River officials need do no more than receive the imperial plan and carry it out with respectful obedience. Only by assiduously reducing unnecessary expenditures and severely punishing bad officials will they be able to avoid wasting [the state's] wealth and [simultaneously] strengthen the construction of defensive revetments."[17]

Li Chun requested a delay in implementing Li Yumei's proposal while an official was sent to the Henan conservancy to question the various circuit intendants and subprefects concerning the feasibility of using brick.

It is clear that the detailed information on dike works in Henan and the well-informed, telling arguments against the brick proposal found in Li Chun's memorial were not based on the author's personal observation. Stationed, like most censors, in Beijing, Li Chun was dependent for his

information on provincial officials.[18] He was only tangentially familiar
with the day-to-day workings of the river conservancy. Moreover, the territory under his purview did not actually encompass the area where most
of the brick dikes had been built. The information in the memorial could
only have come from those with direct knowledge of the river conservancy. Whether it was provided by individuals with sincere concerns
about the innovations or those with an eye to their vested interests, the
arguments against Li Yumei's proposals were meant to provoke an imperial intervention and investigation that would give opponents an opportunity to convey their opposition directly to an imperial representative.

It is almost certain that some of the material in Li Chun's memorial
came from Li Yumei's own subordinates. From the outset, many lower
river officials had decried the new methods of construction as innovation
(chuangxing) and were reluctant to adopt them. That opposition reflected a distrust of new methods that was partly blind conservatism but
also stemmed from a legitimate concern about untried techniques. Exper-
imentation that led to hydraulic failure exposed river officials to severe
penalties, both monetary and administrative. Li's own management style,
which was marked not only by a confidence that brooked no opposition
but also by close personal supervision of construction, probably did little
to endear him to his subordinates.[19]

Li Yumei's biography *(nianpu)* traces the resistance to several sources,
including public works (river) officials *(gongyuan)*, wild rumors, and
spurious objections raised by ill-informed outsiders and by stalk merchants and stone workers who saw Li's proposal as a threat to their
vested interests.[20]

Whatever the composition of the coalition against Li Yumei, it quickly
found a powerful ally in the person of his former mentor and superior in
the river conservancy, Yan Lang. During the investigation, Yan sent a
letter to investigators recalling his earlier association with Li Yumei.
Although he had praised Li and recommended him for promotion in
1820, Yan complained that in 1830, while he was serving as head of the
Henan conservancy and Li Yumei was Kai-Gui circuit intendant, Li had
carried out unauthorized experiments using brick in river conservancy
construction. Yan discouraged these experiments, arguing that brick was
too insubstantial *(songfu,* "loose and buoyant") to be of value. Li Yumei
ignored Yan's opinion and behind his back spent several hundred taels

on brick construction. He halted his experiments only when he was sent to a new post. That obstinate streak, Yan argued, was again evident in Li's recent tenure as head of the Henan conservancy: "Since taking up the post of [governor-general] of the Henan conservancy, Li Yumei has been zealous in his management of affairs. I have heard that what experienced engineers consider impossible, Li Yumei considers a secret revealed only to him. To say that because bricks exist in the world, they must be used on river dikes, this is something never touched upon in Pan Jixun's or Jin Fu's river control [writings]."[21]

Yan Lang's objections differ only slightly from those marshaled by Li Chun, but Yan's condemnation carried the authority of his long and successful career in river conservancy. He could cite instances from his own experience in which brick proved ill suited to river conservancy construction.[22] He also disputed Li Yumei's claim that the use of brick would result in greater economy.[23] Damning with faint praise, Yan said brick could be of some small value when used in locations where the current was weak, but in other applications it would either crack and fall apart or be swept away.[24]

Yan's dismissal of brick as a construction material might have been decisive were it not for his own tarnished reputation. Yan had been removed as head of the Henan conservancy in 1831 when shortages of matériel were uncovered, and he was later demoted when it was discovered that he had taken bribes from rock suppliers while in office.[25]

On June 28 the Daoguang emperor acceded to Li Chun's request and ordered Jingzheng, a president of the Board of Works, to travel to the Henan conservancy and investigate the issue. Li Chun and a department director of the Board of Works named Dechuanshibo were to accompany him. On July 4, after receiving personal instructions from the emperor, Jingzheng visited the Grand Council chambers, where copies of Li Yumei's and Li Chun's original memorials were given to him. On July 6 the trio departed for Henan.[26]

The appointment of Jingzheng is telling and had an immediate impact on the nature and focus of the investigation. Although Jingzheng had some limited experience in inspecting hydraulic construction, his primary skill was as a seasoned investigator in cases involving, among other things, fiscal malfeasance.[27] That reflects the fact that although the main objections to Li Yumei's proposals had been technical, with some mention of fiscal and social matters, the emperor's concerns were different. He was less intent on assessing technical questions than issues of administrative control. Jingzheng's task was to look into the potential for corruption, waste, and administrative breakdown. Technical issues would be secondary.

Before his departure from Beijing, Jingzheng sent a dispatch ordering Li Yumei to respond to Li Chun's charges and to hand over all relevant documents. In his long and reasoned response, Li Yumei makes his case both for the nature of the crisis in Yellow River conservancy in Henan and for the need for brick. The problems in Henan, Li argued, were due to both natural and man-made factors. In Jiangsu the river passed through a narrow gap in the surrounding hills. That created a bottleneck that caused seasonal floodwaters to back up in Henan, collecting in the huge retention basin between the dikes. Stalk revetments had been introduced to protect the dikes from erosion by those floodwaters. "Originally," Li wrote, "stalk revetments in front of the dikes had no difficulty fending off the angry waters. When [use of this method] began, the water [in front of the dikes] was only a few inches deep, so only a few sections of revetments were necessary." But the river's rising bed and the accelerating pace of meander migration created new problems: "Later, as the current in the bends grew more agitated and deeper, they [the meanders] moved many meters, so that places where there was no construction became defensive sites. As the river rose, revetments had to be added [higher up]; as it dropped, they had to be extended to reach it. As the revetments increased in length, maintenance and defense became more difficult."[28]

Stalk revetments had to be monitored constantly. "The greatest danger in river work," Li Yumei wrote, "comes about when stalk revetments, after three or four years, rot and are swept away. This is called 'shedding' (tuotai)." Defensive sites had to be closely watched and regularly repaired. Even old sites no longer near the meander could not be ignored entirely. Should the river again alter its course and return to the same location, a situation arose known as "old works reborn" (jiu gong xin sheng). Unless the rotten revetments were replaced quickly, the current would tear them away and begin cutting through the dike.[29] The expense of maintaining, building, guarding, and restoring that system of stalk revetments was immense. The problem was that "recently, yearly funding and supplies have reached a point beyond which they cannot be increased, but work on stalk revetments can in no way be reduced."[30] That was the river official's dilemma.

In fact, Li Yumei's pessimistic assessment was an understatement. The construction of new defensive sites along the river in Henan was not simply increasing; it was accelerating. In the late Qianlong reign, only some 500 sites existed west of the Jiangsu border. By the first year of the Daoguang reign (1821) there were 931 stalk sections (duan) in place in Henan. In the subsequent seventeen years, that figure had more than doubled to 2,016 sections. Of those, river troops were actively maintaining 1,002, while the remainder had become separated from the current by meander migration.[31]

With stalk revetment construction and maintenance costs on the rise and funding limited, river officials had no choice but to draw funds from another part of their budget. For most, Li Yumei claimed, the choice had been to shift funds budgeted for earthwork to the purchase of stalks for maintenance. Funds designated for earthworks were used primarily to strengthen the main dikes. The shift in spending in favor of stalk revetments resulted in a dangerous weakening of the dikes. Officials met the requirements for dike height by adding small auxiliary dikes (zinian) to the top of the main dike. The result was higher but thinner and weaker dikes.[32]

Li Yumei believed the use of brick would reduce expenditures required for the maintenance and repair of stalk revetments and free up the money to restore the main dikes in Henan to their proper proportions. He claimed that the use of brick revetments had already resulted in substantial savings in maintenance and repair costs.[33]

Li also hoped to draw parallels between his effort to introduce the use of brick in Henan conservancy and the successful introduction of rock in the Jiangsu conservancy by Li Shixu at the beginning of the Daoguang reign. To that end, Li Yumei tried to enlist the support of Linqing in Jiangsu. Li Yumei sent Linqing engineering drawings and requested permission for two subordinates to examine the techniques of rock construction in the Jiangsu conservancy and compare them with brick construction in Henan.[34]

Linqing was cooperative but cautious. He examined the engineering drawings sent by Li Yumei and confirmed that the construction methods using the two materials were similar. But he also warned that since brick was much lighter than rock, it might not serve the same uses. Since the Jiangsu conservancy had no brick dikes, Linqing said, he could not confirm that the two were of equal effectiveness.[35]

Li Yumei chose to interpret the results from Jiangsu favorably, claiming that his two deputies had come to the conclusion that the use of rock in the Jiangsu conservancy and brick in the Henan conservancy were identical *(hao wu er zhi)*. Li did hedge his claim of equivalence slightly— perhaps in deference to Linqing's judgment—commenting that "although brick and rock are slightly different in nature, both can be successfully used."[36]

Before departing for Henan, Jingzheng had also asked other officials in the Henan conservancy to comment on the merits and drawbacks of stone, stalk revetments, and brick. The two reports that survive confirm that lower officials opposed the widespread use of brick. However, both authors admitted grudgingly that brick had some value as a construction material.[37]

While Li Yumei was compiling his report, the imperial investigators were on their way south. Thirteen days after departing Beijing they arrived at Lanyi Temple on the north bank of the Yellow River in Henan.[38] When the Beijing contingent arrived, Li Yumei was at the temple directing flood defense. After some discussion, it was decided that Li Yumei, Li Chun, and Jingzheng would travel together on a tour of the dikes. For two weeks, the trio traveled to construction sites and brick kilns up and down both banks of the river in Henan.[39] After returning to Lanyi, they discussed their findings and the reports from lower officials, most of which were negative.[40]

Jingzheng's own conclusions mirrored those of the lower officials. He prefaced his findings with the comment that "the consequences of river work are great. If Li Yumei has been self-opinionated in his approach to brick construction, then as Censor Li Chun has memorialized, the inaccurate areas should be sorted out."[41] Jingzheng claimed that even Li Yumei had agreed that brick was not a promising emergency repair material.[42]

Although he criticized the efficacy of brick construction, Jingzheng's main concern was the feasibility of the proposed state-operated kilns. He doubted that local kilns could supply the required quality and quantity of brick and questioned the cost of the project, but his fundamental criticism reflected imperial concern with administrative discipline. "Stalks and stones are natural products *(you tianchan)*," Jingzheng wrote, "while making bricks requires human labor. If there are abuses, it is from this that they will arise."[43] Instead of easing the burden on hydraulic officials, the kilns would require constant oversight:

> Although the river governor is conscientious in managing affairs, he is still only the main rope in the net. The subprefectural personnel are therefore important in defense work. How can he [the governor-general] divide his body to oversee manufacture [at all the different kilns]? In my humble opinion, Li Yumei should be ordered to add rock and damp earth to those brick dikes already built to stabilize them. Unused bricks should be stored along the riverbank to be used in case of shortages of stalks or rock. Your slave lacks both talent and experience and is unfamiliar with river defense, but firing bricks and establishing kilns is fraught with difficulties. I fear that we stand to lose more than we gain.[44]

Li Yumei's proposal to use government-operated kilns to produce bricks for river conservancy construction was rejected, and his plan to make wider use of brick in river conservancy appeared to die with it. Li was forced to settle for increased shipments of rock.[45] Li's case had been weakened by the failure of many of the brick dikes he had built and by his own admission that brick was a poor material to use in an emergency. Linqing's cautious comment also underscores the fact that even those willing to consider brick were not certain of its value.

The ultimate question of the utility of brick aside, what is striking in that episode is that the broader hydraulic concerns raised by Li Yumei do not appear anywhere in Jingzheng's reports to the emperor. Li's warnings about the use of auxiliary dikes to meet regulatory specifications, about the burden that the expanded use of stalk revetments placed on river officials, about the changes taking place in the Henan conservancy—all drop from view at the imperial level of consideration. They appear only in Li Yumei's lateral reports to Jingzheng. Like other imperial investigators, Jingzheng was chosen as an outside agent "whose primary loyalty was to the emperor alone" and who was thus immune to the parochial concerns of local and regional officials.[46] Operating as the emperor's eyes and ears, Jingzheng conveyed to the emperor only those matters that fit within the horizon formed by his own circumscribed understanding of technical issues and the emperor's twin fixations: economy and corruption. Although the rationale for sending an outsider was a broader understanding of the issues at stake, the result was a myopia that rendered the larger hydraulic issues invisible and a crisis inevitable.

For almost two years after the rejection of his proposal, Li continued to press for greater attention to the main dikes and more funding for earthwork. His requests were largely rebuffed. Attempts to gain flexibility in funding earthwork were also frustrated. But Li Yumei did not abandon his goal of finding a place for brick in river engineering. In the spring of 1839, Li once more asked permission to use brick, this time wisely avoiding such controversial proposals as state-run kilns. He attributed his renewed enthusiasm to the success of brick dikes in surviving the unusually high floods of 1838. He was now confident that brick dikes could withstand the river's worst.[47]

Li's request might have been ignored again had he not found a new source of support in the gentry of Henan. Gentry leaders had petitioned Li to continue to build with brick and particularly to build brick-and-earth deflection dikes. Li made no secret of the reason for gentry support; the use of brick deflection dikes had forced the current away from the dike and uncovered ten thousand *qing* of agricultural land (one *qing* was one hundred *mou*, or about fifteen acres) for reclamation *(huifu)*. It is unclear how that land would be taxed or who would be able to claim it, but Li put the best possible spin on the matter by arguing that "these people are motivated by a desire to protect their fields and homes." He added, "That which benefits the people is seldom without benefit to the state." Just in case the emperor needed further evidence of the benefits that would accrue to the state, Li Yumei calculated that in the four years of his tenure as head of the Henan conservancy, he had saved 1.5 million taels by replacing stalk revetments with brick and broken rock.[48]

By shifting the emphasis of his argument toward saving money that could then be directed to the maintenance of the main dikes, Li framed his innovation as a minor but important technical adjustment necessary to preserve the system's original design. Dropping the kilns and requesting only funds to purchase five thousand *fang* of brick each for Huangbian and Xia'nan Subprefectures allowed Li Yumei to avoid the appearance, if not the fact, of innovation.[49]

Li also raised the specter of corruption among those who clung to the status quo. "Loose talk and wild stories" were inevitable when a new method was proposed, he wrote. In this case, stalk merchants who hoarded supplies to drive up prices and "floating guests and private secretaries" *(youke muyou)* who used their positions as overseers on work projects to indulge in peculation schemes fanned idle chatter into full-fledged rumors so as to prevent changes that would threaten their vested interests.[50]

Those arguments clearly struck a chord with the emperor, and Li's second proposal failed to provoke the opposition of his initial attempt. On May 2, 1839, an imperial edict approved Li Yumei's request. It cautioned Li that he should keep a close eye on the quality of bricks purchased by his subordinates and that he should not use the bricks in a way that reduced the holding capacity of the retention basin *(yu shui zheng di)*. The edict also specifically prohibited any river official from establishing kilns and ordered the officials to buy all bricks from private sources.[51]

The initial money for brick came from the funds for broken rock. But in the winter of 1839, Li received permission to use 40 percent of the emergency repair funds formerly set aside for purchasing stalks to buy brick. That made a total of 55,500 taels available for the purchase of brick. Li also received more money to buy broken rock.[52]

Those decisions gave Li Yumei most of what he had been seeking. Although setting up state-operated kilns was out, the new regulations established brick as a standard material for construction in the river conservancy. Brick became, along with stalks and broken rock, one of the three standard materials for hydraulic engineering along the Yellow River.[53] Brick continued to be used into the twentieth century, although mechanized transport eventually made the shipment of rock less prohibitively expensive.

The larger issues raised by Li in his advocacy of brick remained unaddressed. Underlying Li's campaign had always been his deeper concern about the condition of the main dikes. His belief that replacing stalks with brick would save money that could be spent to repair the main dikes proved unfounded. The restoration of the main dikes was never undertaken. Shortly before his death, Li Yumei had singled out two areas of particular concern where erosion was cutting away the riverbank near unprotected sections of the main dike. One of those sites was at Zhangjiawan in the lower Xiangfu commandery. Li planned defensive construction, but he died before he could take action. The plans were abandoned after his death.[54] Li's warnings proved prophetic in the fall of 1841 when high waters overflowed at Zhangjiawan and opened a massive break in the southern dike.

Li Yumei's death aroused many public expressions of mourning and appreciation. If the biography of Li in the Hunyuan County gazetteer can be believed, the common people of Henan came out to pay their respects as Li's casket passed through the countryside on its return to Shanxi. Within months of his death, the gentry in several Shandong and Henan towns asked permission to establish temples to venerate Li. The Daoguang emperor added his voice to the chorus, praising Li's conscientious work style and noting that there had been no floods during Li's five-year tenure as head of the Henan conservancy.[55]

In life Li had been confident to the point of obstinacy in his belief that his innovations were valuable and necessary. After his death, support for his views came from other quarters. In an imperial interview before taking up his new post as governor of Henan, Niu Jian praised Li Yumei's knowledge of river engineering. Lin Zexu, who composed Li Yumei's funerary inscription, also eulogized Li's river conservancy work.[56]

Li Yumei's success in keeping the river within its dikes, his involvement in flood and famine relief, and his long and close association with the gentry and other people of the region contributed to his popular reputation as a benevolent and diligent official. The gentry in particular had good reason to recognize in him a champion of their interests. Li's prescient warning of the danger at Zhangjiawan further enhanced his reputation, lending an aura of the supernatural to his legend. Within a decade he was apotheosized in shrines along the river dedicated to Great King Li. In 1877 the former river official was recognized by the state as Li Dawang (Great King Li), a Yellow River god.[57]

Linqing and Technical Mastery in Jiangsu, 1833–1842

Aside from their shared interest in the practical aspects of engineering and a hands-on managerial style, Linqing and Li Yumei had little in common. Born in 1791, Linqing came from a family that claimed descent from an emperor of the Jin dynasty (1115–1234). A member of the bordered yellow banner of the Imperial Household Department (neiwufu), he

Fig. 1   Linqing, age 52.

won his *jinshi* degree in 1809 and was appointed to the post of secretary of the Grand Secretariat. In 1823, after working in several capital offices including secretary of the Board of War and compiler in the Hanlin Academy, he was appointed to the post of prefect of Huizhou County in Anhui Province. His first river conservancy post was as Kai-Gui-Chen-Xu circuit intendant from 1825 to 1829. After several intervening appointments, he was made head of the Jiangsu conservancy in 1833.[58]

Linqing began his bureaucratic career at a time in the Jiaqing reign characterized as "a new era of literati ascendancy within the provincial managerial establishment." Among the men who rose to power at that time were those associated with the ideas of "statecraft," an approach to government that emphasized, among other things, the importance of practical managerial skills. Linqing served under the Jiaqing reformer Xun Yuting (1753–1834) and the noted statecraft official Tao Zhu (1779–1839), both of whom singled him out for praise.[59]

An important component of the statecraft managerial approach was the development of specialized technical skills in areas such as hydraulic engineering. When Linqing was appointed to his first river conservancy post—as Kai-Gui-Chen-Xu circuit intendant—in 1825, the emperor noted with concern that Linqing had not previously served as a river official and asked Xun and Tao for reassurances that Linqing could do the job. Before they could respond, Henan governor Cheng Zulo submitted a memorial recalling that Linqing had distinguished himself in dealing with hydraulic duties while serving as Cheng's subordinate.[60] That apparently assuaged the emperor's doubts.

Linqing set about the task of learning all he could concerning hydraulic engineering, both from books and from experts in the field: "I lined up several books on river control and wrote out summaries of them. I then toured the work sites, inquiring and comparing. . . . Whenever I encountered civil or military officials experienced in river affairs, I questioned them with great humility and care. . . . Thus in intense heat and chilly rain I toured the river banks, and each time I encountered a tool, I looked into it in detail and thoroughly verified its use." Eventually, while head of the Jiangsu conservancy, Linqing put together a reference library of classic writings on river engineering.[61] In 1837, after four years as head of the Jiangsu conservancy, he published his first work on the subject, *An Illustrated Guide to River Engineering Tools,* which was a collection of drawings and descriptions of the tools, boats, and materials used in river maintenance and repair.

Although Linqing was not the first Confucian literatus to take river engineering seriously, his approach was uniquely detailed and thorough. Illustrations accompanied his written explanations because, he noted, "when description is inadequate, illustrations are useful for clarity . . . where a glance [at a drawing] is insufficient, a description is useful."[62] Armed with Linqing's manual, an official could quickly become familiar with the tools and techniques of construction and maintenance and consequently better able to manage subordinates.

In translating the engineering skills developed by military river officials, river troops, civilian engineering experts, and river workers into a format that was accessible to Confucian-educated bureaucrats, Linqing was responding to the demands of the job. His goal was greater managerial competence and defensive vigilance by river officials of every rank. Even the governor-general, whose job included such tasks as personally inspecting construction sites and overseeing the storage of matériel, had to be knowledgeable about the nuts and bolts of river work. But notwithstanding the emphasis Linqing put on technical mastery, he never regarded it as the mainstay of successful river defense; that would always reside in the use of capable people.[63]

Linqing's writings on the technical aspects of river conservancy were not limited to the arcana of tools. After a survey of the Jiangsu conservancy in 1833, Linqing became aware of the long-term changes that had been taking place at the confluence of the Huai and Yellow Rivers at Qingkou. He came to the realization "that the present conditions were not like those of the past, and past practices would not work under present conditions." The result of his investigations was a history of the engineering changes at Qingkou. Titled *An Illustrated Description of the Yellow River–Grand Canal Confluence Past and Present* [Huang-Yun liang he gu-jin tushuo], the book traces developments from the late Ming to his own day.[64] The drawings accompanying the text are powerful evidence of the remarkably baroque engineering solutions that emerged out of the attempt to coordinate the sometimes conflicting demands of grain transport and river control.

Linqing believed that kind of careful study could be used by river officials to educate themselves about the engineering problems they faced. In the introduction he recalled that when he took up his post in 1833, the use of a "transfer reservoir" *(guan tang)* to move grain boats across the Yellow River was a recent innovation and one he was uncertain about. He carried out a survey of the documents, made a careful investigation of the hydrography of the area, and had detailed conversations with knowledgeable secretaries concerning the methods of using the reservoir. As a result, he noted with pride, in the intervening seven years the gates between the transfer reservoir and the river had been opened and closed forty-eight times without incident.[65]

Linqing's success in managing the hydraulic complexities of the Grand

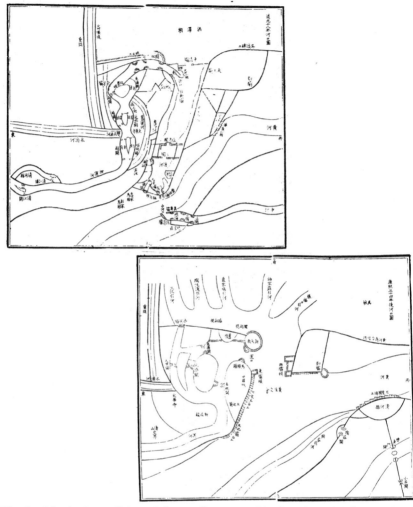

Fig. 2   Linqing's rendition of the confluence at Qingkou in 1796 *(bottom)* and 1838 *(top)*.

Canal and the Yellow River earned him a remarkable degree of imperial trust. In 1838, responding to reports of problems in the Jiangsu conservancy treasury, Daoguang did not send in outside auditors but ordered Linqing to investigate his own treasury. Linqing's investigation found no shortage of cash in the river treasury but noted that several types of expenditure had been misreported for years. He recommended that those officials who had held the posts of governor-general and treasurer of the Jiangsu conservancy between 1828 and 1836 (including Linqing himself) be required to make up any shortfall that might eventually be uncovered.[66] Refusing to exempt himself from responsibility for the fiscal problems of his treasury may have allowed Linqing to confirm the emperor's faith in him, but it was also a mark of his administrative style. During the nine years he headed the Jiangsu conservancy, Linqing practiced what he preached, personally inspecting construction sites and storage facilities, relying on his detailed knowledge of river engineering practices to oversee the work of his subordinates. In those years he managed to successfully facilitate tribute grain transport while preventing floods. For seven consecutive years, from 1835 to 1841, he was singled out for imperial praise for his work.[67]

But even Linqing's exemplary performance at the head of the Jiangsu conservancy could not quiet critics of the river conservancy nor ease the emperor's fear of corruption, a fear fueled by periodic censorial indictments. Linqing was forced to respond to one such attack in 1836. The charges were made by Senior Metropolitan Censor Cheng Guanxuan, who presented a memorial in which he described the county yamens along the river in Jiangsu as overrun by hangers-on and "degenerate secretaries [who] go to and fro seeking their pleasures." Those carpetbaggers lived in rented quarters (emphasizing their transience), threw their weight around, and indulged in various depravities. "Even to hiring prostitutes and smoking opium, there is nothing they will not do," Cheng charged. Meanwhile, the "county magistrates are so stupid or weak, none dares restrain [the miscreants]."[68]

In particular, Cheng criticized "outside workers" *(waigong)*, men hired for their specialized knowledge of the arcana of river conservancy accounting. In some areas, he charged, those accountants had either established control of yearly material purchases or worked in collusion with corrupt subprefects to concoct bogus receipts. In years that required little in the way of repair and new construction, they took advantage of the reduced demand for stalks by buying less than reported and splitting the difference with the subprefects. The result was that the stores of stalks allegedly on hand were nonexistent. When disaster struck, supplies were unavailable. Even if they did not share in the graft, Cheng noted, the subprefects who were dependent upon those men were inclined to cover up and support inaccurate claims of material purchases and work inspections. Thanks to that protection, a knowledgeable accountant could cling to his job for years and do long-term damage to river works.[69]

Cheng proposed to solve those problems by introducing new regulations. Referring to the investigation of finances in the Jiangsu conservancy undertaken by Linqing the year before, Cheng argued that "dismissing officials after the fact is not as good as anticipating problems." He suggested establishing new regulations to control material purchase more tightly. Cheng also thought officials who allowed hangers-on and secretaries to carry out river work and pilfer funds should be investigated and punished.[70]

Cheng was typical of the censors forwarding such charges to the emperor in this period. Like Li Chun, who had opposed Li Yumei's brick proposal, Cheng had never himself held a position in the hydraulic bureaucracy; he had been a capital official since receiving his *jinshi* degree in 1826.[71] As noted in chapter 2, the issue of supernumeraries in the hydraulic bureaucracy was an old one. Linqing was not cowed, however, and responded by putting the role of supernumeraries in the context of beleaguered hydraulic officials' need for technical and administrative help.

The Mencian division of labor that placed the rulers above the ruled was mirrored in the river conservancy in the use of civil officials to manage (and in particular, to manage finances), whereas military officials and river troops were expected to do the actual engineering work. As a result the technical skills of river engineering were primarily the provenance of military officials.

That dichotomy was well established, but the two realms were often linked by the needs of the state.[72] To do their jobs effectively, civil officials in the river conservancy needed at the least to know enough about river engineering to oversee the purchase of matériel and to check on the dimensions and pace of construction. If they were fortunate and if the military officials in their jurisdiction were conscientious, they would likely be able to report success after each flood season. But as defensive sites and subordinates proliferated, civil officials found themselves forced to delve deeper into technical matters in order to prevent corruption and check incompetence.

The problem of technical competence was already recognized in the Yongzheng reign, when a program was developed that required the Censorate, the Office of Imperial Instruction, the Six Boards, and the Grand Secretariat each to send one candidate to be trained in the Jiangsu conservancy or the Henan conservancy. Those who showed talent could be retained as river officials. The assignments were made, the emperor noted, "with an eye to emphasizing river duties." Perhaps fearing that metropolitan bureaus would try to palm off their least promising officials on the river conservancy, Yongzheng insisted that officials of quality be chosen for that training.[73] During a two-year stint in the governor-general's office, trainees were to take part in project planning, matériel inspection, and dredging and construction works, but they were prohibited from handling funds or critical construction jobs. At the end of training, they were examined *(kaoyu)* by the governor-general, then sent to the board for an imperial interview *(yinjian)*. Those who proved inept at river work were sent back to their original posts.[74]

Over the course of the following century, compliance was intermittent and lackadaisical. The bureaus charged with providing candidates were undoubtedly reluctant to send their most promising men, and few capital officials were eager for such training, since many considered the river conservancy a dangerous posting. With capital officials reluctant to serve in the river conservancy, the search for technical competence turned inward: almost half the men who rose to the top posts were themselves products of the hydraulic bureaucracy.[75]

The search for technical competence extended to the lower ranks of the civil bureaucracy. There was a long-standing requirement that all candidates for posts in the hydraulic bureaucracy or for civil posts that involved river conservancy duties be evaluated on their performance during a one-year period of probation. That rule also applied to magistrates of the counties along the river whose duties entailed collection of matériel and management of some hydraulic repairs. A candidate who was unable to master the required hydraulic engineering skills within the three annual flood periods *(san xun)* would not be confirmed in the post.[76]

Low-level officials were also sent to the river conservancy both to meet emergency demands for administrators and as a training measure. In Jiaqing 11 (1806) the Jiangsu governor and two high river officials complained that there were not enough skilled *(anlian)* administrators to handle the construction projects under way on the Gaoyan Dike and along the Grand Canal. They asked that officials dispatched on a temporary basis be retained in river conservancy posts in Jiangsu to help with needed work.[77]

More often, however, temporary service in the hydraulic bureaucracy was justified as valuable training. A program begun in the eighteenth century proposed sending several low-ranking, expectant officials (houbu) to serve a probationary (shiyong) year in the river conservancy. Besides providing temporary employment, that training period would broaden river engineering skills within the bureaucracy and supplement the lower ranks of the river conservancy. The most capable might garner a regular river conservancy post. Such proposals did not always have the intended impact. As the number of successful exam graduates exceeded available jobs in the bureaucracy, capital officials began to dispatch growing numbers to serve as probationary officials in river and canal posts. Although limits were set on the number permitted in each division of the hydraulic bureaucracy, the regulations allowed for flexibility in times of increased demand. The result was that by 1822 the Henan conservancy had over four times the number of probationary officials permitted by the regulations, and the governor-general was asking that no more be sent.[78]

In spite of those problems, Linqing continued to advocate temporary service in the hydraulic bureaucracy. In 1837 he requested that twelve candidates from the lower ninth and unclassed ranks be sent to work in the hydraulic bureaucracy in order "to afford them practical experience" in river work.[79]

In the spring of 1837, Linqing responded to Cheng Guanxuan's charges. The memorial was coauthored by Linqing's former superior Tao Zhu, then serving as governor-general of Liangjiang. The authors did not deny that problems existed, but they urged a managerial rather than a regulatory response. Defending the role played by deputies hired during the busy flood season, they argued that the subprefectures were so extensive that it was impossible for the official in charge to personally oversee every project under his control. Deputies acted as the river official's "fingers and arms" (zhibi), managing certain tasks he could not oversee in person. Although the officials had originally hired only men they knew personally, as the need for deputies rose, the difficulty of verifying each man's "purity" (jie) had allowed some corrupt men to gain positions of trust, but those were exceptions. Linqing and Tao rejected outright the charge that "guests and secretaries," including accountants, were undermining the river work. Such men had little to do with actual river work; their job was largely secretarial, and the reports of their interference in material purchases and depraved and bullying behavior were unfounded.[80]

It was not the supernumeraries who were to blame, wrote Linqing and Tao Zhu, but the regular bureaucrats. They found that both civil and river officials were reluctant to deal personally with the purchase of materials, particularly stalks. Not only were subprefectural officials often deputed to take charge of stalk purchases, but even close friends and family servants were sometimes given that responsibility. Officials sometimes compounded the problem by procrastination, waiting to purchase necessary supplies until prices rose above the government-approved rate.

That laxness at the top of the administrative hierarchy allowed a range of abuses at the bottom. Persons purchasing stalks manipulated prices and falsified quantities or weights, or they colluded with agents and middlemen who bribed them to accept substandard materials (usually stalks). The stalk merchants had their own schemes, which included demanding payment before delivery and then absconding with the funds, hoarding supplies to force prices up, and packing stalks with mud in the center of the bundle to make them heavier.[81]

The solution to those problems was not, as Cheng had suggested, more regulations, but greater diligence in enforcing the existing regulations.[82] To illustrate the approach he wanted to emphasize, Linqing cited an incident that had taken place the year before. During an inspection of stalks stored in Pibei Subprefecture, Linqing discovered that the stacks in the storage shed were below regulation height, indicating a shortage of stalks. He ordered the stores brought up to standard but did not punish the subprefect responsible. Instead, he made a point of remembering him so that he could keep an eye on him in the future.

That undramatic example of managerial attentiveness seems a pale defense against Cheng's dramatic charges and the abuses that Linqing and Tao Zhu admitted were occurring in the river conservancy, but it reflects the belief that administrative dynamism could effectively counter corruption and laxness at the lower levels of the bureaucracy. If that spirit of diligence could be aroused in all river officials, the administration would be reformed. Tao Zhu and Linqing boasted, "We, your ministers, have for years applied ourselves wholeheartedly to investigating these evil practices, seemingly with some effect."[83] Both men acknowledged that abuses were inevitable, but they believed that diligent management was a better safeguard against corruption than a plethora of empty regulations. Linqing and Tao Zhu appear to have won out over the rule-makers, as no new regulations emerged from that case.

When we consider that administrative approach in conjunction with Linqing's publications on river tools and hydraulic engineering, it is clear that he saw those works as an aid to more direct administration by senior officials. The joint memorial underscores that connection, remarking that river officials had some reason to feel confused about inventories, since many of the items stockpiled for river conservancy work had obscure names and it was difficult to verify their meaning. If hydraulic officials were going to practice that kind of direct supervision, they had to know what they were looking at.

The administrative solution proposed by Linqing and Tao Zhu reveals a contradiction at the heart of late imperial Yellow River control; the imperial state remained committed to a task that was outgrowing its available technical, fiscal, and administrative resources. One solution, the creation of a specialist administration of trained river engineers who had the power to set priorities on a systemwide, long-term basis, was both fiscally impossible and profoundly out of sync with the existing bureaucratic ethos and the mandates of imperial rule. The only practicable answer was to squeeze greater efficiency out of the existing system. Both Linqing and Li Yumei saw technology as an important part of the solution to that problem. For Li Yumei, the answer lay in making use of alternative materials that promised to reduce construction and maintenance costs. For Linqing, the answer lay in giving river officials the technical skill to supervise more effectively. Neither man came close to advancing anything that might be considered a comprehensive solution to the crisis of river conservancy; both responded with the ameliorative approach common to late imperial officials.

Linqing's diligent managerial style proved successful in keeping the river under control for almost a decade, but his extraordinary nine-year tenure ended in 1842 when the Yellow River broke through its northern dike at Taoyuan (see chapter 5). Stripped of all his ranks and titles, Linqing left the river conservancy in disgrace. He was called back in 1843 and placed in charge of collection of materials for the repair of the Zhongmou flood. His success in that task won him reinstatement to the fourth rank (he had been second rank before the flood), and he was later appointed emissary to Urga in Mongolia. Illness forced him to reject the post and to retire.

For all their technical knowledge, the Confucian engineers of the late Qing did not see themselves as different from their fellow bureaucrats. They were poets, judges, literati. When they analyzed the failings of late imperial bureaucracy, they did so in terms of Confucian tradition. Thus, when Linqing, whose career was founded on a love and understanding of technology, mused on the pitfalls of bureaucratic life, he made no mention of expertise. Forced by illness to retire, Linqing retreated to his beloved "Half-*mou* Garden," the small estate he owned in the suburbs of Beijing. Surrounded by family, he brooded over the reversals of his career. The penultimate entry in Linqing's autobiography, "Reading at Night in the Tuisi [withdrawing to contemplate] Studio," reveals a man chafing at physical confinement and trying to come to terms with the setbacks and disillusionment of his last years:

> I often sat there reading the *Gazetteer of Famous Mountains* so as to travel vicariously, or the *Classic of the Waterways* as a means of touring far and wide.
>
> One night in the eighth month, I had trimmed the lamps and opened a scroll when suddenly I heard a sound from the southwest that startled me. I rose and looked out on the eastern breezeway. A bright, first-quarter moon was shining and the Jade Rope star still glittered low in the sky. Turning to look, I saw a young [servant] boy, head bowed, sleeping.

Linqing likened the conditions to those described by Ou-yang Xiu (1007–1072) in "The Sound of Autumn."[84] The scene brought to mind the vagaries of bureaucratic fortune:

> I stood still for a time as the night gradually deepened. Then I closed the window, raised the wick of the lamp and continued reading.
>
> I searched out Zhu Geliang's "Admonishing a Son" and read the sentence: "without tranquility, there is no way to clarify one's purpose; without peace, there is no way to extend one's knowledge." I recalled that when I was young and my ambition was still unbounded, seeing that all so-called

worldly affairs and accomplishments were achieved through action, I questioned the place of these two words "tranquility" and "peace."

Now, after more than thirty years of official service, I finally understand.

In the bitter twilight of his own career, Linqing perhaps had some premonition of the turbulent futures awaiting his sons.[85] For the fiery young man who would change the world, Linqing warned, bureaucratic life holds a harsh lesson:

> The man of great talent and broad ambition insists on changing things for the sake of change. [But] he no sooner takes action than obstructions appear everywhere; before many years [his plans] all come to a halt. But before they [come to a] stop, no small amount of harm and chaos result. Truly [such a man] does not understand the meaning of the line in the "Great Learning": "only after tranquility can there come peace."

The bureaucratic world Linqing describes is full of "diseases":

> Those enamored of sensual pleasures fall prey to the sickness of instability; those enamored of profit fall ill with greed; those enamored of achievement become sick with self-promotion; those enamored of fame catch the disease of pretentiousness. They [all] lack tranquility [and thus] cannot clarify their purpose.

Surrounded by the unstable, greedy, self-promoting, and pretentious, Linqing had nonetheless received great honors and risen to high office. In the end he had fallen back. His specialist skills could not protect him from the river's unpredictability. Hearing the boy he had been watching stretch, Linqing was shaken from his reverie. "The fourth watch had already sounded. I rolled the scrolls and left the Tuisi studio, returning to the bedroom."

In the fall of 1846, Linqing died.

4

The Xiangfu Flood and the Siege of Kaifeng, 1841–1842

THE FALL OF 1841 marked a calamitous turn in Daoguang's reign. Both the emperor and the British home government rejected the treaty agreement reached in January to end what turned out to be only the first phase of the Opium War (1839–1842). In August Sir Henry Pottinger arrived in China to prosecute the second phase of Britain's campaign. While the British were preparing attacks on targets around the Yangzi River delta, the Henan provincial capital, Kaifeng, was subjected to a siege of a different sort. During the night of August 2, 1841, the Yellow River broke through its southern dike, trapping tens of thousands of refugees in Kaifeng and inundating vast areas of the densely populated Huaibei region. Just as the Opium War marked a turning point in China's diplomatic fortunes, the flood of 1841 was the first act in a drama that would culminate in a fundamental shift in Qing hydraulic policy.

The break occurred at the Xiangfu lower commandery, one of the sites Li Yumei had warned about. On the evening of August 2 Li's replacement as head of the Henan conservancy, Wenchong, began receiving reports that the Yellow River was threatening to overflow the main dike along its south bank, due north of Kaifeng.[1] The summer flood stage had been unusually high, and incessant rains in the tributary valleys of the loess plateau and in Henan continued to swell the river. On the second, the water level reached the top of the dike near the thirty-first watcher station *(bao)* and began to pour over. From Zhangjiawan—as the area near the thirty-first station was known locally—the waters flowed directly south, covering the 7.5 kilometers (15 *li*) to Kaifeng during the night. Morning found alarmed residents trying to keep out the rising waters by hastily barring the gates of the city.[2]

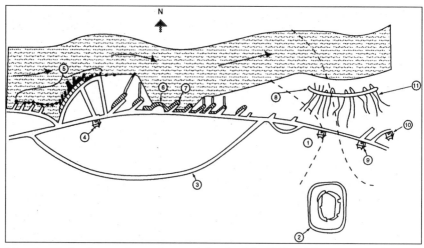

Map 3   Defensive works on the south bank of the Yellow River near Kaifeng, ca. 1840: *1*, thirty-first watcher station; *2*, earth dike surrounding Kaifeng; *3*, "moon dike" *(yueti)*; *4*, "Great King" *(dawang)* temple; *5*, deflection dikes: solid areas are rock or brick; striped areas are stalk revetments; *6*, "fish scale" *(yulin)* revetment; *7*, stalk revetments on earth dikes; *8*, earth levee *(tuge)*; *9*, marker dividing subprefectures; *10*, temple; *11*, erosion gullies caused by high water. The dotted lines show the site of the 1841 breach.

Quick action to repair the break might have averted disaster. Seventy meters of dike had collapsed, but the main current remained several thousand meters away from the site of the break. Unfortunately, the most experienced river official in the area, Kai-Gui-Chen-Xu circuit intendant Bu Jitong, was downstream trying to deal with other weak spots on the dikes. The officials on the scene at the thirty-first station were the subprefect Gao Buyue and a sublieutenant in command of river troops. Neither man was experienced in such extensive emergency repairs. Officers and river troops had also been dispatched to help with problems in two downstream subprefectures, reducing the workforce available in the Kaifeng area. If Gao and his subordinates expected Governor-General Wenchong, directing efforts from his headquarters on the southern dike at Heigang, to take charge of emergency repairs, they were disappointed. Wenchong had been chosen for the post because of his reputation for moral rectitude, not his knowledge of river engineering. A year on the job had given him some familiarity with the basics of river conservancy but had done little to prepare him to respond to an emergency of that magnitude.[3]

Even an experienced official would have found the situation difficult. Repairs were hindered by a shortage of matériel and by transport problems. The thirty-first station was not part of a major defensive site, so limited supplies of construction materials were on hand.[4] Stores of stalks, rock, and brick had already been depleted by emergency repairs at defensive works up and down the river. Even if supplies had been available, the materials could not have been moved quickly because the incessant rains had turned the roads into mud. As the countryside flooded, transport became almost impossible.

The poor condition of the dikes also made repairs difficult. In the months leading up to the 1841 flood season, Gao Buyue had reported that the dikes along the river in the Kaifeng area were eroded and would have difficulty resisting high waters. He requested funding to carry out repairs, but his superior, Bu Jitong, rejected the request. Gao eventually convinced the Kaifeng prefect to supply some money for the project, but not enough to complete it, and work was eventually halted.[5]

Although the gap at Zhangjiawan was small, the erosive force of the flood widened it inexorably. The banks along the river within the main dikes were seven to ten meters above the surrounding plain, and the surface of the swollen river stood another three to four meters above those, so the water gained considerable momentum as it flowed over the dike. As the gap widened, the main current began to shift in the direction of the breach. On August 8 the river, which had dropped slightly in the preceding few days, rose again. Finally, on August 10 the main force of the river was drawn toward the widening breach, tearing a kilometer-wide hole in the main dike and inundating much of the Huaibei plain.[6] For the next two months the capital city of Kaifeng would remain an island battered by the force of the river. In the end it would take eight months and cost several million taels to seal the breach and return the river to its former course.

The Guard Dog

Wenchong would ultimately be blamed and punished for the flood, but the primary responsibility lay with the Daoguang emperor. Increasingly distrustful of his river officials, the emperor had selected Wenchong, known for his incorruptibility but completely unskilled in hydraulic engineering, as Li Yumei's replacement to head the Henan-Shandong administration. Wenchong's mandate was to aggressively police the hydraulic bureaucracy for corruption and waste. The choice of a guard dog over an engineer underscores Daoguang's conviction that technical mastery was less important than administrative and fiscal rigor. The result was disaster.

Wenchong's appointment culminated a shift in the nature of promotion in the river conservancy during the Daoguang reign. As noted in chapter 2, early in his reign the emperor had grilled Yan Lang about corruption in the hydraulic bureaucracy. It must have been discomforting to find later that the same official who assured the emperor that such practices were things of the past was himself taking bribes from rock suppliers. Over the decades of his reign, as censorial indictments repeatedly questioned the honesty of river and canal administrators, the emperor's distrust grew. Although investigations failed to turn up evidence of systematic abuses, cases like Yan Lang's must have had an impact on Daoguang's confidence in his hydraulic officials. After Yan Lang's dismissal and demotion in 1831, the emperor apparently became convinced that promoting officials directly to the top posts from within the hydraulic administration was an encouragement to corruption. Before 1831 internal promotion in the hydraulic bureaucracy had become a well-established practice. Beginning in 1765, when Li Hung (d. 1771) became the first official elevated from river intendant to the head of the Jiangsu conservancy, over half of the men named to the top posts in the Jiangsu and Henan conservancies were promoted directly from circuit intendancies or other river or canal posts.[7] Yan Lang's removal marked the end of that trend. The subsequent appointment of men like Lin Zexu, Wu Bangqing, Linqing, and Li Yumei—all were capable officials and some had prior service in the hydraulic bureaucracy, but none had served predominately in river or canal administration—was Daoguang's attempt to break what he saw as the chain of corruption by which senior officials covered up the crimes of their juniors.

Wenchong's appointment was a further and much more extreme step in that direction, one that ignored the relevance of technical skill and rejected the need for experience in river affairs. Wenchong was chosen precisely because he had no prior contact with the river conservancy and was therefore unsullied. The emperor made that clear in the edict of appointment: "I anticipate that you will remain untainted by the [corrupt] customs of the river works [bureaucracy]." Wenchong's special status is apparent from the fact that his appointment did not follow regular bureaucratic channels but was made personally by the emperor. That was intended to give the posting an extra measure of prestige so that, as Daoguang pointed out, Wenchong would have every possible means to accomplish his task.[8] Prestige was useful in imposing discipline on lax provincial and hydraulic officials but was irrelevant to the task of keeping the river within the dikes.

The appointment of a neophyte in river affairs to clean up corruption in the river conservancy was paradoxical in another way. The emperor expected Wenchong to end abuses and verify that all construction was carried out as reported.[9] That would have been a difficult assignment for an experienced river official, but for the inexperienced Wenchong it was an even greater challenge. Not only was Wenchong untutored in river engineering, but also the emperor's comment about the corrupting influence of river work makes it clear that those with technical proficiency were suspect. Linqing and others had promoted the notion that successful administration demanded close contact with experienced engineers of all ranks. By assuming that those officials were a corrupting influence to be avoided, Daoguang placed a barrier between them and Wenchong that discouraged the upward flow of technical information.

Wenchong was undaunted by his lack of familiarity with hydraulic engineering. Within two months of his appointment, he began exercising his mandate to end corruption. In late June, Wenchong submitted a memorial charging Kai-Gui circuit intendant Zhang Tan with inventing bogus projects that supposedly required urgent attention. In one case in which Zhang had received Li Yumei's approval to spend forty-eight thousand taels for construction, Wenchong could find no record of the work being done or any evidence that Li had inspected the finished work. He asked that as a punishment Zhang Tan be forced to retire *(leling xiuzhi)*. The emperor approved. But Zhang was not to escape so lightly. An edict issued the following month ordered Wenchong and Niu Jian to investigate all construction carried out by Zhang Tan. It noted that during his long tenure in office, Zhang had handled a great deal of money. To allow him to retire without thoroughly investigating his financial dealings, the edict argued, would be to treat lightly the nation's finances.[10]

Wenchong also kept a critical eye on the caliber of work being done by the lower officials under his command. In the winter of 1840, he asked that a magistrate be transferred to another assignment because of a demonstrated inability to master the fundamentals of river defense work. In a separate case, a second-class subprefect who had managed earthworks that proved to be substandard was ordered to return his badge of rank *(dingdai)* in lieu of other punishment. Wenchong could praise as well as blame, and several officials, including Zhang Tan's replacement, Bu Jitong, were selected for special mention after the 1840 flood season.[11]

As far as Yellow River defense works are concerned, Wenchong's record is sketchy. Expenditures for earthworks in Daoguang 20 (1840) totaled 223,046 taels, but those were works planned and approved during Li Yumei's tenure. Similarly, the 157,193 taels spent on rock construction in Daoguang 20 were requested by Li before his death.[12]

When it came time for Wenchong to make his own appropriations, he discovered that for several years running, Li Yumei had requested funding for earthworks almost a year ahead of time, then used those funds wherever he thought necessary. The money budgeted for earthworks to be carried out in 1841 had already been spent. Wenchong requested additional funds, but the emperor disapproved the request as totally without precedent. Only after Wenchong informed the emperor of Li Yumei's creative bookkeeping did he relent and approve an additional 100,000 taels for earthworks.[13]

In his requests for the coming year, Wenchong followed the regulations for matériel requisition established by Li Yumei. Of the approximately 110,000 taels set aside for purchase of supplies, 40 percent went for the purchase of brick and 60 percent for the purchase of rock.[14] Except for the problem with funding for earthwork, it appears that Wenchong did little to alter the cycle of repair and maintenance established by his predecessor.

Between the time of Li Yumei's death in the spring of 1840 and the flood in the late summer of 1841, Wenchong had little opportunity to establish his own engineering program, had such a thing existed. In the fall of 1841, with Kaifeng surrounded and large parts of Henan, Anhui, and Jiangsu Provinces under several feet of water, Wenchong found himself at the head of the list of those who had to take responsibility for the loss of life and the devastation of regional agriculture.

The Siege of Kaifeng

For the people of Kaifeng, the water that encircled the city on August 2 was a harbinger of many months of privation and struggle. Although the flood that struck that morning represented only a small part of the swollen river's total flow, it came with enough force and depth to drown many people. Officials rushed to close the five gates in the city wall—two on the east side and one each on the north, west, and south sides—but they did a haphazard job. The flood swept around the city, forced open the south gate, and poured through an overlooked water gate. In the absence of city officials, it was the local gentry—working around the clock for several days—who took charge of the efforts to close those gaps. By the time the leaks were sealed, Kaifeng was a huge lake where only a few areas of high ground stood above the water.[15] The first wave of the flood had passed, but it would be two months before the flood would recede and the siege of Kaifeng would be lifted.

For those trapped in the city, the situation was desperate. In the early days of the flood, while surface travel was still possible, thousands made their way from the countryside to take refuge within Kaifeng's walls. Even though the city was flooded, as the center of government Kaifeng still offered the best promise of protection from bandits and the most likely source of food and shelter for flood victims. Not everyone chose to stay. As refugees were pouring in, traveling merchants and other visitors, plus local residents who had relatives or lineage members outside the flood area, did their best to get out. Those with the means *(you lizhe)* bought boats at inflated prices and fled, sometimes with unfortunate results: witnesses told of boats that struck submerged trees and overturned, drowning the passengers. Officials also tried to reduce the population of children, the elderly, and women in the city by issuing a proclamation ordering them to leave, but few did. Two months later an official estimated that only about 10 to 20 percent of Kaifeng's residents had departed. Among the steadfast were those who faced serious logistical barriers to escape, including members of very large families and those wealthy residents who were reluctant to abandon their property and possessions. The

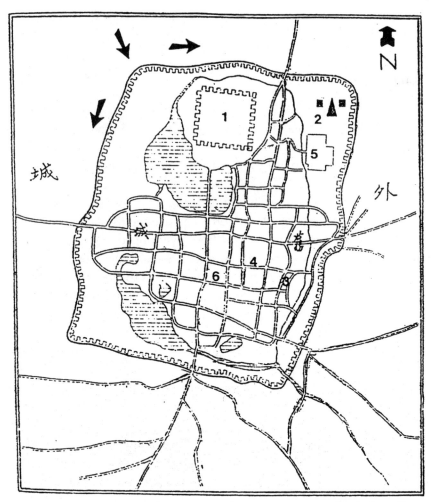

Fig. 3   Kaifeng in the 1841 flood: *1*, Manchu city; *2*, Iron Pagoda; *3*, Great Eastern Mosque; *4*, Prefectural Yamen; *5*, Examination Hall; *6*, Shan-Shaan-Gan Merchants Hall *(huiguan)*. Arrows indicate the route of the floodwaters. Courtesy *Journal of Urban History.*

weak stayed rather than to risk the trek to safety; the destitute hung on because the prospect of work on the inevitable repair project promised to keep them and their families alive through a bleak winter.[16]

   The situation in the city was growing increasingly chaotic by the time Henan governor Niu Jian returned from a trip through the province. On the nineteenth, Niu crossed to the city by boat and began directing relief measures. By that time many of Kaifeng's streets were under ten feet of water and most of its houses uninhabitable. Refugees huddled on the city walls. Markets were closed, and the price of food had skyrocketed. Relying on the Manchu garrison to support him, Niu Jian placed the city under martial law and ordered the markets to reopen.[17]

Local officials were noticeably absent. Some were out at the main dike assisting in efforts to close the widening gap in the dike. Two days after Niu Jian arrived in Kaifeng, expectant prefect Zou Minghe returned from the site of the break and reentered the city by climbing a rope from his boat to the top of the city wall. Niu Jian placed him in charge of relief efforts within the city. Zou set up soup kitchens on top of the city wall to feed the starving flood victims.[18] Boats were sent out to surrounding areas to save those who were stranded on bits of elevated ground, in the tops of tall buildings, or in trees. Apparently optimistic that the people working at the dike would be able to limit further widening of the breach, officials in the city began gathering boats and building rafts in hope of transporting surplus supplies from the main dike to help in shoring up the city wall.

On the twenty-fourth an expedition of troops and officials left Kaifeng bound for the dike. As they approached the site of the break, they observed a mountainous wave of turbid water spouting twenty feet into the air. One superstitious crewman cried out that it was a water demon. Another claimed that it was a *yecha,* a demon that had lived in the Yellow River since early times. Zou Minghe dismissed such alarming explanations: "That is no demon," he said. "The force of the water is stirring up the sand and throwing it into the air so that it resembles a thing." The truth was more depressing. "If the flood has been stemmed," Zou reasoned, "how can this be? It can only mean the main current has broken through." Unable to go on against the powerful current, the flotilla was forced to return to the city without supplies of either food or construction material.[19]

For those trying to staunch the flow through the gap, the failure of the dike had long been a foregone conclusion. Two days before Zou and his flotilla set out, Wenchong reported that the river was rising again and concluded that the measures taken up to that point would probably prove inadequate. The next day his fears were confirmed when the main current began to shift toward the break. On August 15 the emperor stripped Wenchong of his titles but ordered him to remain in his post.[20] Niu Jian and Bu Jitong were punished similarly.

The emperor did not content himself with punishments but also offered engineering advice. Perhaps aware that the inexperienced Wenchong was in a difficult position, Daoguang suggested such unlikely measures as digging a diversion canal in order to guide the river away from the breach. Even Wenchong understood that with the river in flood, digging a diversion canal was impossible. The best that could be done was to attempt to protect the ends of the dike on either side of the breach *(batou)* from further collapse.[21]

Once the river shifted course, the officials and troops downstream were no longer needed to guard the dikes, and Niu Jian requested that every available man be sent to Kaifeng. Since the situation upstream was still precarious, Wenchong sent part of the downstream force to help with emergency measures upstream and the remainder to help with the defense of Kaifeng. Among those sent to Kaifeng was Kai-Gui intendant Bu Jitong.[22]

In the coming month, both Kaifeng's physical geography and the dilapidated state of the city wall would complicate defense. During its heyday as capital of the Song dynasty (960–1126), Kaifeng had been the center of a network of riverine commerce, and the Yellow River had followed a course far to the north. The Mongol invasions in the twelfth century destroyed most of the hydraulic network of which the city was the hub, and the Yellow River's southward shift in the late thirteenth century destroyed the rest. Since that time Kaifeng had been exposed to repeated floods, and the land outside the city stood more than a meter above the level of the streets within the city wall.[23]

The first line of defense against the flood was a protective earth dike *(huchengti)* that encircled the city at some distance from the walls, with gaps at the four compass points to allow for the passage of traffic. Maps from different periods show that dike in varying degrees of repair, but there is no clear indication of its condition before the flood. One source claims that the protective barrier was built in 1320 after a particularly devastating flood. The purpose of the protective dike was not to keep out water but to deflect the current and prevent it from striking the city wall directly. The city wall had last been rebuilt in the Kangxi reign

(1662–1722) and had suffered considerable cracking and erosion in the intervening 150 years. It was known that the wall would be difficult to defend against a strong current.[24]

Once it became obvious that nothing could be done to close the gap in the main dike until the river dropped, Niu Jian sought permission to give priority in labor and matériel allocation to the defense of Kaifeng. His plan was to build deflection dikes to protect the city wall from the powerful current. He assigned each official under his command to a section of the city wall and named Kai-Gui circuit intendant Bu Jitong head of the Defense Coordination Office *(xuanfangju)*. The emperor praised those measures and approved Niu's requests.[25]

At the same time that he was battling the flood, Niu Jian had to deal with the refugee problem within the city. For many of the refugees, the situation was grim. Niu housed the weak and helpless at the Provincial Examination Hall. Located on relatively high ground in the northeast quadrant of the city, the hall was the largest government building in town. Niu also ordered food kitchens to be set up at five locations, but there were many mouths to feed and little food on hand. On the same day that Zou Minghe led his flotilla toward the main dikes, Niu Jian dispatched another group of boats to solicit food and materials from nearby counties and towns that had escaped the flood.[26]

When the river shifted through the break in the dikes, the powerful current tore through the last vestiges of the earth dike encircling the city and placed new pressure on the city wall. Areas that had once seemed secure began to crumble, and new leaks began to appear. Fortunately for those in the city, the current had split into three separate streams, none of which struck the city wall directly. One stream flowed south and passed the city on the west, a second branched toward the southeast and passed the city on the east, and a third flowed past the city's western gate. The third stream represented the greatest danger because it was rapidly eroding the land in front of the wall. Although the floodwaters slowed as they passed south of the city, erosion undercut the wall there and caused large sections to begin to collapse.[27]

In spite of those immediate problems, the defenders recognized that the northwest section of the city wall was the key to the city's survival. If that corner of the wall collapsed, the flood would pour through the city unobstructed, washing away its remaining buildings and burying its streets under meters of silt. With that danger in mind, the city's defenders took advantage of the divided current to shore up the north wall and construct brick deflection dikes to protect it. In the early stages the new dikes proved very effective, prompting Niu Jian to praise Li Yumei's use of brick for dikes.[28]

The situation changed radically on September 2 when the divided current united into a single stream flowing directly at the northwest corner of the city wall. Simultaneously, the river rose twice in the course of the day. The powerful current forced its way through the north and west gates and began to undercut several sections of the city wall. The brick deflection dikes Niu had praised days before were washed away with impunity by the unified current.[29]

The defenders now needed matériel to fill gaps and build revetments in front of the weak spots in the wall and to construct new deflection dikes at the base of the wall. Their supplies of stalks and brick were exhausted, and although Wenchong had been ordered to send supplies to Kaifeng, few had arrived.[30] In desperation, officials issued a public announcement proclaiming their willingness to buy anything that might be of use in preserving the wall. Blankets, straw mats, paving stones, timber, and bricks all went into the gaps in the wall. When those proved inadequate, the officials raided public buildings, including the Provincial Examination Hall and several dilapidated temples, for stones and bricks. Other buildings were torn down entirely. Finally, they bought people's houses and tore them down. When no more brick or stone could be found, the defenders dismantled the battlements on the city wall and sacrificed them to the flood.[31]

Although refugees crowded the city wall, the officials initially found motivated and reliable workers surprisingly hard to come by. As was the usual practice in river work, the few skilled river troops on the scene were augmented by gangs of hired laborers. Since the abandonment of the Ming system and the emergence of a cash economy in the river conservancy, most of the labor required for major projects was hired through labor brokers. Brokers had great influence, however, and even in a crisis such as this one, they could use the threat of work stoppages and slowdowns to demand more money from officials. Hired laborers also were reluctant to risk their lives to construct deflection dikes by wading in the swirling waters below the wall. Labor relations had been soured early on

when officials reneged on a promise to pay fifteen hundred taels to workers trying to salvage the city's protective earth dike. Understandably angry,
the workers walked out. Later, when desperately needed supplies finally
arrived at the city walls, the workers refused to unload the boats until
they were paid.[32]

The labor crisis reached a peak on September 5 and 6, when the wall
threatened to collapse at several points and the indifferent labor of the
hired gangs no longer sufficed. Muslim elders *(huimintou)* saved the day
by volunteering the labor of seven hundred to eight hundred followers.
At the same time, local merchants came forward to offer their own hired
workers to help in the city's defense. Niu Jian and his fellow officials were
delighted to find that, unlike those in the work gangs, these men turned out
to be enthusiastic and quick to follow orders.[33] In spite of the incessant
rain, these volunteers worked waist-deep in the turbid water, braving
exposure and drowning, in order to construct the revetments and deflection dikes needed to fend off the river.

For two weeks the city teetered on the brink of destruction. In mid-
September the situation looked hopeless. With workers and supplies
exhausted and no sign of outside help, Niu Jian turned to the only source
of help left: the supernatural. On September 5 Niu held worship services
to appeal for assistance from the various river gods *(heshen)* of the
region. His prayers were answered on the seventh when the main current
split into two streams and moved fifteen to twenty meters away from
the city wall. The following day a boatload of stalks arrived from the
main dike, and by nightfall all the gaps in the wall had been closed.[34] The
deflection dikes outside the northwest corner of the wall were strengthened against another shift in the current. Kaifeng had survived, but it
stood amid a vast lake stretching for miles in every direction. Inside the
wall, water covered everything to a depth of six feet, and a blanket of silt
lay beneath the water. The restoration of the city would take decades, but
the crisis was past. Attention now turned to the breach itself and to the
huge engineering project required to return the river to its elevated bed.

Wenchong's Demise

While Niu Jian and the people of Kaifeng struggled to save the city,
Wenchong remained on the dike at the Heigang ferry crossing, directing

defense measures and awaiting the arrival of the special envoys appointed by the emperor to take charge of the repair project. Although stripped of rank, Wenchong seemed to believe that he still had the emperor's trust. He did not try to soften his punishment with a show of abject humility or sincere self-criticism but responded to his predicament with a bold proposal. Rather than to immediately repair the break at Xiangfu, Wenchong offered, why not delay repairs for one or two years? That would avoid much of the expense of an emergency repair project, the tight schedule of which would drive up the cost of materials and labor. He cited a precedent for such a delay, noting that in the wake of the Suizhou flood of Jiaqing 18 (1813), repairs had been postponed for two years. In the interim, floodwaters had been channeled into Lake Hongze and then through the confluence at Qingkou. That flow had been used to scour the lower course of the river and to make it possible for the grain fleet to cross.[35]

Of course, the residents of the flooded countryside would have to be given relief aid, Wenchong wrote, but Kaifeng should be abandoned. With its crumbling wall, silt-laden streets, and damaged buildings, the city was a muddy, unlivable hole. The best thing to do would be evacuate the residents and establish the provincial capital at a more secure location.[36]

As if that were not radical enough, Wenchong went on to suggest that the whole system of dikes in Henan be abandoned. His argument was not without foundation. He pointed out that the use of dikes protected by stalk revetments had begun when the riverbed was level with the countryside. As the bed rose, the amount of dike work, the ferocity of floods, and the difficulty of repair had all increased. "Those in recent generations who theorized about river defense utilized the main dikes *(ti)* to protect the land, deflection dikes *(ba)* to protect the main dikes, stalk revetments to protect the deflection dikes, and brick and stone to protect the revetments," Wenchong wrote. The problem was that all those defensive works were encroaching on the river, reducing the holding capacity of the area between the dikes. "Narrowing the waters and using dikes for defense was the inferior policy of Jiarang [of the Han dynasty]." Instead, he argued for "the Great Yu's superior strategy" *(liangmo)* of "'Guiding the stream in accord with the current' *(shunliu shudao)*."[37]

Wang Ding and Huicheng arrived in Kaifeng on September 11 to begin their investigation of the flood and an assessment of Wenchong's proposals. Their initial response to delaying repairs was negative, and they dismissed comparisons with the 1813 flood at Suizhou, pointing out that the break had been much farther downstream, thus flooding much less agricultural land. Nor had it threatened a provincial capital.[38]

The implications of a delay were immense. Although detailed information on the damage done by the flood was not yet in, the turbid waters had swept southeast to cover most of the area between Xiangfu County and the western shore of Lake Hongze, flooding hundreds of thousands of *mou* (a *mou* is one-sixth of an acre) of agricultural land. That land would remain untilled and uninhabitable until the break was repaired. In addition, the silt-laden floodwaters pouring into Lake Hongze would eventually block the confluence at Qingkou, threatening the Gaoyan Dike, causing floods in the Huai-Yang region, and endangering the Grand Canal and the salt fields to the east. Delay would also require the building of new dikes to protect the fields along the course of the flood. Wang Ding and Huicheng concluded that delay would mean greater expense, more suffering, and the risk of long-term damage to the hydraulic structures of the region.[39]

Speculating that Wenchong's primary reason for wanting to delay the project was the fear that he would have to undertake the repairs himself, the memorialists faulted his judgment, competence, and motives. They pointed out that in the fifty days since the flood, the governor-general had yet to make a single visit to the ravaged city; nor had he made any effort to engage in face-to-face discussions with Niu Jian. Everywhere they went in the stricken region, Wang and Huicheng found deep bitterness toward Wenchong.[40]

The envoys also found Wenchong profoundly ignorant of both the consequences of the flood and the progress of the repair project. He was unable to answer simple questions about the status of construction or the purchase of materials, and he did not know the approximate length of the section of river below the breach that was now dry.[41] The emperor's special representative was revealed as incompetent, his attitude so Olympian that it left him completely ignorant of the basics of river engineering.

Convinced that Wenchong's proposal to delay repairs was nothing more than an artful scheme, Wang and Huicheng criticized the plan's indifference to the suffering of the people and the destruction of agriculture in an entire region. Wenchong was just trying to dodge the consequences of his failure.[42]

The emperor was enraged. The man he had handpicked to clean up

the river conservancy was now revealed as an incompetent and an embarrassment. Wenchong's punishment was harsh. He was sentenced to stand
each day on the riverbank wearing the cumbersome wooden collar known
as the cangue. After three months of that humiliating treatment, he was
exiled to Ili. Wang Ding was ordered to take over Wenchong's duties until
the new governor-general of the Henan conservancy, Zhu Xiang, could
take up his post.[43]

Wenchong was disgraced, but his proposal to abandon Kaifeng and
move the provincial government continued to get serious consideration.
There was precedent for such a move. The state's primary concern was
fiscal. The issue was whether it would be more expensive to rebuild the
dike that encircled the city and the city wall and create a drainage system
than it would be to move the provincial government to another city in
Henan, such as Loyang.[44]

Naturally, the people of Kaifeng universally opposed such a move.
Wang Ding and Huicheng found the idea of a move unpopular with everyone they interviewed. They pointed out that the gentry and the people of
Kaifeng had struggled hard to save the city. With the city safe and the
refugees returning, it made no sense to send the populace fleeing with all
they owned across the countryside. Not only would that make them easy
prey for thieves, but also bandit gangs would find a ready following among
the dispossessed. The result would be to turn the upright people who had
so courageously resisted the flood into bad elements who plundered and
looted.[45]

After considerable inquiry and public outcry, it was the willingness
of the people of the region to contribute to a subscription campaign for
the rebuilding of the city wall and the other needed repairs that resolved
the issue. As money began to pour in, the emperor consented to allow
Kaifeng to remain the provincial capital.[46]

The Scope of the Disaster

As hard as the Xiangfu flood had been on the people of urban Kaifeng,
it was in the countryside that the suffering was the greatest. The peasant
who managed to avoid drowning faced a long winter that threatened
starvation, exposure, and the predatory assaults of roaming bandit gangs.
The emperor's oft-repeated insistence to his officials that no peasant be

displaced *(shisuo)* reflects the imperial psyche's deep-seated fear of rootless peasants. That fear was not irrational. Linqing described the people of the flooded regions as "violent and fierce" *(piaohan)* and pointed to the Henan-Anhui border as an area where Nian bandits, smugglers, and sectarians had formerly united to cause trouble. An edict of October 19 cautioned Governor Duo Hunbu to guard against the possibility that flood victims fleeing areas bordering Cao County might join with Nian bandits who were active there.[47]

The main technique used to immobilize peasants and keep them out of trouble was to distribute relief in the villages. Before that could be done, officials needed to assess exactly which areas were flooded and how much damage had been done. Investigators were ordered to report the route of the flood, the number of villages affected, and the degree of agricultural loss that was likely to result.

The investigators also took careful note of the impact of the flood on the rivers and lakes in the region.[48] Their primary concern was with the situation of Lake Hongze. Silt from the flood flowed into the lake through its numerous tributaries, raising the lake bottom and threatening to block the confluence with the Yellow River at Qingkou. The lake was already high from the floodwaters; blockage at Qingkou would put further strain on the Gaoyan Dike. That situation was particularly dangerous in the winter, when storms from the northwest sent huge waves slamming into the dike. When it became clear that the breach at the thirty-first station was not going to be closed quickly, the officials at Xiangfu decided to dredge at Qingkou to drain lake waters into the Yellow River downstream of the flood. Feeder streams were also to be dredged for quicker drainage. Contingency plans called for the opening of several strategically located reduction dikes along the eastern side of Lake Hongze. Since they protected valuable agricultural land, opening those dikes was a last resort to prevent the failure of the whole of the Gaoyan Dike. The emperor ordered officials to devise a system to warn residents of the area if it became necessary to open the dikes. At the same time, officials were ordered to track and report the route of the floodwaters.[49]

Keeping tabs on the flood was no simple task. The disruption of transportation and communication systems made information-gathering difficult, and the threat of banditry discouraged officials from making investigative forays into the countryside. The emperor had little sympathy for those problems. When Anhui governor Cheng Rocai presented a memorial on the extent of the flooding in Anhui Province, his vague statistics on the depth of the water and the extent of crop damage brought a sharp rebuke from the emperor. Daoguang accused Cheng of handling affairs like a man in a dream and of being ignorant of important matters. The emperor ordered the board to recommend punishment.[50]

In contrast, the comprehensive reports forwarded by the conscientious Linqing were rich in detail. In spite of Linqing's many responsibilities involving the Yellow River in Jiangsu, the Gaoyan Dike, and the hydraulic system at Qingkou, he took great pains to put together a detailed report on flood conditions not only in Jiangsu, but in Anhui and Henan as well. According to Linqing's investigation, the two streams that flowed around Kaifeng reunited south of the city and then diverged again at a small village called Sucunkou. The smaller stream, carrying about 30 percent of the flow, followed the course of the Huaiji River and flowed southeast past Chenliu, Qi, Sui, and Zhe Counties, entered the Wo River south of Luyi, then moved into Anhui Province, eventually emptying into the Huai and other streams feeding into Lake Hongze. The larger stream flowed south past Tongxu, Taikang, and Luyi, finally joining the Qingshui River and turning east toward Lake Hongze. The low-lying lands between those two flows were covered by a vast sheet of water one to seven meters deep and ten to fifty kilometers wide. The water level had already dropped a meter since the peak of the flood. Linqing noted that the color of the water showed it to be heavily laden with silt. In areas where the current was slow, the silt was already beginning to settle out.[51]

The areas in Henan hardest hit *(zuizhong)* by the flood were Chenliu, Tongxu, Qi, Taikang, and Luyi Counties, whereas Suizhou and Zhecheng Counties suffered second-level *(cizhi)* flooding, and Huaining suffered only light *(jiaoqing)* damage.[52]

In Anhui Province, Taihe, Fengtai, and Wuhe suffered major damage. Guyang, Haozhou, Yingshang, Fengyang, Huaiyuan, Xiuzhou, Xuyi, and Lingbi all suffered second-level damage. Huoqiu, Mengcheng, and Shouzhou were only lightly hit.[53]

Those trapped by the flood on islands of high ground could not afford to wait for government officials to gather precise information on the flood. They needed immediate help. As funds began moving from the provincial treasuries toward the countryside, officials dispatched fleets of small boats to deliver emergency rations, mainly steamed buns made with rice flour *(mantou)*, to the trapped victims.

Initial relief funds were drawn from land tax moneys stored in the Henan, Anhui, and Jiangsu provincial treasuries. On October 11 the emperor authorized Niu Jian to use those funds to provide nine counties in Henan with one month's supply of rations *(kouliang)*, regardless of whether they had suffered primary *(jipin)* or secondary *(cipin)* impoverishment.[54]

The state's basic goals in disaster assessment were to guarantee social stability, to control the distribution of aid to affected areas, and to guard against wasting funds on regions unaffected by the flood. Provincial officials had a different agenda. Although they, too, were concerned to use relief as an aid to social stability in disaster-stricken regions, they sometimes exaggerated both the scope of the disaster zone and the degree of damage done to agriculture. Long after emergency needs had been met, provincial officials continued to submit detailed claims on the crop losses suffered by counties in each of the affected provinces. Those memorials were attempts to appropriate additional funds for further relief measures while simultaneously establishing claims of agricultural loss that would qualify those areas for tax reductions in the coming year.

The levels of disaster were assessed according to the percentage of crop loss, with anything below 50 to 60 percent dismissed as not constituting disaster *(bucheng zai)* and thus not requiring relief. The total number of villages affected in each county also contributed to the assessment.[55] Each area received one, two, three, or four months of rations, based on its assessment. Although it was in the interest of local officials to exaggerate losses, their reports were subject to oversight by higher bureaucrats and had to accord with earlier reports of flood damage. For the nine counties in Henan Province, losses were assessed as follows:

Degree of Crop Loss	Number of Villages/Units
100%	376
90%	4,152
80%	2,242
70%	1,199
60%	725
50%	275[56]

The surviving memorials describing conditions in Anhui provide fewer specifics, but parts of thirteen counties were considered to have suffered over 60 percent damage and thus qualified for tax remission and other forms of disaster relief. A map of the flood lists a total of twenty-four counties in Henan and Anhui and gives the degree of damage suffered by each. Nine counties suffered heavy *(zuizhong)* damage, ten suffered moderate *(cizhong)* damage, and four only light *(jiaoqing)* damage. Two of the areas shown suffered no flooding.[57]

Refugees and Work Relief

Relief was also used to control those who sought refuge on the dikes or in urban centers. The use of "work as relief" *(yigong daizhen)* was common in cases of natural disaster. It was particularly useful in cases of flooding. Unlike a famine, in which many of the victims were weakened by malnutrition, floods displaced large numbers of able-bodied men. By offering work relief, the state drew them into a circumscribed area where they could be controlled by limited military forces until their land drained and they could return to agriculture.[58]

Of equal importance was the supply of cheap labor afforded by work relief. Anxious to cut costs wherever possible, the officials in the region wanted to apply work relief as broadly as possible. They requested that it be the only form of relief offered flood victims in Jiangsu, Anhui, and Henan and suggested that refugees unable to find work at the site of the breach could be sent to work on related projects downriver.[59]

Work relief had drawbacks as well as advantages. If relief rations were available only at construction sites, there was the danger of mobs or starving people migrating to the dikes in search of food. That would encourage the very social dislocation the state hoped to avoid. It was that fear that led the emperor initially to reject work relief and order increased aid to be sent to the interior areas of the three flooded provinces. Eventually the emperor approved work relief only for the digging of the diversion canal at Xiangfu.[60]

Officials also had to plan for the demobilization of the workers after the project was completed. That could be as dangerous a situation as the initial flood of refugees to the work sites. For example, when the diversion canal was completed in the early months of 1842, demobilized workers began to steal wood and grasses for fuel, and fights over food broke out. The emperor ordered the officials to find out how many refugees *(youmin)* remained. Those with homes to return to or relatives to rely on were to be sent away on their own recognizance. He also insisted that they find some method to deal with the elderly and the weak and with unemployed youth who might drift into banditry when the repair project ended. Fortunately, such instances of conflict proved temporary, and most workers and their families returned to their native places without incident.[61]

Preparation for Repairs

While the details of the relief effort were being hammered out, officials began to plan repairs. Normally, that would have included the preparation of a detailed budget for each component of the project. The major tasks included closing the breach, digging a diversion canal, constructing deflection dikes, and dredging the downstream section of the river. Detailed estimates would have been prepared on the length and dimensions of all dikes and canals, and regulations would have been laid down to govern the costs, sourcing, and distribution of matériel. The triumvirate in charge of repairs in Henan was convinced that it was too late in the year to go about the planning of the project in that way. They pointed out that Kaifeng was still surrounded by the flood, the gap in the dikes was a kilometer wide and growing, and several hundred kilometers of riverbed needed to be dredged. The delay required for thorough investigation and planning would push the start of construction into the winter months and make the timely completion of repairs more difficult.[62]

Citing earlier repair projects as budgetary models, the trio compared the Maying project of Jiaqing 24 (1819), which had been carefully planned and budgeted, with the Lanyi project of Jiaqing 25 (1820), which had been undertaken without extensive planning. The former had cost 12 million taels, whereas the latter had cost only 4.7 million taels. Although the conditions at Xiangfu were worse than those at Lanyi and the project would likely be more expensive, Wang and his fellow officials agreed that the Lanyi project was the model to follow. They asked the emperor to approve an initial budget of 4.75 million taels so that they could begin work as soon as possible.[63]

The use of precedent-based budgeting was not new, and in an emergency it made sense as a way to get money moving toward the flood site with the least delay. Only minimal discussion of hydraulic circumstances was required. One risk of that approach was that if the project proved to be more complex than the cited precedent, funds for additional work might be hard to justify. When the officials later found it necessary to modify their initial estimates, they indulged at length in comparison of such variables as the length of the break, the quality of the soil, the availability of repair materials, and other factors that justified further funding. The Board of Revenue complained that the provincial treasuries all were extremely short of funds but did not object to the initial proposal. In giving his approval, the emperor warned, "On no account should the arbitrary wastefulness of earlier projects be emulated," and he reiterated that the lower officials must be forcefully reminded of the need for economy.[64]

Though approval came easily, the funds themselves were slow to arrive. By November 19 the moneys delivered to the river conservancy treasuries had been exhausted, and Wang was forced to ask the emperor to prod the governors and governors-general of Zhili, Liangjiang, Shandong, Gansu, Shanxi, and Shaanxi to send their share of the required funds as soon as possible.[65] Money problems continued to plague the project for another month.

Whether funds were on the way or not, the officials knew they could not delay the construction needed to stabilize the situation around the break. Prior to his ignominious departure, Wenchong had managed to stop the collapse of the dike (guotou) on the east side of the breach, but the current had continued to erode the dike on the west side. Every meter that collapsed was a meter that would have to be won back from the river at great expense in labor and materials. As the water level began to drop, Wang Ding made "wrapping" (bao) the western end of the broken dike his first order of business.[66]

With the start of construction, the purchase of materials became an issue. The officials once more appealed to precedent to set the price of construction materials and to estimate the cost of the dredging projects, but the unusual circumstances of the Xiangfu flood rendered earlier examples less useful. Most of the floods of the Jiaqing reign had occurred in years of good harvests and in the late fall when crops had been harvested and sorghum stalks were already on the market.[67] The break at

Xiangfu had come before the millet and sorghum crops reached maturity and had destroyed them when the fields were flooded. Other stalk-producing regions, including the most accessible counties upstream of Kaifeng and those across the river in Zhili Province, had seen crops reduced by drought in the summer and excessive rains in the fall. Since matériel was going to be scarce, Wang suggested that the best way to meet the demand would be to widen the source area. The officials at Xiangfu had already requested that the magistrates of forty nearby counties give an estimate of their available stalk supplies. They would then be required to supply an assigned quota of from one hundred to four hundred *duo* of stalks to the repair project.

Aware of Daoguang's sensitivity to cost, the officials set prices unrealistically low, well below what had been paid in earlier floods, when supplies had been more plentiful. The lowest price offered for stalks in the Jiaqing period was 180 taels per *duo,* with 190 to 200 taels being more common. For the Xiangfu project, the prices were to range between 160 and 185 taels per *duo,* depending on the distance sellers had to ship the stalks.[68] The low prices were bound to cause friction with stalk producers and suppliers.

Time limits on stalk shipments were also a source of tension. Worried that matériel shortages might delay construction, the officials required that those counties closest to Xiangfu deliver their stalks to the work site within eight days; those farthest away were to complete shipment within fifty days. The magistrates received the money to purchase their quota of stalks beforehand, and any magistrate who fell behind in his shipments risked punishment.[69]

Wang Ding and his fellow project managers knew that high demand for materials and low government prices might provoke hoarding by suppliers and strong-arm collection tactics by runners and troops. Although Wang suggested heavy punishment for any official or runner caught extorting materials, he clearly did not sympathize with the producers. "People of conscience" *(tianliang),* he wrote the emperor, "would not take advantage of this situation to raise prices." "Dishonest traders" *(jianfan)* should be dealt with harshly.[70] In other words, anyone who resisted selling at the government-ordained price was to be treated as a dishonest trader.

Not surprisingly, that approach did not eliminate any of the many

紅搶河引

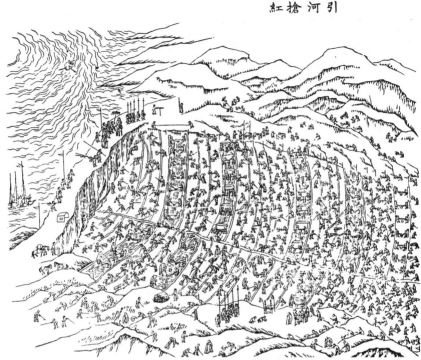

Fig. 4   Digging a diversion canal.

abuses associated with material collection. Although most magistrates supplied the matériel on schedule, the process was plagued by complaints of forced contributions, confiscation of private stocks of firewood, and the commandeering of carts. Early in the spring of 1842, a censor named Lu Xianji reported that in several counties along the Yellow River, mobs had gathered to protest to the local magistrates the extortionate methods used by runners and soldiers to collect materials.[71] But when the magistrates themselves were under heavy pressure to help in procuring matériel, they could do little to resolve those complaints.

Dike construction also required large quantities of hemp, wood palings, grasses, and other materials. Hemp in particular presented problems. It was grown locally only in Chengzhou, Runing, and Guide Counties, all of which had been flooded. Officials in those and other areas were ordered to investigate available supplies and prices in their locales.[72]

Perhaps the single most urgent task officials faced was digging the diversion canal, a huge, deep trough carved out of the riverbed to connect the top of the bend near the site of the breach to the lower course of the river. As its name implies, the diversion canal was designed to draw off the main current when the gap in the dike was being closed. At the crucial moment, the bank separating the canal from the river would be broken open and the river would rush in, diverting water away from the construction site and allowing officials to plug the breach. Delaying the canal's excavation would not only result in workers having to dig frozen ground in the middle of winter but could also threaten the timely completion of the entire project.

Excavation also had to be done downstream of the diversion canal, to remove obstructions and facilitate flow. When the Yellow River left its course *(duanliu)*, water in the downstream section of the river came to a standstill, and its entire silt burden settled to the bottom. In some areas that sedimentation could reshape the bed and cause the river to move in unpredictable ways. Those changes might not become apparent until the following flood season, when high waters pushed the current against unprotected portions of the dike. The result could be another flood. The task of digging out the sediment was complicated by the fact that the trapped water had to be drained before the bed could be dredged. In this case, officials eventually found it necessary to excavate almost the entire bed from the site of the breach to the confluence at Qingkou.

Once again, Wang Ding appealed to precedent to justify his cost estimates for the required dredging. Wang calculated that the site of the Xiangfu flood was forty kilometers farther west than the Yifeng flood and seventy-five kilometers farther west than the Suizhou flood, thus requiring proportionally more dredging. Wang also claimed that deeper deposits of silt in the riverbed than in earlier floods justified increased expenditure.[73]

As with material collection, dredging required organization, coordination, and expenditure on a vast scale. The payment for hauling earth, which was based on the rates for earlier repair projects, was set at five cash *(qian)* per *fang* of earth for dredging work and three cash per *fang* for dike work. (One thousand cash was theoretically equal to one ounce of silver.) Those are tiny sums, but with a total of 4 million *fang* of earth to be moved, even small-scale peculation—minor manipulations of the distance earth was carried or the amount dug—could add up to substantial costs. Wang and his associates proposed dividing the project into sections, with county magistrates responsible for those sections of the river that passed through their territory. Troops and river workers stationed along the river would oversee and carry out the actual digging. The lieutenants in charge of each district military post *(xun)* were ordered to give an accounting of all available able-bodied men under their command and would be responsible for recruiting additional workers. In a remarkable argument on the benefits of nepotism, Wang claimed that allowing military officers to handle the recruiting would be beneficial because anyone recruited by them for the project would be either a relative or a neighbor, and thus it was less likely that those in charge would abscond with the funds. On the technical side, Wang pointed out that those officers were familiar with the soil and river conditions in their areas and could both assure quality control and guard against misuse of funds.[74]

Anxious to avoid delays, Wang early on dispatched Bu Jitong to take charge of the digging of the diversion canal and related work. According to Bu's reports, the total length of the area that would require excavation was around 120 kilometers. That included the diversion canal proper, which was divided into 225 sections *(duan)*, each approximately 170 meters in length. Two additional sections of the riverbed, each roughly the same length as the canal, would require less extensive digging to ease the flow and guide the current away from unprotected sections of the dike.[75]

By far the most demanding engineering task faced by the officials at Xiangfu was the construction of the dikes that would cut off the flow through the breach. Trained personnel were needed to undertake such tasks as *zhuangsao* (driving palings to keep stalk revetments in place), *xiangkun* (binding the huge bales used to create a new dike), and *jinzhan* (placing the stalk sections in the water). Ironically, thanks to the success of river defense measures in the two decades since the Ma and Yi projects, the Henan conservancy lacked troops or officers skilled in repairing a dike break.[76] Wang Ding requested that troops and officers from the Jiangsu conservancy with the requisite skills be sent to the Xiangfu work site. Wang requested three or four officers of the rank of lieutenant colonel or major who were familiar with river work and four hundred "vigorous and experienced" *(jingzhuang ganlian)* troops. He also asked specifically for one man who was known to possess the needed engineering skills, a seventy-year-old retired lieutenant colonel named Zhang Zhao.

Linqing reported that Zhang was ill and could not travel to Xiangfu until his health improved.[77]

The fact that the officials felt the need to call the aging Zhang Zhao out of retirement underscores the paucity of men experienced in flood repair. It also points to the symbiotic nature of engineering management. Projects were run by civil officials appointed on a temporary basis, usually high-ranking bureaucrats, few of whom possessed more than limited engineering skills. To undertake repairs of this magnitude, they were dependent on the low-ranking but highly skilled engineers, often military officials, who had spent their careers in hydraulic work. In place of the feeble Zhang, Linqing dispatched another lieutenant colonel and six other civil and military officials.[78] Zhang eventually showed up at Xiangfu, but his health was so poor that he was soon forced to return to Jiangsu.

The competence of the administrative team at Xiangfu was bolstered unexpectedly when Lin Zexu arrived at the work site on October 10. Lin's fall from grace after the outbreak of hostilities with the English had culminated in his exile to Ili. As partial atonement for his failures, he was ordered to stop along the way and help with the dike repair. Lin's experience in dike repair was limited, but it was greater than that of the other civilian officials at Xiangfu. He had supervised repairs on the Yellow River in Jiangsu in 1825, had been financial commissioner of Henan in 1830, and in 1831–1832 had briefly headed the Henan conservancy. Perhaps most important, he was a skilled and knowledgeable manager who understood provincial finance. After his arrival, the burden of organization and management fell almost entirely upon him.[79]

Organizing and housing troops and workers were major tasks. In particular, housing and food had to be found for the specialists in the construction of stalk revetments, for the troops transferred from other areas to maintain security, and for the clerks and runners *(tingchai shuyi)*. To prevent incoming troops and workers from harassing or burdening the locals, the officials decided to house them along the banks of the river (inside the dikes), where common people were forbidden to build houses. They were also given pay subsidies to compensate them for the fact that grain prices were much higher than usual.[80]

Besides providing housing, the officials set up workshops to manufacture such items as candles, paper, and rope. Ferries were put in service to take workers and materials across the river or from site to site along the dike, and special boats and skilled boatmen were hired to help in the repair project. Collection centers for each type of raw material that went into the manufacture of stalk sections *(xiangsao)* functioned as supply depots during the project. Carts and horses or mules were found to move those materials, and each center was put under a manager, whose duties included purchasing materials and directing shipments to the dikes.[81]

Engineering the Repairs

The system of dike repair that had evolved over the centuries called for engineers to construct two halves of the repair dike out into the current, beginning simultaneously from bases along the main dike on either side of the breach. Sometimes using smaller parallel dikes as secondary support, the workers extended the main dikes out into the current one stalk section at a time *(jinzhan)*. Gradually, those dikes closed on the current to pinch off the flow through the breach. Obviously, as the two halves of the arc moved toward each other, the flow through the gap became swifter and progress more difficult.

At the same time that the repair dikes were being built, workers excavated a diversion canal at the top of the bend where the river turned toward the break. The entrance of that canal remained blocked until time for the closing of the breach *(helong)* drew near. Upstream of the repair dikes, engineers built a long deflection dike extending out from the main dike on the same side as the breach. That dike pushed the current away from the repair dikes and toward the mouth of the diversion canal.

When the two ends of the repair dikes drew close enough together that a single huge bundle of stalks and earth could be forced into the gap to seal it, the diversion canal was opened. The diversion of the river into the canal reduced flow through the breach and allowed engineers to place the massive stalk plug into the space between the two ends of the repair dike. Once the plug had been pounded down to the bottom, the river was back in its course. Then workers strengthened the repair dikes and the various support dikes and rebuilt the main dike. If the river had shifted its course, new deflection dikes and stalk revetments were constructed to keep the current at bay.

The complexity of the operation matched its scale, particularly in the engineering involved in placing sections *(jinzhan)*.[82] The process began at the point where the sandy bank ended and the dike entered the river. Up to that point, from the main dike to the water, the repair dike was mainly constructed of rammed earth. From that point on, stalk sections *(xiangsao)* replaced earth as a construction material. In a highly organized ballet, workers on the riverbanks carried bundles of stalks and wheelbarrows of dirt up each section of the earth dike and out to its terminus. An endless stream of workers stacked great piles of stalks on a special work platform at the end of the dike, with successive waves of workers climbing on top of the pile to flatten the stalks. When an amount sufficient for a layer was ready, workers used ropes laid beneath the stalks at the outset to bind them loosely, then rolled them off the end of the dike into the water. A boat moored across the head of the dike (the "binding the *xiang*" boat) would loosen a series of ropes leading over its side, under the layer of stalks, and to the shore. That would create a rope net into which the bundle of stalks would fall.

Simultaneously, boats stationed upstream and downstream of the working end of the dike maintained tension on ropes strung laterally through the bundle of stalks. Eventually the entire section was wrapped by a network of ropes. If the current was strong, long wooden stakes were driven into the bottom along the upstream side of the new section to help anchor the materials in place.

To counter the buoyancy of the stalks, earth was dumped on top of the bundle, resulting in successive layers of stalks and earth. It was crucial to compress the mass enough and give it enough weight to anchor it firmly to the bottom. Stones might be added to increase the weight, or wooden stakes might be driven through the sections into the river bottom. The section was also anchored to the earth dike or the preceding section by ropes tied to stakes driven into the dike.

As the work progressed, huge stalk bundles were fixed to the upstream side of the dike to protect it from the current, while earth was built up behind it. After the dike had advanced into the current several sections, the boats would be repositioned and the work started again.[83]

The officials gathered at the Xiangfu work site made the necessary preparations to put that entire operation in motion, but the actual start of construction had to await both a drop in the water level and the selection of a propitious day *(zhuoji donggong)*. On October 29 Wang Ding, Huicheng, Zhu Xiang, and E Xun'an made offerings to the river gods and signaled the start of construction. The total dimensions of the project that confronted them were immense. The plan called for the eastern repair dike to be approximately 3,000 meters long and the western dike over 13,000 meters long. Most of that consisted of "dike tail" *(bawei)*, rammed-earth dikes about 3 meters across the top, 25 meters at the base, and 3 meters high, built out over the sandy flats of the riverbank. Those culminated in two segments 45 meters across the top and approximately 150 meters in length called the "dike bases" *(baji)*, which functioned as work platforms and staging areas from which workers began the placement of stalk sections into the river. The distance between the two bases was almost the same as the width of the break in the main dike.[84]

As the process of placing sections got under way, it was Lin Zexu who took de facto charge of the operation, visiting the work site each day to see that all went as planned. Initially, progress was slow. A month after work began, matériel stores were still only 20 percent of the required total, and the placing of sections had not yet begun. A light snowfall on November 27 served as a reminder of the coming winter. The difficulties of digging frozen soil and trying to construct a dike across an icy river urged speed, but shortages of money and matériel interfered with large-scale projects. As a result the officials decided to divert most of the available labor to the digging of the diversion canal. An initial sixty sections were singled out as particularly difficult and given priority. All dredging was scheduled to be completed in forty days.[85]

Wang Ding's subsequent bimonthly reports chart the progress of the project in terms of four elements: the weather, the length of dike completed, the percentage of the needed materials collected, and the amount of dredging completed. Of those, the dredging seems to have presented the least difficulty. By December 13, 30 percent of the diversion canal was done, and work on the less demanding dredging downstream was also under way. Two weeks later the diversion canal was 50 percent completed, and areas downstream reported their dredging projects 30 percent to 60 percent complete. By the end of the month, 90 percent of the diversion canal was finished.[86]

Because unusually warm weather kept the ground from freezing, work on the diversion canal had gone more quickly than expected. Unfortunately, the same was not true of work on the repair dikes. Matériel and money shortages delayed the start of work until mid-December. Even

坝 啟 蕭 豐

Fig. 5   Breaking up ice on a tributary stream.

then, only on the western dike could workers start the placing of stalk
sections. The first section of the eastern dike did not go into the water
until December 16. Nevertheless, the weather was clear, and a full moon
allowed work around the clock. By the end of December, the western dike
was over two hundred meters long and had begun to encounter the force
of the main current.[87]

Although the repair dikes were half completed by early January of
1842, increasingly cold weather began to hamper construction. Ice formed
on the river and interfered with the operation of the "stern grasping" and
control boats. To combat the formation of ice around the work site, officials prepared several dozen small ice-breaking boats *(da bing chuan)* and
equipped the crews with long wooden poles. Those boats patrolled the
base of the dike and the waters around the work boats; with the poles the

crews agitated the surface of the water in order to keep ice from forming. The poles were also used to capture and redirect floe ice drifting down from upstream so that it would not collide with either the dikes or the work boats.[88]

A sudden shift of the wind to the east on January 14 brought some relief from the cold but led to breakup of ice upstream. Ice floes sped downstream and slammed into the boats and the ropes. The thinner floes, perhaps one-third of a meter thick, floated high enough to be easily visible and could be fended off. Much more dangerous were the thick floes of "black ice" *(heiling)*, which lay so low in the water that they were invisible. On the fifteenth, floes of black ice damaged four boats protecting the western dike and cut the moorings holding two large binding boats, setting them adrift downstream. A turn to colder weather eventually put a stop to that bombardment, but the loss of the binding boats halted work on the western repair dike. To avoid delays, the men working on the western dike were transferred to the eastern dike until the boats could be recovered.[89]

After initial delays, matériel deliveries began to pick up. By the end of December, 80 percent of the total quota was on hand, and all of it was available by mid-January. Only hemp continued to be hard to come by. To urge officials to ship the required quotas, Wang asked that tardy officials be temporarily removed from their posts until they came up with the goods. The threat appears to have had the desired effect on hemp supplies, and by the end of January quotas were being met.[90]

Timing was crucial at that stage. The two repair dikes were drawing close. By the second week of February, their combined length was almost nine hundred meters, and the "golden gate" *(jinmen)*—the gap between them—was only twelve meters wide. As the gap narrowed, the water depth increased to twelve to thirteen meters and the current grew more forceful, making construction more difficult. Some protection from the current came from the completed deflection dike, which extended five hundred meters out into the river and pushed the main current in the direction of the diversion canal.[91]

Everything was ready for the final push. On February 4 officials opened the diversion canal. The river poured into the new channel, lowering the water level at the gap by almost a meter and diverting 70 percent of the flow back into the river's old course. The plan was to close the gap in two or three days and complete the repair. In the early morning hours of February 6, workers began pressing the stalk and earth plug into the "golden gate" to seal it. Success seemed imminent. Then the weather changed. Before daybreak, an unusually violent storm came in from the northeast. For the next several hours, a relentless wind sent waves pounding against the dikes. By the time the storm passed, it had destroyed over one hundred meters of the eastern repair dike. River troops struggling in the darkness to save the dike were trapped when it began to collapse. "Several hundred" drowned, along with the official commanding them.[92]

After the storm, officials assessed the destruction. Besides the damage to the eastern dike, the western dike lost twenty to twenty-five meters to the storm. In places the storm had washed away tons of earth and brought the top of the dike level with the river. Fortunately, sufficient materials were on hand to repair the damage. By doubling wages and instituting around-the-clock construction, officials repaired most of the damage in a brief six days.[93]

The weather was not yet finished with its work. On the third morning of the lunar new year, as officials and workers again sought to close the gap, another storm as fierce as the first struck the work site. For the next three days, work continued in spite of a blinding snowstorm and freezing winds. A constant stream of workers moved back and forth across the dikes depositing earth. On February 14, when it seemed that the current was slackening, a third storm came up and destroyed another thirty-five meters of the eastern dike. But the rest held, and the situation gradually stabilized.[94]

On the surface, the damage from the later storms was small, but when engineers again began the process of placing sections, they discovered serious problems. The high water accompanying the storms had increased the flow through the "golden gate," cutting deeply into the river bottom. Where the water had been twelve meters deep, it was now twenty to twenty-five meters deep. That meant that constructing each stalk section required three to four times as much material.[95]

Unfortunately, material supplies were exhausted. Faced with the need to replenish them quickly, Wang requested permission to suspend price controls and asked for funding to purchase an additional two thousand *duo* of stalks and other materials.[96]

Other problems began to appear. As the flow through the "golden gate" increased, the current in the diversion canal slowed, causing rapid sedimentation. In similar cases in the past, engineers had closed off the mouth of the canal with a levee *(lanhuang ba)* until preparations to close the gap were again nearing completion. That also required additional funding. Officials requested 1.1 million taels to get the project back on schedule.[97]

Without waiting for approval for funding, officials went forward with the job of closing off the mouth of the diversion canal and purchasing new stocks of matériel. By the middle of the first month, the situation had improved. Supplies were streaming in from surrounding counties and the area north of the river. An estimated 800 or 900 *duo* was on hand by February 28, enough to make a new start on closing the breach.[98]

A survey of the diversion canal also brought welcome news. After blocking off the mouth, officials found only minor silting and only a few sites that would require the digging of ditches to clear newly deposited sediment and trapped water. Wang estimated that the gap could be closed within ten days but reiterated his request for 1.1 million taels. The emperor ordered the funds transferred with all possible dispatch.[99]

Another crisis arose on March 8, when an express rider from an upstream station brought word that rising waters were on the way. The question confronting officials was whether it was better to open the diversion canal before the work was completed or risk losing sections of the repair dikes. They decided to open the canal, with good results. The flow returned unobstructed to the downstream course of the river. Teams on the eastern and western sections of the repair dike also reported progress.[100]

By the end of the month, there was no longer room between the two ends of the dike for two binding boats to operate. Engineers halted work on the eastern dike and conducted the final stages of construction from the western dike. A storm on March 15 threw a scare into everyone but passed without damaging the dike. Finally, on March 17, the gap between the two sections of the repair dike was again twelve meters. The ends of the dike stood ten meters above the level of the water, which was twenty-five meters deep at the gap.

On the morning of March 19, officials again offered sacrifices to the river gods, then began the last phase of the repair, closing the breach *(helong)*. Workers passed ropes across from each end of the dike and secured them in place, constructed the great stalk plug, and rolled it onto the ropes. As it sank down into the breach, they piled earth and more stalks on top. Binding ropes kept the current from washing away the stalks and earth inside the bundle. Work continued at a feverish pace. In half a day the bundle touched the river bottom; the flood was at an end.[101]

Finishing Up

The flood was over, but construction was a long way from being completed. The final phase of any major repair project was the finishing (shanhou) work that had to be done to consolidate the repairs and protect them from any future damage. The primary dikes had to be strengthened and supporting dikes constructed. Deflection dikes also had to be built to direct the water away from weak spots. All those tasks required money. Since the start of construction, a total of 5.85 million taels had been dedicated to the project. Wang Ding now asked for an additional 422,000 taels for finishing the work.[102]

Consulted by the emperor, the Board of Revenue suggested the following sources for the needed funds:

Shaanxi	50,000 taels from the spring land tax
Shandong	50,000 taels from the land tax arrears for 1841
Shanxi	50,000 taels from the land tax arrears for 1841
Lianghuai	100,000 taels from the 1842 salt tax
Anhui	20,000 taels from the sale of degrees (*juanjian*)
Jiangxi	50,000 taels from the sale of degrees
Jiujiang customs	30,000 taels
Hushu customs	40,000 taels
Linqing customs	12,000 taels[103]

With that final infusion of money, the total expenditures for the repair of the Xiangfu dike came to over 6.5 million taels, more than the Lanyi project had cost but well below the cost of many other flood repair efforts. Added to that was another 500,000 taels spent on the defense of Kaifeng. That money had been drawn from the land taxes of ten provincial treasuries, from salt taxes, and from a variety of lesser sources, including *yanglian* (nourishing goodness) funds and money from the sale of offices and ranks.[104]

The consequences of the Xiangfu flood touched every aspect of life in the region. Kaifeng was left a muddy pit whose streets lay two meters lower than the surrounding countryside. Heavy rains in Daoguang 30 (1850) again turned the city into a lake, damaging homes and public buildings and forcing government offices to move to barges. The land within the walls became so saline that one could see the white powder on the soil when the water receded. Not until the 1870s was a method of drainage devised that would allow rainwater to flow into the Huiji River.[105]

The destruction of agriculture in the areas covered by the flood was extensive, with over eighty-five hundred villages in Henan and probably an equal number in Anhui and western Jiangsu suffering 50 percent or greater crop loss. Although no reliable numbers are available, the loss of life from drowning and starvation was no doubt extensive. Elizabeth Perry has written about the impact of repeated natural disasters on the Huaibei peasant mentality. Fatalistic in the face of nature's ravages, they struggled constantly with each other for the scarce resources of the region. The fact that for twenty years the Yellow River had not intruded into their struggle for survival may have given the residents of the region a small reserve of resilience in the face of disaster. The Xiangfu flood seriously depleted that reserve.[106]

For those held responsible for the flood, the price of failure was humiliation and exile. Besides Wenchong, four other river officials were forced to wear the cangue and stand exposed on the riverbank, then were exiled to do hard labor in Xinjiang. They included Gao Buyue, who had tried to get funds for the repair of the dike before the disaster occurred.[107]

The emperor, of course, took no responsibility for the flood. The impact of his decision to appoint an inexperienced official is unremarked (who, except for the emperor himself, would have had the audacity?). Daoguang's embarrassment is evident only in the harsh punishment inflicted on Wenchong. An official with more experience than Wenchong might not have been able to prevent the flood once it began, but he would have been more sensitive to the dangers before the flood and would have known how to take decisive steps to limit the scope of the damage. More damaging than the decision to appoint an inexperienced man was the conflicted assignment Wenchong was given. Faced with continuing fiscal problems and a burgeoning river conservancy budget, Daoguang set Wenchong loose to root out corruption and waste. That was a task that could have been best undertaken by an official familiar with the realities of the job, but by definition such men were tainted. The untainted were ipso facto the ignorant. Wenchong was sent to ride herd on the very men whose knowledge and support he needed to perform the engineering aspects of the job. Unable to trust his subordinates, unwilling to spend the funds they requested, breathing down their necks and hounding them into retirement, Wenchong alienated many of his most experienced officials. Little surprise that the chorus of condemnation was so resounding.

The glaring miscalculation on the part of both the emperor and his guard dog—the assumption that an upright and intelligent man could master the technical demands of the job well enough to second-guess more experienced subordinates—reflects most harshly on the emperor, whose experience with an earlier hydraulic crisis should have made him aware that technical skill was central to the control of the river. For the first twenty years of his reign, Daoguang took a pragmatic approach that recognized that some corruption and waste was part and parcel of effective engineering. His loss of flexibility in 1840 seems to reflect a change in Daoguang's attitude. Perhaps budgetary pressures and the state's weakening fiscal system took a toll on Daoguang's patience. If so, his irritation provoked decisions that would mushroom into a fiscal crisis of even greater proportions.

Not everyone suffered from the flood. For some officials it represented a career opportunity. Six officials were awarded the peacock feather for their work at Xiangfu, among them Zhang Liangji. Another ninety officials were singled out for their performance and rewarded with promotions. Those burdened more with money than talent were also given an opportunity to advance their careers by contributing funds for repair or relief. The contribution of thirty thousand strings of cash by a department director in the Board of Punishments brought him a peacock feather, whereas a first-class licentiate contributing ten thousand strings of cash was promoted to be an official of the ninth rank. Others benefited in a similar fashion.[108]

The rewards garnered by the officials in charge of the repair point to the fact that most had performed effectively. Niu Jian's timely imposition of martial law had quieted popular unrest and hysteria in Kaifeng and saved the city from chaos, whereas Wang Ding and Huicheng had proved to be capable overseers of a vast and complex project. Lin Zexu had added much-needed experience to the administrative team. Lin earned plaudits from Wang but no immediate leniency from the emperor. When the project was completed, he continued his journey into exile.

The emperor had some reason to be pleased. The Xiangfu flood, although a disaster of immense proportions, was handled with relative competence, dispatch, and a minimum of social dislocation. The efficiency of the repairs and their early completion reduced the risk of banditry by allowing peasants to return to their fields in time for spring planting. The officials had shown initiative in making repairs, the emperor flexibility in funding. Everyone understood that it was impossible to guarantee that the river would never flood. The Xiangfu repair was an example of emergency response at its best.

By the summer of 1842, the region was beginning to get back to normal. Crops were planted, and the repair work was completed. Given a few years, the region would have been restored to health. But the river was merciless. A flood in the following year in the Jiangsu conservancy, near Taoyuan, further undermined imperial confidence in the river conservancy. Then, in the fall of 1843, the same areas afflicted by the flood at Xiangfu were again inundated by a breach of the southern dike thirty kilometers upstream at Zhongmou. For the emperor and the people of the Huaibei region alike, the Zhongmou flood would leave wounds that would not heal.

5

The Taoyuan Flood and the
Zhongmou Debacle, 1842–1845

THE QING RIVER OFFICIALS understood that Yellow River floods often came in series.[1] In the wake of a flood, sedimentation raised the bed of the river and reduced the holding capacity of the area between the dikes. Although river officials carried out extensive dredging in the dry downstream bed, those measures were aimed at deepening the channel or cutting across meander loops to facilitate the flow. Little could be done to remove the millions of tons of silt deposited in other parts of the riverbed. When the river returned to its old course, it did so at a time when the flow was reduced and the reshaped and deepened channel could contain it. Danger came with the first high water. As the river overflowed its prescribed channel, it sometimes moved in unanticipated directions and eroded unprotected sections of the main dike. The reduced holding capacity of the area between the dikes could also bring floodwaters to the top of the dikes sooner than anticipated. Experienced officials like Linqing, head of the Jiangsu conservancy, were aware of those dangers and kept a close eye on the river as the first postrepair flood season approached.

When the Yellow River settled into its old bed east of Xiangfu in the spring and summer of 1842, Linqing and others responsible for river control were distracted by the war with Britain. As British forces returned to the lower Yangzi region in the summer of 1842, top regional officials were called upon to assist in defense. The post of Yellow River–Grand Canal governor-general still retained military responsibilities arising from its origins in the Ming military structure. Linqing left behind his duties in the North and went south to defend the northern bank of the Yangzi. It proved to be an untimely distraction. Unable to carry out his usual careful seasonal survey of the dikes, Linqing was forced to rely upon subordinates less skilled and possibly less conscientious than himself. The result was the second Yellow River flood in two years, a breach of the north dike near Taoyuan in northwestern Jiangsu.

Taoyuan, 1842–1843

In the summer of 1842, unusually heavy seasonal rains and the sedimentation of the river channel resulting from the 1841 flood caused the waters of the Yellow River to rise to unprecedented heights. By mid-August the river was fourteen meters deep at the Xunhuang Dike, two-thirds of a meter higher than the record set the previous year. Near dawn on August 22, 1842 (DG 22/7/17), a thunderstorm accompanied by high winds created huge waves, which smashed a hole in the north dike in Taoyuan County, northern Jiangsu Province.[2] The floodwaters cut through the Grand Canal, traveled north and east to capture the Liutang and several smaller rivers, and disgorged into the sea some sixty kilometers north of the Yellow River's normal outlet at Yuntiguan. When the storm abated, investigation revealed a gap of six hundred meters in the main dike.

Compared to a cataclysm like Xiangfu, Taoyuan was a minor disaster. The area through which the floodwaters passed was sparsely inhabited.[3] For the dynasty, the main issues were the cost of repairing the dike and the impact on Grand Canal transport.

For Linqing, the Taoyuan flood brought the end of a long and successful period as head of the Jiangsu conservancy. Perhaps in deference to Linqing's past successes, the emperor ordered only mild punishment—removal from office and loss of rank. More anomalous was the emperor's injunction that Linqing, perhaps the dynasty's most experienced and technically proficient hydraulic official, be excluded from all subsequent discussions on the handling of the Taoyuan breach.[4] The exclusion of Linqing seems to offer further evidence of Daoguang's deepening distrust of his hydraulic bureaucracy.

The Taoyuan flood is also of interest for the debate it provoked over changing the river's course. The prospect of abandoning the silted bed of the old course for a new, lower bed was appealing: grain boats could cross more easily, the water level in Lake Hongze could be lowered to relieve pressure on the Gaoyan Dike, and upstream floodwaters would drain to the sea more quickly.[5]

As tantalizing as the prospect of a ready-made solution was, the idea of changing the river's course was an old one, which had been debated since the Ming dynasty. Advocates pointed to the obvious advantages—improved downstream flow, easier dike maintenance and repair. Opponents decried the equally obvious shortcomings—the immense cost of building new defensive structures, the dislocation of a large number of people, and the inevitability that the river would quickly silt up the new bed and the same old problems would arise.[6]

The emperor appointed Board of Revenue president Jingzheng and Board of Works president Liao Hongquan to take charge of the repairs and to evaluate the possibility of leaving the river in its new course. When they arrived at the work site two months after the break, they found Linqing had completed much of the work needed to stabilize the break. Their survey of the hydraulic situation was not encouraging. They found deep layers of new sediment in the river's old bed. The Xiangfu and Taoyuan floods had together added a meter or more of sediment to the deepest part of the river, creating blockages from Qingjiangpu to the sea.[7] The situation along the river's new course was not reassuring, either. Well before the river reached the coast, it lost coherence and dissolved into a profusion of small, turbid streams flowing through sandbars to the sea.

The imperial commissioners found many drawbacks in the plan to allow the river to remain in its new course. Building new dikes alone would cost an estimated 10 million taels (as opposed to 6 million to repair the break).[8] Moreover, since the flow to the section of the Central Transport Canal *(zhong yun he)* below the breach would be lost, grain boats would have to use the transfer lake *(yitang)* method to cross the old bed of the Yellow River. The transfer lake was essentially a huge lock created by blocking off the eastern side of the river's former channel and filling the resulting basin with water sufficient to allow the grain boats to exit Lake Hongze and cross to the northern portion of the Grand Canal. Finding a source of water to fill the transport lake deep enough to float fully loaded grain boats was problematic. The most likely source, the Qing River, did not always have adequate flow.[9] The commissioners concluded

that although returning the river to its old course involved many difficulties, leaving the river in the new course would be expensive and would
not resolve any of the river's serious hydraulic problems.[10]

The repair schedule established for the Taoyuan break was leisurely.
Unlike the Xiangfu project, the Taoyuan flood offered few reasons to pull
river officials away from the task of transferring the empty grain boat fleet
south across the Yellow River. Since it was already too late in the year to
complete the needed dredging before winter began to freeze the water
standing in the riverbed, Jingzheng and Liao proposed extending the
project over a one-year period. The final closing would take place after
the empty grain boats had returned south the following fall. Work relief
and tax remissions would be granted to help the residents of the disaster
areas. In their final proposal, Jingzheng and Liao Hongquan reduced their
estimate of the costs for dike construction to 2,790,000 taels. Combined
with dredging costs and funds for the transfer pond, the total amount
required for the project was 5,741,000 taels. The emperor finally gave his
approval and ordered the transfer of the needed funds.[11]

At the same time that he approved the repair plan, the emperor named
Pan Xi'en, a *jinshi* of 1811 with considerable river experience, to replace
Linqing. Pan was the Huai-Yang circuit intendant, and his appointment
represented a momentary return to the earlier pattern of appointment from
within the river conservancy.[12]

No sooner was the decision to go ahead with repairs made and everything planned than the entire project was thrown into doubt by the memorial of a censor named Lei Yixian. Lei was convinced that the government
was missing an opportunity to "take advantage of existing conditions."[13]

Lei proposed using the part of the old bed between the breach at
Taoyuan and the confluence at Qingkou as a section of the Grand Canal.
The Yellow River would be allowed to find its own path to the sea through
the channels of the small streams it had captured. When it rose too high
for those streams, the overflow would be guided back into the old channel
downstream to join with the Huai River. Dredging boats would combat
silting. Following that plan, Lei claimed, would cost less than a third of
the cost of restoring the river to its former course.[14]

Prepared for a hostile reaction to his proposal, Lei sought to get a
jump on his opponents. He charged that high river officials were too
dependent on subordinates, too fearful of anything outside the accepted

consensus, and too mired in old methods to be able to clearly assess the situation. At the lower levels of the river bureaucracy, river officials, clerks, and craftsmen all stood to benefit from extended repair projects. The longer a job lasted, the more supervisory officials *(chaiwei)* would be dispatched, the greater the amount of money that would be spent, and the more opportunities there would be for peculation.[15]

Lei also brandished the specter of social unrest, warning that extending the work over a long period would encourage displaced commoners *(liumin)* to band together by the thousands. It would then be difficult to keep salt smugglers *(yanxiao,* literally "salt owls") and Nian bandits from mixing with them and stirring up trouble.[16]

The task of responding to Lei's proposal and criticisms fell to Pan Xi'en. Taking no chance that he might be accused of failing to take a personal hand in the investigation, Pan not only dispatched lower officials to investigate the conditions along the Yellow River's old course but also personally boarded a boat and followed the floodwaters from the site of the breach toward the east. At the coast Pan questioned local fishermen about the impact of tides on the river's ability to flow into the sea. He then returned to Qingjiangpu, where he read the reports of his underlings.[17]

Pan's dismissal of Lei's proposal was blunt: "What this censor . . . considers acting according to circumstances, your minister calls inventing; what [he] considers economizing, your minister calls profligacy *(fei)."* Pan dismissed the notion that the Yellow River would eventually dig its own channel along the new course. Along much of the new route, Pan wrote, there was "nothing distinguishable as a river." Instead, a sheet of muddy water from two-thirds of a meter to two meters deep and from five to fifty kilometers wide covered the region. Within a year or two, Pan predicted, silt deposits would block the existing channels, and the river would seek a new, lower path to the sea.[18] The only solution to the silt problem was building dikes close together to "restrict the flow to attack the silt." The existing dikes were so far away that they would be useless, and the expense of the new dikes would be massive. Pan bridled at Lei's suggestion that workable solutions were thwarted by the conservatism of or the venality of river officials. Calling Lei's proposal "a plan for disaster," Pan asked, "How is it [that Lei] does not know that in proposing to change plans, if one does not understand matters, one dare not make frivolous suggestions?" Pan's arguments carried the day. The emperor ordered the project to go forward.[19]

One cannot blame Lei Yixian for trying. To be able to turn a disaster into a solution to the knotty problems of the lower course was an attractive fantasy, particularly for a government without the resources to repair its hydraulic infrastructure. With his natural parsimony exaggerated by a real fiscal crisis and his manifest distrust of river officials, Daoguang was willing to believe that a lucky disaster might be the solution to the problem of Yellow River control. But the Taoyuan flood was not the right disaster: the river's new course would solve too few hydraulic problems at too great a cost. As it turned out, events rendered the question moot. Repairs had hardly begun at Taoyuan when the Yellow River again broke through its southern dike in Henan. Once again the attention of the emperor and his river officials turned to the Henan conservancy. The memory of the Xiangfu flood was still fresh, but as difficult as that experience had been for the state and the people of the Huaibei region, Zhongmou was to prove worse. Overshadowed from the outset by fiscal problems that provoked administrative jealousies, created delays, and resulted in unwise cost-cutting engineering decisions, the repair project at Zhongmou became an example of everything that was wrong with imperial river control.

The First Repair at Zhongmou, 1843–1844

Beginning in the last years of the Yuan dynasty (1260–1368), the county town of Zhongmou suffered from frequent Yellow River floods. The trouble continued in the early Ming, with major floods in 1382 and 1393. One observer commented that "since the river's southward shift, Zhongmou has been most subject to its blows and injuries; over time [the river] has completely scoured [the city]. The people work on the river, are impoverished by the river, then die in the river."[20] Defense consisted of an extensive dike system along the entire forty-five kilometers of Zhongmou County's northern border. Like most rural areas in China, Zhongmou suffered a variety of natural disasters, including locust plagues, violent rain and wind storms, famine, and drought, but "of all the disasters afflicting Zhongmou," wrote the author of the local gazetteer, "none is greater than [the flooding of the Yellow River]."[21]

The river conservancy had also become deeply embedded in the economy of the area. The switch from corvee labor to wage labor that took place in the Kangxi reign relieved localities of some of the direct financial responsibility for river control. That burden was partly reintroduced through taxes, but some of the taxes found their way back into the local economy through payments to suppliers of matériel and to river workers for their labor.

The number of river officials stationed in Zhongmou increased as the river defense sites proliferated.[22] Three river officials—two subprefects and an assistant district magistrate—and fifteen members of their staff represented the civilian side of the river conservancy in Zhongmou. They were paid out of local taxes at a cost of slightly over two hundred taels per year. Four military officers were also stationed along the river. They commanded the 196 river troops *(hebing)* and 78 river workers *(baofu)* stationed along the south bank of the river.[23]

In spite of the huge amounts of money being expended on Yellow River conservancy in that period, the men who staffed the bureaucracy were mainly low-ranking officials, with most posts held by men with licentiate degrees.[24] Most of them were natives of neighboring provinces, with a few from southern Jiangsu and Zhejiang.[25]

Civil and river bureaucracies tended to remain separate at that lowest level, but the barrier was not absolute. For example, Ding Zhuo, a licentiate from Zhejiang who served as assistant district magistrate of the Zhongmou lower commandery from 1826 to 1829, was appointed to head the Shangnanhe Subprefecture from 1842 to 1845.[26] There appears to have been no regular term of office for officials in those posts, and periods of tenure varied widely. Some assistant district magistrates moved back and forth between posts in the upper and lower commanderies. Others served in a post more than once, sometimes at intervals of several years.[27]

Although the bureaucratic status of river conservancy officials and military personnel was not high, their sacrifices were noted and honored. Accounts of their heroics can be found among the biographies of notables in the Zhongmou Gazetteer. One such case involved a sublieutenant named Xin Decheng, stationed at Zhonghe Subprefecture, who helped in the repairs after the Xiangfu flood. He impressed his superiors by his refusal to interrupt his labors for sleep and his vigilant supervision of the workers under his command. Xin took charge of the dangerous task of overseeing the placement of stalk revetments, which exposed him to repeated dunking in the river. Exhaustion finally caught up with him, and he fell ill and died at the work site. Not mentioned in the hagiographic gazetteer account is the fact that Xin was one of the officials held responsible for the flood. Stripped of his hard-earned rank, his frenetic work habits were fueled by a desire to redeem himself and salvage his career. Nevertheless, he is honored in the gazetteer not only with a laudatory biography but also by a poem written by the then assistant district magistrate Wang Yufan.[28]

If the river was a trial for the people of Zhongmou, it could also be an opportunity. Lu Yi, a Zhongmou native who grew up in the shadow of the Yangqiao Dike, joined the river troops and worked on the Mayi and Yifeng flood repair projects, among others. He eventually made second captain and was posted to Suining. Lu was awarded the blue plume for his work on the Xiangfu diversion canal. Ironically, his career came to an end in Zhongmou County in 1843. Assigned to the Zhongmou repair project, Lu was forced to work in the wind and rain. Eventually he fell ill, began coughing up blood, and died. He was accorded the same posthumous honors as a soldier fallen in battle.[29]

By the late Daoguang reign, the defensive structures serviced by those soldiers and officials included thirty kilometers of the main dike and its complex of deflection and defensive dikes of earth, stalk revetments, stone, and brick.[30] The bulk of those defensive structures were concentrated in the Zhongmou lower commandery. Between there and the defensive site at Heigang, the river paralleled the dike at a distance. Beyond Heigang the river executed a series of radical turns that brought it into contact with first the north and then the south dike at locations heavily fortified against the current.[31]

In 1843, perhaps as a result of changes in the flow resulting from the Xiangfu and Taoyuan floods, several meanders moved closer to unprotected sections of the southern dike between the Zhongmou lower commandery and Heigang. In July the Kai-Gui circuit intendant Fu Mei noticed a silt spur forming across from the eighth watcher station in the Zhongmou lower commandery. The spur was pushing the current in the direction of the southern dike. Fu began constructing stalk revetments to counter the current, but those were washed away when the Yellow and Bian Rivers rose simultaneously on July 18. The current then shifted eastward toward the ninth watcher station. On the night of July 22, heavy rains and strong winds pushed the swollen river against the dike. As dawn broke on the twenty-third, the river gradually overwhelmed the dike and opened a gap three hundred meters wide.[32]

At the moment the Yellow River was broaching its dikes for the third time in three years, Governor-General Huicheng was working 150 kilometers downstream. Throughout the month, incessant rain and repeated surges of the Yellow and Bian Rivers had caused the highest water levels in several years. Huicheng had been kept busy responding to the emergencies that sprang up all along the river as stalk revetments, brick dikes, and even stone dikes were washed away. When news reached him of the Zhongmou break, Huicheng rushed to the site of the flood but arrived after the situation was already beyond saving. All he could do was to wrap the ends of the broken dike with stalk revetments to prevent further erosion.[33]

Those living near the dike had been lucky. The flood came during daylight, and advanced warning had allowed most of them to take flight. Huicheng reported that damage to fields and homes was widespread, but he claimed that the loss of life had been minimal. Relief efforts were quickly initiated, and food and money were dispatched to the flooded areas. Officials were also sent to investigate the route of the flood.[34]

The emperor wasted no time pointing the finger of blame. Huicheng, Henan governor E Xun'an, Zhonghe second-class subprefect Wang Mei, Zhongmou lower commandery assistant district magistrate Zhang Shihui, Sublieutenant Xin Decheng, and Zhongmou magistrate Gao Jun were held responsible. Zhang Shihui and Xin Decheng were removed from their posts immediately. Punishment for the rest was to be decided by the board.[35]

For a fisc already drained by war and repeated floods, the Zhongmou flood came as a heavy blow. Early in 1843, confronted with a shortfall of 9 million taels in the treasury, the emperor instructed the Imperial Clan Court, the Board of Works, the Board of Revenue, the Imperial Household, the Court of Sacrificial Worship, the Office of the Gendarmerie, and Xuntian prefecture: "In every large or small construction [project] and all disbursement of funds, where reductions are possible, reduce; where economy is possible, economize. If every effort is made to economize, small economies will result in abundance, to the benefit of the public fisc."[36]

The version of the edict that made it to the Yellow River conservancy noted that capital offices had been ordered to economize; Huicheng and

Pan Xi'en were to consult with experienced officials on their staff to see where cutbacks could be made without endangering important defensive works. "Moreover," the edict continued, "officials cannot be allowed to use public works as an excuse for extravagance. At present, for the sake of the nation's finances, it is necessary to greatly increase efforts at economy over those of recent years. After one or two years, when the nation's resources are again abundant, it will be possible to return to normal."[37] Anyone familiar with the fiscal difficulties of the Qing state cannot help but be struck by Daoguang's Pollyanna economics. After the flood at Zhongmou, that absurd optimism could not be sustained.

Even before Zhongmou, the state's machinery of extraction was working overtime. For example, the sale of degrees, which had been declining since Daoguang 6 (1826), began to rise again in Daoguang 21 (1841). Approximately seven thousand degrees and ranks were sold nationally in Daoguang 21. By Daoguang 23 the figure exceeded eleven thousand. Moreover, Henan's percentage of the national sales was rising steadily from a low of 4 percent in Daoguang 9 (1829) to an average of around 10 percent in the years between Daoguang 17 (1837) and Daoguang 25 (1825).[38]

Huicheng clearly understood that recourse to the sale of ranks and titles to fund the Zhongmou project was inevitable. He proposed a one-year subscription campaign for "river works funds" *(hegong jingfei)*. Contributions would be open to "those gentry and officials in Zhili, and those in the Henan conservancy and Jiangsu conservancy who want to contribute funds for river repairs." Contributions for each rank or title would be the same as the amounts required in contributions to the coastal defense fund.[39]

When Jingzheng and He Rulin arrived at the Zhongmou work site on August 14, they found Huicheng struggling to accommodate the flood victims. Although Henan governor E Xun'an had already dispatched to the countryside food, money, and straw mats for building temporary housing, refugees continued to stream into the cities and unaffected areas. The sight of "flood victims supporting their elders and carrying children" as they wandered in search of food and shelter convinced the investigators that additional relief would be necessary.[40] By the beginning of the following month, more than ten thousand people crowded the main dikes, "calling for food like nestlings." Jingzheng appointed Guide prefect Hu Xizhou to head a group of officials and gentry chosen to deal with the problem. They divided the refugees into four groups, constructed two hundred tents to house them, and distributed food to each victim by name.[41]

Unlike Kaifeng in 1841, Zhongmou city had escaped the direct impact of the flood. The waters had passed to the northeast, devastating the area and leaving it buried beneath a blanket of sand.[42] The waters then turned east, skirting Kaifeng and flowing southeast into Anhui.

The emperor, concerned that downstream regions had not yet recovered from the 1841 flood, pressed his officials for information on conditions in the countryside. In particular, he chastised Anhui governor Cheng Maocai for his tardy response. After another month's delay, Cheng finally reported. The news was not good: emergency rations were exhausted and the flat lands lay submerged beneath a sheet of water two to three meters deep. In some areas, Cheng wrote, the flooding was worse than in 1841.[43]

There were a few hopeful notes. Since the flood had come early in the fall (three weeks earlier than the Xiangfu break), officials were hopeful that if the flood receded there might still be time to plant and harvest a crop of vegetables (caishu) before the arrival of winter. Also, forewarned of the breach at Zhongmou, peasants had managed to save more than half of the sorghum crop.[44]

Unfortunately, the flood did not subside. Weeks later the area along the banks of the Huai River near Fengyang County was "still like one vast sea," with the plain covered by sheets of water thirty kilometers across. Not only had the flood failed to recede, but beginning in early September, repeated rainstorms visited further misery on the countryside. Only in late October did the waters finally begin to retreat.[45]

DELAY AND INEFFECTIVENESS were also evident in the measures taken at the flood site. Wrapping the dike heads to keep the gap from widening had been a priority from the outset, but the efforts proved unavailing. By August 15 the breach had widened from three hundred to over one thousand meters. It was another two weeks before the erosion was finally stopped.[46]

While that struggle was going on, the emperor's overseers were attempting to assess the work needed to restore the system. The usual

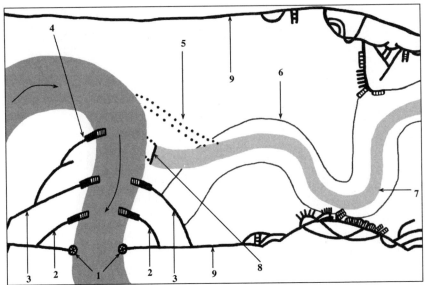

Map 4   The second repair project at Zhongmou, 1844: *1*, dike heads wrapped in stalk revetments *(guotou ba)*; *2*, secondary repair dikes *(erba)*; *3*, primary repair dikes *(daba)*; *4*, deflection dike *(tiaoshuiba)*; *5*, site of proposed diversion channel *(yinhe)*; *6*, former river course; *7*, standing water in the lower channel; *8*, earth embankment blocking off diversion channel; *9*, main dikes.

model, the one followed successfully at Xiangfu, called for constructing a primary dike *(daba)* backed by a secondary dike *(erba)* and a deflection dike *(tiaoshuiba)*, digging a diversion canal *(yinhe)*, and dredging the river channel downstream. The Taoyuan breach also had to be closed and the dike strengthened. The Xiangfu repairs had cost a total of 6,582,000 taels, with a further 1,600,000 spent on dredging the river downstream in the Jiangsu conservancy.[47]

In some ways the Zhongmou flood was worse than the 1841 flood. On the technical side, the breach was almost one hundred meters wider, and the soil at the construction site was loose and sandy, making it more difficult to build stable dikes. As for the social consequences, the area flooded was greater, and the populace, still struggling to recover from the last flood, was worse off than two years earlier. He Rulin and Jingzheng complained that the repairs, maintenance, and relief connected with the succession of floods had left little money to respond to the current crisis.[48] Clearly under pressure from Daoguang to reduce costs, the two men made a crucial engineering decision: the repair project would not include a secondary dike. By excluding that safety measure, Jingzheng and He Rulin were gambling that the project could be completed before winter storms threatened the repair dike. It was a gamble that allowed them to propose a budget of only 6 million taels for the repairs.

Funding

In the climate of fiscal crisis that existed in the wake of the Opium War, even that modest budget provoked a contest over financial resources that threatened to undermine the repair project and destroy any cooperation between the Jiangsu and Henan conservancies. Many of the normal sources used to fund Yellow River repairs—transfers from the treasuries of neighboring provinces, the salt monopolies, various customs offices, "voluntary" contributions from officials, restitution (peixiu) funds from officials held responsible for the failure of the dikes, and the sale of ranks and titles (juanna, juanshu)—had been depleted by the earlier flood repairs and the war.

The first salvo in the battle for resources was the Zhongmou officials' request that the funds sent by neighboring provinces to Jiangsu for the Taoyuan project be diverted to Zhongmou. They argued that those ready moneys were needed so that repairs could get under way quickly. Although some important construction (yaogong) could be started using work relief (yigong daizhen) laborers, the officials at Zhongmou feared that work would come to a halt without a rapid and substantial infusion of funds. They asked for the immediate transfer of 2.3 million taels from neighboring provinces and from the customs and monopolies. Pan Xi'en was ordered to forward his cash reserves to Zhongmou in the form of silver. The emperor also approved the additional request for 2.3 million taels.[49]

Pan Xi'en was slow to comply. After a second edict upbraided him for his tardiness, Pan aired his complaints against the officials at Zhongmou. At issue was the exchange rate of silver to copper. Much of the money Pan had on hand was copper cash. At Qingjiangpu the rate was 1,600 cash per tael of silver. The official exchange rate, however, was 1,000 cash to 1 tael of silver. The officials at Zhongmou had used the latter figure to calculate how much silver the Jiangsu conservancy should ship to Zhongmou. Pan pointed out that if he complied and converted his copper cash to silver, the Jiangsu conservancy treasury would be forced to make up a difference of over 71,000 taels. Pan also argued that he needed all the copper currency he had on hand to pay for emergency defense against the winter storms that had begun to buffet the Gaoyan Dike. He offered instead to forward 600,000 taels in cash and redirect another 900,000 taels allocated for the Taoyuan project but not yet received. The emperor gave his approval.[50]

It was now the turn of the officials at Zhongmou to fume. Pan's funding plan essentially stuck them with the task of trying to collect funds from treasuries that were already tardy in their payments to the Taoyuan project. Meanwhile, Pan kept the ready cash in the Jiangsu conservancy. On October 1, when Jingzheng and his associates finally presented their comprehensive budget for the Zhongmou project, they complained that among the moneys ordered transferred to their control were "budgeted land and poll taxes *(ying zheng diding)* and stipulated customs taxes *(yuezheng guanshui),* as well as funds from such distant provinces as Jiangxi and Fujian. It is feared that it will not be possible to effect timely transfer of these funds to the work site."[51]

Those complaints do not appear to have altered the disposition of funds from the Jiangsu conservancy, but the emperor did order Pan Xi'en to reconsider his proposed budget for repairs at Taoyuan and make cuts where possible. Daoguang also dispatched two officials from Beijing to double-check Pan's calculations. Under their watchful eyes, Pan managed to trim another 141,700 taels from his initial estimate.[52]

The funds from the sale of ranks and titles also became a focus of rivalry. When the Taoyuan flood occurred, a subscription campaign was already under way for coastal defense. A similar fund was established for the Taoyan repairs, and the remaining funds from the coastal defense fund were shifted to the Jiangsu conservancy. After the Zhongmou flood, Huicheng was given permission to begin the sale of ranks and titles to benefit the Zhongmou project. The existence of two subscription campaigns left both officials and contributors confused about where contributions should go. Early in September, officials in charge of the Zhongmou project asked that funds collected from all provinces be directed to Henan. The only exception they supported was to allow contributions from gentry and officials of the immediate area of Taoyuan to go to that repair project. The emperor went along with that request, giving the Henan conservancy priority.[53]

For meeting the short-term needs of the Zhongmou project, those were hollow victories; little money was available from either contributions or provincial treasuries. As the time to begin repairs approached, the Henan treasury had received less than half of the funds budgeted for the project. Some funds were in transit, but more than one-third, a total of 2,168,560 taels, had not yet been sent. Once again the emperor urged dispatch in shipping the required moneys, demanding that the funds be at the Zhongmou work site before mid-December.[54]

As the starting date for the repair work approached, the tardy arrival of funds caused the officials at Zhongmou great concern. Fearful that delays would undermine the entire project, Liao Hongquan took the unusual step of requesting 1.5 million taels from the Imperial Household Department treasury. He offered to repay the debt when the remaining funds arrived at Zhongmou. As remarkable as the request was Daoguang's acquiescence. Within days the emperor gave his approval and ordered the funds transferred.[55] Although that ended temporarily the funding problems at Zhongmou, the shortage of cash created a cost-cutting mentality that adversely affected matériel collection, labor practices, and engineering decisions.

Matériel Supply

The lack of cash at Zhongmou also slowed the collection of stalks and other materials needed in the repair. Several officials proposed creative solutions. Among them was Lei Yixian, who again waded into the murky waters of hydraulic policy to propose that stalks and rations be accepted in lieu of cash to purchase degrees, ranks, and titles. The value would be calculated according to the market price of the materials or grain contributed. The emperor forwarded the suggestion to the officials at Zhongmou and asked for their response.[56]

The officials at Zhongmou had mixed reactions to the proposal. They rejected matériel contributions as impractical, but some saw merit in accepting grain, which could be used to reduce the cash outlay for rations and salaries (since workers could be paid in grain). Grain could also be used to supplement relief efforts.[57]

Grain contributions would help the cash flow but would do little to solve the problems of matériel acquisition. As the pressure to find supplies increased, abuses appeared. A censor named Chen Tan reported that deputies sent to collect stalks from prefectures and counties outside the stricken area were using strong-arm tactics, including forcing peasants to contribute based on the amount of land they owned, requiring contributions from some (well-off) families, confiscating people's firewood, and requisitioning (without authorization) private carts to haul stalks. Those depredations were particularly gratuitous, Chen argued, since stalks from areas unaffected by the flood were available for purchase in the markets.[58]

Concerned that the harsh collection tactics would provoke social unrest, Daoguang ordered the officials to investigate ways to stop local bullies *(tugun)* and deputies *(weiyuan)* from colluding in such types of extortion.[59] And perhaps recognizing the need for an experienced hand to manage the process, the emperor called upon Linqing, whom he deemed "capable of self-renewal" to take charge of the Zhongmou collection centers.[60]

Upon his arrival at Zhongmou, Linqing discovered that fiscal shortages were only part of the problem. In spite of government reassurances, a legacy of suspicion from forced exactions and defaulted payments for materials collected during the Xiangfu project made the villagers reluctant to sell their crops. The deputies in charge of collection often viewed that as a subterfuge designed to drive up the prices, and they responded with aggressive tactics that only compounded the popular distrust. Linqing felt that further measures were needed to encourage stalk merchants to bring their supplies to the centers, including closer supervision of collection center employees and more vigilant efforts to prevent troops and local toughs from interfering with merchants.[61]

At the eastern center, things quickly improved; within a week of Linqing's arrival, its daily intake had jumped from ten *duo* per day to around one hundred *duo* per day. The western center continued to lag behind, bringing in only half as much. Linqing noted that materials coming to the western center from Hebei had to first be transported by land, then loaded on boats to cross the river, then off-loaded on the south bank, and again transported by land to the collection site. The resulting high transport costs discouraged merchants from shipping their supplies. He suggested ordering local magistrates to improve the roads along the shipping route as an inducement to stalk merchants.[62]

捷 聞 廠 料

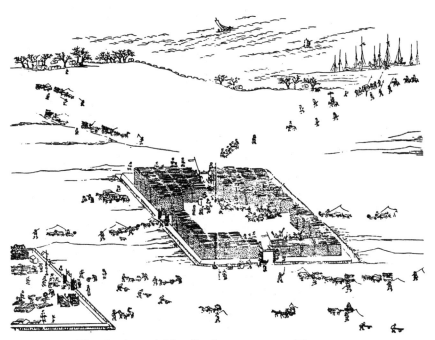

Fig. 6   A matériel collection center near Zhongmou.

Whether because of those measures or for other reasons, collections did pick up. By early December the eastern center reported enough stalks on hand to begin construction. A month later the western center followed suit.[63] Although reports of abuses resurfaced in early January, this time in the collection of hemp, investigators were unable to confirm the charges or discover the names of those involved. Again the emperor issued a stern warning to officials high and low that abuses would not be tolerated.[64]

Labor and Refugees

The fiscal urgency that was manifested in other aspects of the project also dominated the management of labor at Zhongmou. The emperor harried the officials about peculation in the payment of workers, and he fretted about the danger of social unrest when workers were demobilized, but neither Daoguang nor his officials seemed much concerned about the welfare of the refugees and laborers employed on the project. Their lack of comment on that issue perhaps reflects an admirable aversion to empty rhetoric. The stark reality was that no surplus to ease the plight of refugees existed; what relief there was would have to be provided through work on construction projects. When winter slowed construction, the workers struggled to survive bitter weather on starvation rations. The result was a demoralized and at times truculent workforce whose reluctant labor added to the woes of those managing the project.

Peculation was no small matter at Zhongmou. With tens of thousands of workers engaged in a wide range of tasks, the amount of money paid out daily was substantial in value and, since it was all copper cash, in bulk. There were many schemes to steal it. Pay tables *(paizhuo)* set up on the dikes on either side of the breach were used to pay daily wages. Depending on the pace of work, twenty to forty tables might be in operation at once, each paying out as much as one hundred thousand copper cash *(zhiqian)* per day. The deputy in charge of disbursement at each table received the day's supply of copper cash from a central office, and other deputies were assigned to tour the work site and watch for peculation by paymasters.[65]

Problems arose when the paymasters and those assigned to watch them cooperated. The resulting losses might run as high as one thousand to two thousand cash *(wen)* per table. With the pay of thousands of laborers at stake, ignoring the embezzlement of trivial amounts would effectively legitimate those practices. Losses could total tens of thousands of taels a day.[66]

The officials at Zhongmou sought to reassure the emperor that they were taking precautions against such practices. To limit the amount of money out in the field at any time, two wooden buckets *(paitong)* would be assigned per table, each labeled with an identifying character, to supply cash as needed. They were filled to the top with cash and then carried to the table for disbursement. After all the cash in the two buckets had been paid out, they were brought back to the central office to be refilled. Roving inspectors would oversee the process. Those measures could not be entirely effective, they noted, because many of the men in charge of the pay tables volunteered for that difficult job just for the chance to steal. To remedy the problem, project managers proposed to replace the usual appointees, most of whom were ninth-rank or unclassed officials, with assistant district magistrates *(xiancheng)* and registrars *(zhubu)*. Besides their normal pay of 1.2 taels per day, they would be given a subsidy of 0.8 taels per day and a staff of eight workers *(genyi)*, each of whom would receive 0.25 taels per day. Similar salary subsidies and controls applied to the military officials in charge of moving matériel to the dikes. Those caught pilfering were to be severely punished.[67]

The emperor remained dubious. He questioned whether paying officials more would guarantee their honesty. The officials at Zhongmou, of course, had little choice but to respond in detail, describing the security measures used at every level of the disbursement operation. In addition to using marked buckets, the workers assigned to carry the buckets had their clothes labeled with large matching characters, which made their movements easy to track. In order to discourage them from handing off cash to accomplices, they were searched if they appeared to be consorting with idlers or laden with hidden objects. In order to keep closer tabs on the servants and subalterns of the paymasters and military officials, a list was compiled of their names, and each trip they took to the dikes was noted. Any worker, servant, or soldier discovered cheating or stealing was to be severely punished on the spot as a warning to others. The extra salary for paymasters was intended to encourage a sense of obligation and self-esteem that might reduce peculation. In the event that more money and stricter punishments did not do the job, local officials would be recruited to beef up the numbers of officials patrolling the dikes.[68]

Somewhat mollified, the emperor nevertheless ordered high officials to make surprise visits to the dikes in person to ensure that the safeguards were functioning as promised. The security system seems to have been a success. Though some cases of peculation came to light during the project, none involved the construction at Zhongmou.[69]

While the emperor worried about the distribution of copper cash, much more was at stake, both in financial and in social terms, in the distribution of disaster relief and the treatment of refugees. According to one rough estimate, the number of refugees affected by the flood totaled several million *(shubaiwan)* people. As late as November, the flood still surrounded Taihe County in Yingzhou Prefecture and Huaining County in Chenzhou Prefecture. The most heavily damaged areas were in northern Henan, including Zhongmou, Xiangfu, Chenliu, Tongxu, Weishi,

Huaining, Fugou, Xihua, and Taikang Counties. Investigators reported widespread destruction of houses and general displacement. Officials urged that repair work begin soon so that victims living in the areas near the dikes would have a source of income.[70]

As heavy rains and the Yellow River's continued flooding extinguished hopes of salvaging part of the growing season, tens of thousands of peasants from northern Henan and Anhui gravitated to the repair site seeking work. One official commented, "The area affected by this year's disaster was comparatively broad and the starving are many; the number who have come to the work site to hire on as laborers is incalculable."[71] Most found employment digging the diversion canal, a task that required large amounts of unskilled labor.

Events at Kaifeng had shown that a large captive labor force did not mean a compliant one. To undermine labor resistance, Linqing, now involved in the excavation of the canal, offered prizes of money, cloth, wine, and meat to those workers who were the first to finish digging their section. For river troops, boots and hats were added incentives. Otherwise, Linqing wrote, there were "those who [would] dupe the supervisors, causing embankments to collapse as a pretext to stop work and argue for higher wages."[72]

Officials also worried about what the workers might do when the diversion canal was completed. A few workers could be used in constructing repair dikes, but dike work demanded fewer and more skilled workers than did dredging work. Understandably nervous at the prospect of gangs of unemployed workers roving the devastated winter countryside in search of food, the officials proposed various projects to keep the men occupied. Those included construction of an earth dike to connect the deflection dike with the western repair dike and constructing raised platforms behind the eastern and western dike heads for use as storage and staging areas. The emperor approved those suggestions but stressed the paramount importance of security, ordering the general in charge of troops in the area to guard against outbreaks of trouble.[73]

As winter approached, the living conditions for the workers and refugees deteriorated. The workers lived in tent cities built on the sandy banks of the river. Many did not possess adequate clothing for cold weather, and their meager pay did not allow them to purchase adequate food to meet the caloric demands of the hard labor they performed. Things turned hellish in late January. Powerful winds from the northwest blew ceaselessly for three days, churning up huge waves on the river and raising clouds of sand dense enough to blot out the sun. At one point all the tents housing the workers were blown down. Then the wind shifted to the northwest and three inches of snow fell.

When emergencies arose, the professional river troops could still be counted on, but the refugee labor force proved reluctant to brave the elements. When a slight warming trend loosened the ice upstream and sent black ice floes careening into the stalk repair dikes and the binding boats, professional river workers manned a fleet of small boats and traversed the dike base, using long poles to fend off the floes and beating the water at the base of the dike to keep ice from forming. They used special iron-tipped poles to break up frozen sections. But on February 12, when winds from the northwest damaged small sections of both the eastern and western repair dikes and officials tried to muster workers to move earth up to the dikes to repair the damage, most of the refugee labor force remained huddled in their tents and refused to come out. Those who did emerge often fared badly. One official described seeing the bodies of desperate workers, "clothes thin and bellies sunken, forced by hunger to come out in search of food, lying frozen where they had fallen." At the time, the officials showed little concern for the workers. Only after the project encountered repeated setbacks did charges of worker mistreatment surface.[74]

The failure of the officials in charge of the Zhongmou project to provide the refugee labor force with adequate clothing and rations to survive the winter stemmed from the same pervasive lack of funds that made the emperor so anxious to control peculation. The consequences were dire.

Things Fall Apart

The lack of funds did not initially prevent steady progress in the repairs. Work began on the main repair dikes on November 22. Lieutenant Colonel Lu Yongsheng (transferred from the Jiangsu conservancy at Lingqing's request), in command of several hundred trained river troops, was assigned the difficult task of "advancing by sections" *(jinzhan)*. By January 2, both the eastern and the western repair dikes had advanced some 350 meters into the current. Two weeks later 650 meters of the deflection dike had been completed, the western dike advanced another 150 meters, and the eastern dike advanced 100 meters. The diversion canal and other dredging projects were close to completion.[75]

The progress was encouraging but deceptive. The stocks of matériel had been reduced by 60 to 70 percent, and there was no money to purchase more. To cover immediate needs, the emperor approved ad hoc expenditures for purchase of materials, although without making clear where the money was to come from.[76]

In late January, the same violent storms that blew down workers' tents also damaged ninety meters of dike. Fortunately, the winds died before the situation became critical, and workers quickly repaired the damage. By mid-February, the distance between the two dikes had been reduced to seventy meters, and officials were confident enough of the pace of repairs to predict that the gap would be closed around February 27.[77]

The progress slowed when deep water and silt on the river bottom near the center of the breach prevented the successful placement of stalk sections. Whereas earlier sections of the repair dike had been built in water ten meters deep, with each section taking approximately two days to complete, the water was now more than twice that deep; each section required four or five times the material and four or five days to complete.[78]

The most serious problem continued to be bad weather. High winds blew for days at a time, creating waves that crashed incessantly against the unstable repair dikes. Work crews could do little but protect the sections already in place, putting down stone rubble revetments and adding earth to the top of the dikes. Placing new sections was impossible.[79]

On February 25, two days before the scheduled closure of the gap, a storm from the northeast destroyed some forty meters of dike and sank several boats. After a week the storm abated. Workers dragged out the sunken boats for repairs and restarted work on the dikes. Although the damage had been moderate, the force of the current through the break had dug a trench forty-five meters deep, making the placement of sections even more problematic. But the officials continued to report progress.[80]

On March 20 the "gate section" *(menzhan)* for the eastern repair dike was completed, and work on the western dike's gate section was under way. Only thirty meters remained between the two dikes, the diversion canal was ready for opening, and officials expressed confidence that "'linking the dragons' *(helong)* will be comparatively easy."[81]

On March 25, the diversion canal was opened, causing the water level at the breach to drop almost a meter. Linkui reported that 60 percent of the current was flowing into the diversion canal and predicted that the break would be closed on March 31.[82]

Disaster struck the same night. Without warning the river began to rise. Waves began to wash over the tops of some sections of the dike, eventually overturning section 37 of the eastern repair dike and washing it away. As the officials struggled to halt the collapse, a (somewhat tardy) report arrived from Xiazhou warning that on March 23 the river was up over half a meter and continuing to rise.

As the river rose, the wind began to blow from the north. The combination was devastating; sections of repair dike that had stood ten meters above the water were suddenly awash. Within two days, 150 meters of dike had been lost to the wind and waves. Linkui and Liao Hongquan accepted responsibility for the disaster and abjectly requested punishment. No doubt with an eye to minimizing their culpability, they also requested that officials familiar with river affairs *(shu an he wu)* be sent to replace them.[83]

The emperor was incensed. He blamed Linkui and Liao Hongquan for their dawdling and delays. "If [the repairs] had been handled with dispatch and the breach closed in the first month, then the spring waters would not [yet] have risen," he wrote, adding that the present failure was unforgivable.[84]

Although the collapse of 150 meters of repair dike out of a total of approximately 1,260 meters does not seem an insurmountable loss, other complications made the setback decisive. Matériel shortages and the need to clear newly deposited silt out of the diversion canal and the riverbed made it unlikely that repairs could be completed before the summer floods. Even protecting the existing dikes would be difficult. Linkui reported that the completion of the project would require a further 2 million taels, with no assurance of success.[85]

The same day that Linkui sent that memorial, the emperor dispatched Niu Jian to the Zhongmou flood site to act as E Xun'an's deputy. The emperor recalled Niu Jian's popularity during his tenure as governor of Henan and characterized the people of Henan as "pure and virtuous," then got to the point: "Previously, when restoring the wall of the provincial city, they enthusiastically contributed [funds], and it was not necessary to expend any [government] money. This indeed shows a love of duty and concern for public welfare." Niu's unenviable job was to coax more blood from Henan's much-squeezed merchant and gentry turnip in order to finance the Zhongmou project.[86]

The failure at Zhongmou also brought forth the bureaucratic buzzards. Within a few days of the collapse of the repair dikes, the emperor received a memorial harshly criticizing the conduct of the project and the treatment of workers. That indictment followed by only a month a memorial charging corruption in the Jiangsu conservancy. Although none of the charges were aimed at Henan, the emperor, with characteristic suspicion, remarked, "If it is found that such abuses exist in the Jiangsu conservancy, the Henan conservancy will be unable to avoid them."[87]

The emperor ordered a transcribed but anonymous copy of the memorial critical of the Zhongmou project sent to the officials in charge. Among other things, it charged lax supervision in matériel collection and in the digging of the diversion canal. Delays had come about because neither suppliers nor laborers had been paid the money owed them. As a result, the workers had begun to flee the work site and merchants were reluctant to come forward with construction materials.[88]

The memorial disparaged the high officials at Zhongmou as "humble and yielding" and charged that "when it comes to handling problems, they are indecisive." The memorial also criticized the lower officials. In particular, it singled out former Kaifeng prefect Zou Minghe, "well known as an [official of] talent (caineng)." The author claimed that higher officials had allowed control of the project to slip from their grasp, to the extent that all planning and personnel appointments for the project were in Zou's hands.[89]

Some of the charges, such as the assertion that the bottom of the diversion canal was three feet higher than the riverbed, were clearly absurd (the canal had worked as designed when it was opened). Other charges, however, echoed earlier difficulties in matériel collection and the treatment of workers.[90]

Although the project was officially under the control of Liao Hong-quan, the official whose name headed the memorial responding to the censor's indictment was Linkui, a Manchu of the bordered white banner and president of the Board of Rites who had been dispatched to assist at Zhongmou. In spite of the fact that he had no experience in river affairs,

Linkui's special status is evident in that from the time of his arrival, his name appeared at the top of most of the memorials from Zhongmou.[91]

Linkui's assignment was vague. The only specific reference to his role appears in an edict of December 11. In it the emperor notes impatiently that "Linkui at this time should already have arrived at the work site" and orders him, "together with" Liao Hongquan and the other top officials at Zhongmou, to keep a close eye on subordinates and make sure that the need for haste does not lead to carelessness.[92]

Linkui's career to that point had been remarkable. After distinguishing himself in the *jinshi* exams of 1826, he moved rapidly through a succession of increasingly important posts. Among them was his appointment in 1842 as minister of the Imperial Household Department. Linkui was thus an imperial insider, a talented Manchu trusted by Daoguang. A second Wenchong, he was sent to Zhongmou as Daoguang's eye on the suspect river conservancy.[93]

And like Wenchong, he quickly found himself in trouble. Clearly stung by the censorial assault, Linkui's initial reaction was defensiveness. He claimed that because he and his associates had had no experience in river affairs, they had no choice but to ask advice of knowledgeable people; what appeared to be indecision was simply justified caution. Those claims of inexperience were true enough for Linkui but were overstated for the other officials in charge at Zhongmou: Huicheng and E Xun'an both had taken part in the Xiangfu repair. One of the ironies of the censor's charges is that the most experienced river official at Zhongmou, Linqing, was excluded by imperial order from any part in policy discussions. His role was confined to managing matériel collection and the digging of the diversion canal.[94] Linkui and his fellow high officials would have been well served by being allowed to freely consult Linqing.

Not all of Linkui's rebuttal was defensive. He flatly dismissed the charges against Zou Minghe, pointing out that he and his fellow high officials still approved all appointments. The fact that the central office and the branch offices each were responsible for personnel on separate parts of the project made it impossible for any single official to control appointments. In the aftermath of the flood, Linkui's attempts to dispute the charges must have seemed little more than excuse-making to an angry emperor. The delays the emperor pointed to were actually minor; the Zhongmou break occurred ten days later in the year than the Xiangfu flood, and construction began a little more than two weeks later.[95] More harmful was the slow pace of matériel collection, which never brought work to a halt but did slow each phase of construction. The result was that the repairs were still under way in late winter, when conditions were deteriorating and the river was beginning to rise. The dilatory transfer of funds also delayed the start of construction. Pan Xi'en's reluctance to part with hard cash and instead to pass along to the Henan conservancy only promised funds was typical of the territorial mentality that marked most fiscal dealings in the provinces. The resulting recourse to the emperor's own treasury was an exceptional move that underscored the urgent nature of the state's concern and the pressure on the officials who made the request.

In the end, Daoguang deserves a measure of the blame for the failure of the first repair project. His emphasis on limiting expenditures, though understandable in the context of the state's deteriorating fiscal condition, led to poor engineering decisions. In particular, the decision to eliminate a secondary repair dike left the main repair dike extremely vulnerable to the wind and waves.

Even without those many problems, the men in charge at Zhongmou would have faced a difficult task. The conditions at the site were bad from the outset. The break was larger than that at Xiangfu, poor weather was a constant hindrance to progress, and the river seems to have remained high longer than in 1842. Nor was the sudden rise that finally spelled disaster something that the officials could have predicted or prevented.

The question hanging over the officials at Zhongmou was what to do next; should the project continue or be put on hold until the following year? The conditions for continuing work did not look good. Stalk supplies were exhausted, and only five to ten carts of stalks were arriving at the collection centers each month. The new crop would not be ready for harvesting for some time. Spring floods would soon cause the river to rise again, cutting a wider gap in the dikes. As the weather warmed, peasants returned to their fields; by the end of the second month, over half of the labor force had dispersed.[96]

Linkui's sensible suggestion that the project be postponed only provoked imperial outrage: "Linkui and Liao Hongquan were officials specially appointed to manage [the repairs]. [Their] procrastination and ineffectiveness are unspeakable offenses. I have already sent an edict removing them from office. [Now] they are also stripped of the seventh rank they were formerly awarded and ordered to come to the capital and await further orders."[97]

The emperor gave Zhongxiang and E Xun'an joint responsibility for the project and ordered them to consult with each other on all matters. Daoguang was especially concerned about the laborers who had no fields to return to and might cause trouble when the work came to a halt.[98]

As if to add to the emperor's fears, another memorial charging corruption in the river conservancy now appeared. Echoing charges made by earlier critics, a censor named Jiang Hongsheng wrote accusing river officials of peculating from the river works to support extravagant lifestyles.[99] According to Jiang, that had become so commonplace that the two or three honest officials who pointed out the excesses were themselves condemned as troublemakers. The emperor again ordered officials to investigate.[100]

The cost of the setback had been high. Nearly 7 million taels had been transferred to the construction project at Zhongmou, almost all of which had been spent. Most of the moneys were from other provincial treasuries. The sources included the following:

Source	Amount (in taels)
Provincial and customs treasuries (*guan*)	5,199,000
Central government treasuries	1,500,000
Contributions (*juanshu*) for matériel purchases	34,000
Interest on commuted taxes from Kaifeng Prefecture	96,920
Savings from matériel purchases	21,840
Other contributions (*juanshu*)	4,000
Total	6,855,760[101]

Linkui's original estimate had been 5,182,000 taels. Cost overruns resulted from the need for repair dikes 180 meters longer than originally estimated and the extra material required to construct sections in deep water at the center of the breach. Of the 6.85 million taels received for the project, only 60,000 taels of silver and 28,000 strings of cash remained.[102]

The emperor was determined that the state would not bear the costs of the failure alone. Regulations covering the guarantee *(baogu)* of works carried out on the Yellow River held officials responsible for part of the cost of construction that failed within one year of completion. On May 4 the emperor asked the Board of Works to suggest a breakdown of the responsibility of the various officials at Zhongmou. The board replied that the statute called for "government expenditures to cover 60 percent, compensation by officials to cover 40 percent" *(xiao liu pei si)*. The board determined that Linkui and Liao Hongquan together had to pay 10 percent and that Zhongxiang was responsible for 20 percent and E Xun'an for another 10 percent. The remaining moneys due were divided among the lower officials in charge of the project. Applying those percentages to the total costs, the breakdown of money owed would be Linkui and Liao Hongquan, 123,338.5 taels each; Zhongxiang, 493,355.5 taels; E Xun'an, 246,677 taels; lower officials, 1,480,066 taels.[103]

With the repairs stalled, the officials turned to the problem of facing the coming flood season without losing everything accomplished during the winter. They estimated that a gap of six hundred meters was necessary to handle the summer and fall floods. With the gap reduced to only ninety meters, the coming high water would almost certainly destroy both repair dikes and would probably break through the levee closing off the mouth of the diversion canal.[104]

The alternative was to strengthen the deflection dike to protect the western (upstream) repair dike. The eastern repair dike would be dismantled, opening the needed gap but allowing workers to salvage the materials for use in the fall. Those plans were approved by the emperor.[105]

The dismantling of the Zhongmou operation also necessitated finding alternative work for the demobilized laborers. The officials decided that work relief would be provided for the needed repairs in the four upstream subprefectures—Huangbian and Weiliang on the north bank and Shangnan and Zhonghe on the south bank.[106]

As part of the demobilization, river troops from the Jiangsu conservancy were ordered to return to Jiangsu with their officers. In addition, since the laborers had been dispersed and no longer required policing, all Henan troops except those needed to protect the repair works from the coming floods were sent back to their original posts.[107]

From that point on, the activity at the work site slowed to a crawl. The only ongoing construction was that designed to reinforce or protect existing repair structures. Because of those efforts, the western repair dike, the original deflection dike, and the diversion canal all survived the summer floods.[108]

Xiangfu had been a mixture of tragedy and triumph; Taoyuan was an unlucky setback. Zhongmou was a harbinger. The first repair attempt had cost lives, careers, and precious resources. More importantly, it exposed Qing river engineering at its most disorganized and inept. But the time was not yet right for a reassessment of the state's commitment to river control. That would come in the next decade. For the moment the only response possible was to wait a year and clean up the mess.

6

A Change of Course, 1844–1855

IN SPITE OF THE COSTS—both fiscal and administrative—of the Zhongmou debacle, it was still seen only as a setback. Questions of delay and issues of construction and funding aside, there was no real alternative to completing the repairs. In August of 1844, preparation began again for closing the breach. A comprehensive estimate called for shifting the "golden gate" to a site east of the earlier location and building 650 meters of repair dike.[1]

The report was also blunt about the need for a secondary dike *(erba)* to prevent a repeat of the earlier collapse: "Last winter the project office *(zongju)* recommended that a secondary dike be built, but because the cost of supplies was increasingly heavy, permission was refused. This time it is imperative [that funds be] budgeted [for it]."[2] The planned dike consisted of an earth base 1,250 meters long, to be built out from the main dike over the flat silted plain along the river. After the dikes reached the water, they would begin "entering by sections," according to established practice. The shallows between the secondary dike and the main repair dike would be filled with earth, further strengthening the overall structure.[3]

The total estimated cost of closing the breach, including those repairs and several other smaller projects, was 6.3 million taels, with 4.5 million to be sent as soon as possible to prevent delays like those of the previous year.[4] Ordered to comment on the budget, the Board of Revenue in turn ordered various treasuries to prepare the needed funds.[5]

Even at that late stage, however, the emperor's distrust of river officials and fiscal shortages left him unconvinced that the repairs were necessary. In an edict both wary of and weary with river affairs, Daoguang foreshadowed the state's withdrawal from Yellow River control a decade later:

Before beginning a great undertaking, it is necessary to calculate its beginning and its end and to accurately weigh its light and heavy [aspects]. In the year since the Zhongmou flood, there has not been a day that the inability to close the breach and the continued displacement of the disaster victims of three provinces has not been on my mind. . . . [Now that the needed funds are ready] I order that [Zhongxiang and E Xun'an] again closely examine the actual conditions at the work site. If, after funds are transferred to the work site, [they] can be sure that the situation is under control and that the work can be finished in a timely fashion, then [they] naturally should follow the original plan [of] buying materials and beginning work, so that with one great effort the problem can be solved.

But should things become difficult and success uncertain and, as before, it becomes necessary to constantly request more money and supplies, then continuing to carry out the imperial mandate and undertake repairs would only be ignoring the warning of last year's mistakes.

As for the disaster-stricken people of these provinces, if they temporarily cannot be returned to agriculture, work relief *(yigong daizhen)* is the best plan [for dealing with them]. If the repair project is [again] delayed, then funds for relief and ways to deploy [the refugee labor force] can be recommended and discussed. In particular, [the refugees] cannot be allowed to migrate elsewhere and stir up trouble.

[Because] the nation's fiscal resources *(jingfei)* are limited, those using them must stretch them out; in that way [the nation's] wealth will be adequate. Year after year, military and river repair funds have been needed at the same time. No area of state finance is free of constant worry over shortages. If this major repair project could again be delayed and work restarted in the fall of the coming year, everything would benefit from greater convenience.

Zhongxiang and E Xun'an have received great favors. Both are men of conscience. Moreover, they live each day at the work site and can closely observe [conditions]. Upon receipt of this edict, they are ordered to secretly memorialize on the total situation. They cannot be hesitant, and must not bend to compromise. They especially should not consult river officials [about the situation]; who among the civil and military officials in the river conservancy would not want the project to go forward? Everything must be reported accurately without delay.[6]

His faith in the river conservancy completely eroded and his watchdogs disgraced, Daoguang had no choice but to entrust the question of the feasibility of river repairs to two provincial administrators. For their part, what other reply could Zhongxiang and E Xun'an give except that the project must go forward as soon as possible? Their reasons were varied and convincing: disaster victims who "already had passed one winter and two summers" as refugees needed to be returned to agriculture and again made self-sufficient. Delaying the repair would leave them demoralized and agitated.[7]

Delay would also waste the work done and the materials collected up to that point. The stalks would begin to rot, and rain and erosion would fill the diversion canal. Postponement also would threaten urban centers in northern Henan and Anhui. If the coming flood season was a bad one, cities like Kaifeng stood a good chance of being flooded once again.[8]

There were also fiscal reasons not to postpone the repairs. The cost of relief had reached nearly 2 million taels in the current year, not counting tax remissions. Another year's delay would require the expenditure of several million taels in Henan and Anhui. Closing the breach would not only reduce the need for relief funds, but it would also return the population to agriculture, reducing the need for tax remissions.[9] In spite of his misgivings, the emperor finally accepted the need to finish the job and ordered that the repairs proceed.[10]

As in the previous year, the officials at Zhongmou faced funding delays, but rigorous collection efforts and a broadened use of subscription campaigns allowed the work to continue unimpeded.[11] By December 14 all phases of the repairs were well under way. Over 90 percent of the dredging had been completed, and 40 percent to 50 percent of the diversion canal was dug. The repair dikes, now called "large dikes" (daba), and the secondary dikes (erba), were pushing out into the current, with 100 meters of each completed.[12]

Cold weather brought the usual problems; ice floes cut ropes and sank boats, storms damaged sections of the dikes. In one particularly gruesome episode, a large ice floe came downstream with such velocity that it damaged or sank thirty vessels, drowning many crew members. The work halted as crews were dispatched to fish out the bodies of the drowned. In spite of those setbacks, by December 29 another 70 meters of the large dike and 100 meters of secondary dike had been completed, and 300 meters had been added to the deflection dikes.[13]

The diversion canal was opened on January 25, and the water flowed through into the old course without obstruction. By the twenty-eighth the gap between the repair dikes had been reduced to seventy meters. Matériel shortages had briefly threatened delays, but stepped-up purchasing had kept pace with repairs, and the closing of the breach appeared to be just a matter of days.[14]

Labor problems threatened momentarily when workers carrying stalks and earth up to the repair dikes seemed to slow their efforts. Zhongxiang and E Xun'an, anxious to complete the "door sections" *(menzhan)*, urged them on with higher wages.[15]

It was also important to placate the river gods. On January 30 the collected officials on the project sacrificed to those gods. They also cast five-colored rice cakes *(zongzi)* into the river to exorcise bad influences.[16] "Nine lotus lanterns" were hung to help the souls of those who had drowned on the project cross over into the other world.[17]

The final phase of closure began on January 31. Ropes were stretched across the gap between the two dikes to form a huge net into which stalks and earth were piled to create a massive plug. An unending stream of workers carrying bamboo baskets of earth and loads of stalks moved up the dikes to drop their burdens into the gap. As the bundle rose above the repair dikes, it was pressed down, the earth and stalks packed tightly together. On the night of February 2, the officials in charge of the project got a scare when heavy waves washed away the upper portion of a section of the repair dike. But the dike held and work continued. After five days and nights of unceasing effort, the closing section was finally pressed into the bottom of the river. The plug stopped the flow and sealed the breach. Zhongxiang and E Xun'an immediately sent a memorial to the emperor reporting that the Yellow River again flowed east.[18]

The emperor's satisfaction was manifest. He ordered Zhongxiang to burn incense in the temple of the river gods to express his gratitude to those deities. More important to the officials at Zhongmou, the emperor lifted earlier punishments and rewarded those who had worked on the project. Zhongxiang and E Xun'an were restored to the second rank and awarded the peacock feather. Huicheng was to be returned to one of the six boards as an assistant department secretary. Linqing was raised to the fourth rank (still two ranks lower than before the Taoyuan flood),

龍合工牟

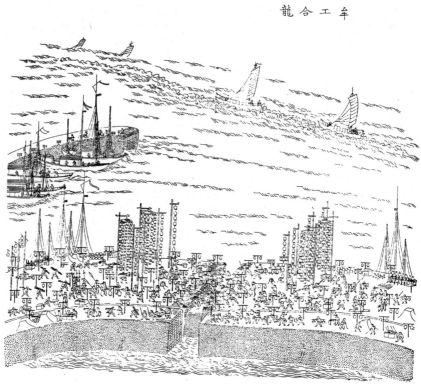

Fig. 7   Closing the final gap at Zhongmou.

and Niu Jian was made an official of the seventh rank. Both Linqing and Niu Jian were ordered to return to Beijing after their work at Zhongmou was completed, ostensibly to receive new assignments.[19]

Although much remained to be done, the closing of the breach brought to an end the long nightmare of Zhongmou. The cost of the second repair project was 4,704,900 taels, but during the repairs the project treasury had taken in a total of 6,029,700 taels. Of that amount, 1 million was to be refunded to the board treasury *(buku)*, whereas 256,300 was to go to finishing the work.[20]

Including the 7,707,800 taels spent on the initial repair attempt, the total cost of repair construction on the Zhongmou flood was 12,412,700 taels. But that hardly tells the whole story. There are no overall statistics for the relief expenditures for the Zhongmou flood, but as already noted, Zou Minghe estimated the cost for three months of relief granted in the spring of 1824 at 800,000 taels. He also reckoned the combined tax remissions given to the affected counties and prefectures in Henan for the first year of the flood at more than 1.2 million taels and the relief and tax remissions for Anhui and Jiangsu at around 1 million taels. The total cost in lost tax income and relief expenditures for the two years of the flood was certainly over 7 million taels, giving a total estimated cost of almost 20 million taels.[21]

The Xiangfu flood had been a disaster for the state and the people of the region; Zhongmou was a cataclysm from which neither the region nor the river conservancy would recover. It devastated the Huaibei region, drained provincial treasuries, decimated the ranks of experienced river officials, and completed the alienation of the Daoguang emperor. Although a gloss of normalcy was restored in the years after 1845, the Yellow River control system and the bureaucracy that maintained it were living on borrowed time.

THE RIVER CONSERVANCY BUREAUCRACY quickly resumed its routine, although not without some slight innovations. Jingzheng suggested that since river duties were such an onerous part of the job of the governor-general of the Henan conservancy, he should no longer keep his main office at Jining in Shandong but should instead reside at the Lanyi Temple in Henan. The emperor asked Zhongxiang, E Xun'an, and Shandong governor Chongen to respond to the suggestion.[22]

They were not entirely in accord with the proposal, noting that when the grain tribute fleet passed through Shandong, the sixteen hundred troops under the governor-general's command were needed to keep the thousands of grain boatmen in line. If the governor-general was at the Lanyi Temple, it would be difficult for him to train and deploy his troops effectively, they argued. Instead, they suggested that the governor-general transfer to Henan and begin his inspection and preparations to meet the coming flood two weeks before the summer flood season arrived. After "first frost" (*shuangjiang,* in late October or early November) he should return to Jining to take up his duties there. The emperor accepted that proposal.[23]

Although the river conservancy bureaucracy soon returned to routine, the areas in Henan province that had suffered the most from the flooding were unable to quickly regain their former level of vitality. Late in 1847

E Xun'an memorialized for permission to again solicit subscriptions to provide relief to the Henan peasantry. He explained that besides the repeated floods, shortages of rain and snowfall in 1846 had made it impossible to grow a second wheat crop, deepening the hardship of the farmers in the area. The drought had continued into 1847, with only a few locations able to escape its effects. He requested permission to open kitchens to provide rice gruel to those who needed it. If relief was not provided soon, he warned, the weak might begin to migrate in search of food, whereas the strong might turn to banditry.[24]

The provincial officials did not have the resources on hand to deal with the situation, E Xun'an wrote. There was no ongoing work to provide work relief for those people. Moreover, because of the tax remissions awarded to the Henan peasantry in the wake of the 1841 and 1843 floods, the treasury had no funds to use for relief purposes. In its response to the emperor's request for comments, the Board of Revenue gave its support to the proposal. Contributions from those wishing to purchase degrees were to be sent to the Henan treasury under the same guidelines that had prevailed during the Zhongmou project. In order to provide aid, the board recommended that funds be immediately advanced from the central government.[25]

Those measures were largely cosmetic; the fundamental problems of the river conservancy and the tensions they provoked between river officials and the central government soon reappeared. Charges of corruption again were leveled, and a new generation of river officials was forced to defend the integrity of the river bureaucracy. In DG 30 (1850), board president Qiying complained that money was being wasted in the Yellow River conservancy by officials who would falsely report problems in order to garner emergency repair funds. He also charged that bribery (lougui) was widespread. Yan Yiyu, governor-general of the Henan conservancy, became the latest in a long line of river officials called upon to reply to such charges. Not surprisingly, he denied them.[26]

Foremost among the problems facing river engineers remained the issue of funding. The tension between the cost of the Yellow River control system and the fiscal constraints under which the central government was operating continued to dominate the relationship between the two. The documents relating to river costs show that the officials were under great pressure to reduce their expenditures. For example, the practice of comparing each year's supplementary works *(ling'an)* costs with those of the three previous years had been introduced to track those costs and pressure officials to either hold the line on them or reduce them. Records for the 1840s show that such costs did remain fairly steady. The total supplementary work expenditures in Henan were as follows:

Year	Total (in taels)
1841	1,207,938
1842	1,621,986
1843	1,309,709
1844	716,467
1845	1,938,296
1846	1,834,954
1847	1,686,766
1848	1,777,841
1849	1,558,580
1850	1,496,201[27]

As with the earlier efforts to control expenditures through tighter accounting, a way was found to circumvent those controls, and the total cost of river repairs, including regular maintenance and emergency repairs, continued to rise. The rising costs made a confrontation between river officials and the central bureaucracy inevitable.[28]

The crackdown came in DG 29 (1849), in an edict that ordered river expenditures to be kept to no more than 3 million taels per year in each of the Henan and the Jiangsu conservancies. Both governors-general consented to the limit, although they no doubt had little choice. In any case, their consent proved more strategic than sincere; within a year they began requesting additional funds. At one juncture, the emperor demanded that river officials make up for any spending above the limit. Following the earlier method of tracking supplementary expenditures, the emperor ordered river officials to verify in detail and record the amounts of annual overruns. When the Jiangsu conservancy spent 3,300,000 taels for river repairs, the emperor ordered the extra 300,000 taels subtracted from the coming year's budget.[29]

Those attempts to put a hard ceiling on river conservancy expenditures were tardy and, with the emperor's death in the following year, ineffective. Although they were on file as policy, the appropriations continued to rise. A flood in 1851 and the partial collapse of the repaired dike in 1853 further undermined efforts to limit expenditures.

At the same time, the Grand Canal was becoming inoperable. In 1849 the state began once more to experiment with sea transport of tribute grain. Finally, in the sixth month of 1855, the Yellow River ruptured its northern dike and captured the course of the Daqing River. The new course approximated one of the river's old routes to the Bohai Gulf.

The Xianfeng emperor, pressed by the war in the south and no longer reliant on the Grand Canal for the transport of tribute grain, was anxious to find an easy solution. With funds in short supply, he asked whether there was not some way to "take advantage of the circumstances" *(yin shi li dao)* and thus delay the closing of the Lanyang break.[30] He ordered Li Jun, head of the Henan conservancy, to investigate and report.

Having made his preference clear, the emperor could hardly have been surprised that Li Jun responded favorably. The river official pointed out that with funds in short supply, building dikes along both banks of the river's new course was out of the question except where they were necessary to protect cities endangered by the river. For the other areas subject to floods, Li Jun suggested that the common people be mobilized to build levees no more than three feet tall. Li explained that "when the water is low, those will be adequate to restrain it. When the water is high, it will flow over those dikes, dissipating its force. The more the river floods, the more sediment it deposits, so that the surface of the land will gradually rise." In that way, the river would build its own banks. And what of the impact on the peasants of the region? Li showed that he understood his role as Pollyanna, commenting that "moreover, the sandy margins [along the river] will be turned into fertile borders"![31]

In spite of the language of delay, the decision to allow the Yellow River to remain in its new course ended the state commitment to the control system. Six years later, the Jiangsu conservancy finally was abolished and the system formally abandoned.

Conclusion

> A technology is the expression of man's working relationship with the natural world, the point at which environment and society meet and shape each other.
>
> Mark Elvin, *The Pattern of the Chinese Past*

THE CONSTRUCTION OF THE Grand Canal in the Yuan dynasty and the Ming decision to confine the Yellow River to its southern channel for the sake of inland grain transport together created the conditions for a complex interaction between the river, the state, and the bureaucracy—an interaction that changed all three. Two views of the relationship between the state and the river have prevailed. One treats the river as a perennial problem responsive to efficient management. From that perspective, Yellow River floods were the product of administrative laxity, corruption, and imperial inflexibility, and the river's change of course in the mid-nineteenth century was a symbol and a symptom of dynastic decline. What that approach cannot explain is how Daoguang's engineers overcame supposedly enfeebled dynastic institutions to produce two decades of successful river control, a record equal to that of any of their predecessors working in more virtuous times.

According to the second view, the Yellow River's flooding and change of course was a natural and inevitable product of geologic and hydrologic forces against which human institutions could not prevail. The second view ignores the fact that by the end of the Ming dynasty, the Yellow River—"cribbed, cabined and confined"[1] in a network of dikes that stretched from the coast to the western hills—had long since ceased to follow "natural" cycles. Although the natural forces that complicated management of the Yellow River—heavy siltation, erratic flow, sudden flooding—remained unchanged, the dikes and other components of the system disrupted and contravened the river's natural tendencies. Even so profound an event as a change of course was neither natural nor inevitable. The Yellow River changed course every time it breached its dikes; and with every successful repair by river officials, the river's course was changed back again.

The crisis that created the river's shift in the 1850s signaled neither dynastic decline nor an irresistible natural cycle, but the administrative, technological, and economic limits of the late imperial state. Ming and Qing engineers succeeded in constructing a system that defied nature for two and a half centuries, but at a high price both in environmental and monetary terms. The yearly cycle of flood and siltation that raised the river's bed also lengthened the dikes, added to the number of defensive sites, and raised the stakes and the costs of control. By the nineteenth century, the fiscal strain was becoming insupportable. The legacy of precedent and the dictates of dynastic prestige affirmed the strategic and economic necessity of the Grand Canal, even as its engineering costs soared. Daoguang and his predecessors sought to shore up the system in spite of its obvious limits. In the 1850s, with the Grand Canal silting up and the Taiping rebels rampaging through the Yangzi River valley, the Qing leadership finally abandoned the Yellow River, allowing it to follow its new, northern course. The Yellow River–Grand Canal hydraulic system was perhaps the most ambitious imperial enterprise of any age, but it was costly and, with the South in revolt, irrelevant to the state's immediate survival.

The (Neo-)Confucian engineer personified the imperial state's quandary over how best to handle the Yellow River. A hybrid literati-technologist, he was expected to bridge the gap between Confucian administrative ideals and practical hydraulic decisions. The blending of bureaucrat and technologist was nothing new in Chinese history, but the men who worked in the river bureaucracy in the nineteenth century were unlike their predecessors in many ways. For most early technobureaucrats, technological accomplishments were a sideline, not a career. They were amateurs. In contrast, late Qing Confucian engineers were chosen primarily for their ability to manage technological tasks, not their achievements as literati-bureaucrats. Unlike their early Qing counterparts, nineteenth-century river officials seldom had the prestige to affect national policy. The elevation to positions of great responsibility of men whose skills were technical was a mark of both the flexibility and the limits of the dynastic system: the Confucian engineers were a compromise; they were as far as the late imperial state could go to accommodate the need for a technical meritocracy.

The ability of Confucian engineers to effect broad, meaningful changes in hydraulic policy was undermined by the institutional weakness of the Board of Works, the metropolitan bureau that represented their interests. The Board of Works served less to focus the power of river officials than to check them. The river conservancy has often been depicted as a monolithic, self-interested bureaucracy. In reality, there was no Yellow River conservancy except as a subdivision of a much larger hydraulic bureaucracy. And that bureaucracy, like its metropolitan overseer, the Board of Works, was fragmented by the administrative and functional divisions designed into the Qing administration. The close and direct attention paid by the emperor and the Grand Council to the Yellow River–Grand Canal system further diluted the influence of the Board of Works. Like the salt monopoly, the hydraulic bureaucracy suffered from a lack of strong executive leadership.[2] The concomitant weakness of technical or professional forces meant that hydraulic policy turned more on bureaucratic and fiscal issues than on engineering strategy. When a strong emperor or minister and a skilled engineer cooperated, the drawbacks of that institutional atomization could be minimized, as in the cases of Zhang Juzheng and Pan Jixun, or Kangxi and Jin Fu. In the long run, however, such happy convergences were too uncommon to guarantee continuity or strategic focus.

Nonetheless, it is not true that the Chinese state killed technological innovation by an emphasis on "routine, traditionalism and immobility." On the contrary, most emperors welcomed innovation within limits. River officials were expected to be flexible, rejecting precedent when circumstances demanded it and "on guard against the charge that they were unreceptive to new proposals because they held *cheng-jian* (closed viewpoints)."[3] The innovating official had to prove that his innovation would work, but success could add immensely to his prestige. Furthermore, opponents could not simply rely on precedent or established regulations to counter innovation. They were expected to present practical arguments against new practices and policies.[4] The innovations of Pan Jixun succeeded, as did less dramatic measures such as the introduction of stone in the Jiangsu conservancy and brick in the Henan conservancy, in part because they were demonstrably beneficial and effective but also because they were given at least limited support by the emperor. And it must be remembered that the same imperial caution that sometimes circumscribed innovation also served to counter particularism and corruption and prevent the squandering of state resources on wild and impracticable schemes. For every rejected proposal that (in hindsight) seems a missed opportunity, one can find another, and probably many others, that was unrealistic, wasteful, even potentially ruinous. Caution did not mean immobility. Innovation took place throughout the Qing period, and the importance of technical proficiency was recognized. That is evident in the Yongzheng program, which sent promising capital officials to the river conservancy for training; in the use of probationary officials in river posts; and in the "three floods" trial period required of civil officials appointed to posts along the Yellow River.

During the early years of his reign, the Daoguang emperor welcomed reform and entertained suggestions for innovations of all sorts. Even when proposals were rejected, their authors suffered no loss of status. For those whose proposals were accepted, rewards often followed. Tao Zhu was promoted after his work to reform the salt monopoly. Other officials associated with reform, including Wu Bangqing, who headed the Henan conservancy from 1832 to 1836, were also rewarded with high posts.[5] The emperor's outpouring of gratitude after Li Yumei's death shows that the brick controversy engendered during Li's tenure did nothing to undermine his reputation in the emperor's eyes. Even Lei Yixian, whose hydraulic proposals were harshly rejected by Pan Xi'en, was not censured by the emperor.

Indirect evidence from the technical writing of the period also shows a strong literati interest in technology. Traditionally, technological skills were concentrated in the hands of semiliterate artisans, craftsmen, and technicians. The exception was in technical knowledge directly related to state power, such as astronomy and hydraulic engineering.[6] The proliferation in the late imperial period of publications on subjects such as mining and river engineering reflects increased state concern with those subjects.

The interest in practical statecraft also encouraged the study of technology. The statecraft movement elevated mundane administrative concerns such as water conservancy to a new level of intellectual importance and thus made them acceptable subjects for literati attention. Statecraft leaders encouraged their subordinates and members of their secretarial staff to study and write about practical matters such as hydraulics, giving those who were technically inclined an opportunity to follow their interests.[7] That resulted in encyclopedic compilations like the *Huangchao Jingshi Wenbian* (1827) and the *Xu Xingshui Jinjian* (1832), as well as individual explorations such as the works of Linqing. By the nineteenth century, a growing corpus of detailed and sophisticated writing on technology allowed even the least technically oriented official, with a little study, to achieve a modicum of competence in an area such as river engineering. Engineering canons such as the works of Pan Jixun and Jin Fu, often long on philosophical speculation, were supplemented by new works that focused on historical development and on the nuts and bolts of hydraulic engineering.

The influence of statecraft ideas was not uniformly positive. Regional and patronage loyalties led to divergent political agendas that precluded a unified movement. The administrative philosophies of statecraft officials also differed, separating them into two groups variously labeled the moralists or radicals and the moderates or realists. Those divisions hindered the development of consensus solutions to problems such as how best to manage the Yellow River.[8]

There were also limits to what books could teach officials about the practical demands of hydraulic engineering. Without hands-on experience, the officials had to rely on their own grasp of technical materials to convert what was found in books into effective engineering solutions. Officials without the engineering gift were forced to rely on lower officials and skilled commoners, whose arcane knowledge made them invaluable but also made effective supervision by technologically unsophisticated superiors difficult.

Literati who rose to high positions because of their technical competence also risked being assigned to extended service in dangerous posts. Linqing's long tenure as head of the Jiangsu conservancy was not unique; during the Qing, successful river officials often served for long periods. Not only was an extended stay in the river conservancy dangerous in itself, but it also marked an official as the possessor of specialized technical abilities rather than the more highly prized general administrative skills.[9]

Although the state was eager to utilize technical competence and took measures to ensure that hydraulic officials possessed it in some measure, technical specialization presented the state with problems of control. Censors and imperial commissioners sent to investigate river affairs were at a disadvantage when it came to technical issues. They were seen as objective judges because they were not veterans of the hydraulic bureaucracy, but unfortunately, they were also ignorant of the knowledge required to assess technical issues or ferret out corruption. Imperial watchdogs like Wenchong operated at an even greater disadvantage, since they were expected to both administer and investigate, a role that put them at odds with the very subordinates whose expertise they needed in order to succeed in their job. Those same shortcomings made it difficult for the officials appointed to oversee major repair projects to prevent waste and peculation.[10]

Conversely, specialization could be used as a barrier to ward off censorial attacks. Hydraulic officials sought to blunt censorial charges of corruption by claiming that outsiders could not accurately assess the situation and by dismissing censorial proposals as preposterous and based on "rumors circulating among those outside the center of affairs."[11] Though not an absolute defense, that argument carried weight because the special technical knowledge required to undertake management hydraulic engineering was recognized. But that strategy also exacerbated the imperial suspicion that hydraulic officials were using their expertise to screen corruption.

The separation of hydraulic engineering work into two spheres, civil and military, was one of the functional divisions intended to prevent corruption. By assigning to the military the actual work of engineering while civil officials remained in charge of administration and funding, the state hoped to create a check-and-balance system. The result was instead a barrier between administrative and technical realms that weakened the control of both. Civil officials could not judge the necessity or the efficacy of repairs they did not understand, whereas military officials had difficulty justifying expenditures to civil officials ignorant of engineering realities. One consequence of that unworkable division was the weak oversight of military officials evident in the corruption cases cited in chapter 2. The gap could be bridged by motivated and capable officials, but it also provided civil officials who were too busy or disinterested to take a close interest in the technical aspects of river affairs with a measure of insulation from such duties.

With the Qing unalterably opposed to expansion of the upper echelons of the bureaucracy and the administrative responsibilities of the hydraulic officials expanding, the emergence of an intermediate layer of semiofficial administration was inevitable. Some officials chose to delegate responsibilities to family members or friends. High officials became dependent on hired secretaries *(muyou)*, often chosen from among their friends, to carry out many technical and administrative tasks.[12] That reliance on privately employed support staff created an "irregular bureaucracy," an expanding cadre of more or less specialized supernumeraries. Motivated by self-interest constrained only by personal loyalty, those men were beyond the reach of administrative sanction. They were thus more susceptible to collusion with stalk merchants and unscrupulous military engineers than were regular bureaucrats. Such men were less likely to undermine construction, which would threaten those who employed them, than they were to overpay for materials, authorize phantom construction, and engage in petty peculation in ways that inflated the overall cost of engineering. Their superiors were understandably reluctant to criticize those assistants because of their value, but they were also restrained from doing so by bonds of patronage or family and by the desire to avoid embarrassment.[13]

Contemporary problems of literati unemployment fueled the growth of the irregular bureaucracy. Reduced opportunities in legitimate paths to success in the early nineteenth century "enhanced the appeal and the importance of illegitimate routes, particularly among men of wealth and influence." The Yellow River conservancy, with its massive budget and its reliance on supernumerary personnel, became a particularly attractive destination for those men.[14] The effect was not all bad. If some aimed at self-enrichment, many members of the irregular bureaucracy carried out important, even essential work.

Fiscal problems also forced high officials to manipulate accounts to their advantage. In a bureaucratic system in which salaries were inadequate to the demands of office and the division between public and private funds was vague, peculation was neither unusual nor necessarily venal. The Jiaqing emperor's remark that some self-enrichment was acceptable as long as river control remained effective was typical of an imperial attitude that offered little incentive to establish a clear barrier between public and private funds.[15] The threat of financial ruin posed by restitution statutes made a measure of peculation no more than rational economic strategy. If the river breached its banks, an official had reserves to pay punitive fines. If the funds went unused, the departing official could pocket them with only minor qualms, satisfied that he had done the job asked of him. If the fear of loss of rank, impoverishment, or exile kept some officials in line, it must be remembered that moral and ethical values restrained others. However much honored in the breach, the Confucian idea of service to the people and the emperor also had the power to motivate some officials and circumscribe the venality of others.

Critics of the river conservancy have charged that the corruption of river officials extended to intentionally causing floods in order to enrich themselves on the repair projects. Considering the ruinous impact of a flood on the finances and careers of those responsible, such charges appear absurd. Even Linqing's nine-year record of success could not protect him from the consequences of a single failure. No documentary evidence exists to support such assertions. Like the exaggerated accounts of feasting, they were products of the propaganda war waged by opponents of the Yellow River–Grand Canal system.

Fiscal Crisis

Technological systems are always sensitive to fiscal realities. The Yellow River control system not only cost a great deal to construct and maintain but also was an important link in the tax system and interregional trade. As dynastic fiscal administration matured, the ad hoc financing of Yellow River construction in the early Qing inevitably gave way to a more rational system of accounting. As the state's economic problems compounded, a new emphasis on fiscal restraint lent greater urgency to efforts at cost control. In that new climate of fiscal concern, the Yellow River conservancy began to develop a reputation for corruption and waste. River officials found themselves caught between the realities of hydraulic engineering and imperial demands for reduced expenditure.

The same hydraulic developments that demanded a larger bureaucracy also caused costs to spiral upward. As stalk revetments multiplied, yearly maintenance costs soared. At any time, about half of the existing defensive sites were active. As many as one-third required replacement each year. In addition, the river's rising bed required that the dikes undergo periodic raising and strengthening. The river's rising bed also made closing breaks more difficult and expensive.

The shift from corvee to wage labor that took place in the early Qing was a mixed blessing for the river conservancy. On the plus side, it made possible better accounting, which improved the control of expenditures and enhanced fiscal rationality. The acquisition of construction materials through the market rather than through requisition eased the burden on the peasantry and created a substantial economy involving the production and transport of sorghum, hemp, willow, stone, and eventually brick.

The primary drawback of a money economy was that the cost of labor and materials was more sensitive to economic fluctuations. The reliance on cash in the river conservancy was almost absolute. Even in work relief projects, workers usually were paid cash rather than being supplied with food. Hoarding by merchants and work slowdowns by laborers became established tactics for forcing up prices and wages. In cases of major flood repairs, the demand for large amounts of copper cash opened the door to currency manipulation and resulted in higher matériel and labor costs.

In the first four decades of the nineteenth century, the state hovered on the brink of insolvency. The depletion of silver mines in Yunnan and the outflow of silver used to purchase opium exacerbated those problems. Inflation beginning in the late eighteenth century added to the cost of construction materials, labor, and the salaries of private secretaries and clerks.[16] An edict of April 26, 1843 (DG 23/3/27) proclaiming the state 9 million taels in the red marked a new low in the Qing's fiscal fortunes.

One response to price increases and related economic problems was to seek supplementary income through the expanded sale of ranks, degrees, and offices. Many subscription campaigns were directed toward collecting funds for emergency river repairs. Occasionally, contributors received posts in the river conservancy. Since those purchases were not only a political but also an economic investment, the officials who made them undoubtedly expected to reap economic benefits from their new posts. Even if many such men performed ably, an atmosphere of opportunism hung over the river conservancy.

Long before corruption became a primary issue in the river conservancy, a battle was under way between river officials and the central bureaucracy over the rising cost of maintaining the river system. Throughout the late eighteenth and early nineteenth centuries, the state sought to regulate spending by imposing more precise accounting rules. River officials, eager both to enlarge their budgets and to retain flexibility in their allocations, resisted and succeeded in circumventing some of these restrictions. Their budgets continued to grow, but they lost much of their freedom to make discretionary use of funds. The emperor and his advisors acquiesced in the river conservancy's demand for more resources but failed to establish a long-term hydraulic strategy linked to and supported by coherent fiscal planning. The system did not become more rational—merely more regulated.

Perhaps the most unfortunate result of that fiscal contest was the tension it engendered between the river conservancy and the central government. Heightened distrust is evident in the expanded use of guaranty *(baogu)* and restitution *(peixiu)* statutes, both as punitive tools and as a way of recouping part of the cost of repairs. As noted in previous discussions, those measures were often counterproductive, only serving to encourage peculation as a form of self-protection, with the cost passed on through padded budgets and phoney construction.[17] The fact that the state proved unable to force officials to pay up further undermined the punitive force of the regulations.

Daoguang's understandable concern with the deteriorating economy found two expressions in his dealings with the river conservancy. One was a cautious openness to reform. The other, based on his belief that the dynasty's wealth could be restored through fiscal rigor, was a nearly obsessive insistence on economy. Where the two conflicted, the emperor and his advisors emphasized reducing waste and corruption rather than improving engineering strategies. That hindered a broader approach to hydraulic issues and made impossible any comprehensive program of river control.[18]

Monarchy

The direct involvement of the emperor in administrative affairs is decried by those who see it as evidence that the imperial institution became more despotic in the Ming and the Qing. That analysis echoes Wei Yuan's complaint, similar to the comment by Balazs quoted above, that imperial oversight robbed local officials of initiative and encouraged lackluster performance.[19] As a consequence, that theory goes, the average bureaucrat, hemmed in by red tape and detailed regulations, deadlines and paperwork, became a timid timeserver whose primary goal was avoiding mistakes.

No Qing institution came under closer imperial scrutiny than the Yellow River conservancy. Yet, as this study has shown, river officials were neither timid timeservers nor rule-bound sycophants. They risked innovation, fought tough bureaucratic battles to get their ideas accepted, and sometimes found the emperor as much an ally as an opponent. Rules, regulations, and routine were not only tools of monarchical control; they also protected officials from the arbitrary power of the emperor. Innovative officials ran risks not because they defied regulations but because they were willing to abandon the security of routine and venture into uncharted realms where no regulations existed to protect them. That was especially dangerous for high river officials, whose failures were interpreted as a "personal affront" to the emperor.[20] Failure jeopardized their career, wealth, family, and reputation and could lead to humiliating punishments and exile. The willingness of many hydraulic officials to innovate and gamble arises in part from the immense pressure they were under to solve difficult problems; but it also reflects a belief that the emperor was not inherently opposed to innovation.

One consequence of the increasing-despotism thesis, particularly when combined with the assumptions of the dynastic-cycle model, has been an exaggeration of the importance of the imperial personality. Early emperors must be described as effective, later emperors as lacking. No emperor has suffered more from this syndrome than Daoguang. Described as a "cautious, even . . . timid ruler," his reign is rarely associated with success.[21] Daoguang inherited a set of problems, including a troubled economy and a belligerent and militarily superior West, that would have challenged a Kangxi or a Yongzheng. There is little question that he was not the equal of either of those. But there is equally little likelihood that either of those would have found solutions to Daoguang's problems.

Sincere if unimaginative, cautious but not closed-minded, Daoguang began his reign determined to improve the dynasty's situation. The evidence suggests that, contrary to Wei Yuan's complaint, the emperor's early and sustained interest in river conservancy contributed to two decades of exceptional success in Yellow River control. Only later, surrounded by the defeats and failures of the 1840s, did Daoguang allow suspicion to replace caution and frustration to decide policy.

Daoguang's progress is evident in his approach to river control. His early efforts to reform the hydraulic bureaucracy took a short-range approach to both fiscal and engineering problems, emphasizing reduced or controlled expenditures and the elimination of corruption. Although Daoguang repeatedly showed his willingness to listen to radical proposals, particularly if they promised to cut costs, his overall policy remained short-sighted and piecemeal. It was not in Daoguang's character to entertain grand schemes that ran counter to his own compulsion to economize or to the pressing economic realities of the day. When partial efforts proved ineffective in reducing expenditures, Daoguang's early suspicions of the river conservancy were reborn.

Shifts in the imperial attitude were important bureaucratic weapons. Unwary officials might find them dangerous traps, whereas the savvy might view them as opportunities.[22] Daoguang's early concern with hydraulic issues helped elevate the subject to a new level of importance and induced a spirit of activism in some officials. Similarly, the imperial ire with river officials acted as a lightening rod for censorial indictment. The motives for such attacks ranged from sincere concern with policy issues to the petty pursuit of vested interests. But their unfortunate impact on hydraulic policy was to highlight the issue of corruption at the expense of a deeper exploration of technical matters.

The spate of censorial assaults on the Yellow River conservancy that began in the 1830s deepened Daoguang's already serious doubts about the reliability of river officials. In the 1840s those doubts led the emperor to select river officials not for their engineering skills but for their perceived honesty and loyalty. In the years between 1763 and 1820, seventeen of the twenty-three governors-general appointed to head the Jiangsu or Henan conservancy were promoted from the posts of river circuit intendant or governor of Henan or Jiangsu. In the Daoguang period (1821–1851), only four of twelve came from those posts, and three of them were early Daoguang appointees.[23] Although most of Daoguang's appointees, like Linqing and Li Yumei, had experience that qualified them for the post, others did not. In the selection of Wenchong in 1840, Daoguang showed clearly that he had greater faith in a reliable watch-dog than in his proven but tainted Confucian engineers. Both the Xiangfu flood and the problems encountered during the Zhongmou repair project can be blamed in some part on Daoguang's willingness to believe the worst about river officials.

Confucian Engineers

The governors-general of the Jiangsu and Henan conservancies were successors of a long line of men whose professional service combined Confucian ethical and moral concerns with practical engineering skills. In the towns along the Yellow River and the Grand Canal, notable river officials were honored in public temples and stele inscriptions. Lauded for their service to the emperor and their concern for the welfare of the people, Confucian engineers were respected and rewarded.

Linqing and Li Yumei were inheritors of that mantle. They sought to control the Yellow River by extending and refining a long tradition of moderate technical innovation. Contrary to the stereotype of the bureaucrat trapped by Confucian ideals in a stagnant imitation of the past, both were aware of the historical changes taking place in the river conservancy.[24] Arguing that changed circumstances called for new methods, both criticized their opponents for being "stuck in the mud" of the past.

Of course, many bureaucrats were unwilling to risk innovation. Fearing that new techniques would bring new dangers, opponents of change were able to close ranks against technical reforms and convey their fears to the emperor.[25] One technique was to funnel opposition through censors. Taking advantage of patronage ties and the isolation of censors in Beijing, opponents could and did introduce wildly one-sided condemnations of proposed reforms. That tactic was particularly effective because the support river officials might have expected from their metropolitan counterparts in the Board of Works was uneven, and its top officials were rarely knowledgeable about the realities faced by river officials in the field.[26] Thus, even when they sympathized with line officials, board officials often were unable to grasp the full dimensions of the hydraulic problems that made innovation necessary.

In spite of the weak support they received from the Board of Works and the heat sometimes generated by their attempts at innovation in technique and administration, both Li Yumei and Linqing were ardent in their belief that the reforms they offered were within the scope of acceptable change. Both men clearly belong to the moderate or realist category of reformers. That approach allowed them to "grapple with difficulties and stretch their organizational resources while retaining their ideals."[27] Li Yumei promoted brick as a construction material in full awareness that the resources for a more comprehensive change were not available. Similarly, Linqing's emphasis on technical competence and administrative efficiency recognized the monarchy's reluctance to expand the ranks of the regular bureaucracy. Instead, Linqing sought ways to help officials achieve greater efficiency with fewer resources.

Criticism of moderate reformers came from both conservatives, who found them too radical, and moralists, who saw them as fainthearted. The charge that such men were inadequately radical in their approach finds echoes in recent research that argues that Qing officials, afraid of confronting the "real" problems of the day, instead sought to tackle problems "where retrenchment seemed possible."[28]

Successful hydraulic officials were nothing if not masters of the art of the possible. Like all provincial officials, they were expected to promote the economic well-being of the state; mediate between regional, local, and state interests; and guarantee the tranquility of the populace—all of that as they were being buffeted by the battles that constantly whirled through the Qing body politic. Added to those distractions was the wild card of the Yellow River itself. A county magistrate was unlikely to be held personally responsible for a famine or a plague of locusts, but a river official knew that a flood, whether caused by record high water or incompetent dike maintenance, would always be interpreted as a dereliction of duty.

Considering their tenuous position, river officials might be expected to be cautious and routine-addicted. They were not. Linqing and Li Yumei, far from manifesting "an unshakable preference for routine procedures,"[29] sought to move both the emperor and their fellow bureaucrats in the direction of reform and technical innovation. They did so knowing that they would be attacked, and they took on their bureaucratic foes without flinching. Their motives remain their own. Perhaps they were spurred by a moral compulsion to transform the world or perhaps by desire for fame, glory, and wealth; or they could simply have wanted to do their job well—probably they were driven by some combination of those. In the end, their successes were as moderate as their mode of action. Neither was able to solve the conundrum of Yellow River conservancy. As their counterparts in the self-strengthening movement were to discover in the second half of the nineteenth century, large-scale innovation could only succeed with strong imperial backing. Without strong support from the center, the setbacks and failures that inevitably accompany experiment represented too great a career threat for most officials. Both Daoguang and his best hydraulic officials wanted reform, but for the most part it was a defensive approach to reform, one that fit within the limits of the late imperial state's fiscal and bureaucratic structure.

Fiscal, bureaucratic, and technological problems weakened the state's commitment to Yellow River control, but it would take a rebellion and another round of floods before the monarchy could bring itself to abandon the system. When, in 1855, the Qing made the decision to leave the river in the new northerly course, it did so not because the vast hydraulic machinery of Yellow River control was decaying but because the state could no longer afford to keep the system operating. With the loss of the Yangzi valley to the Taiping rebels and the virtual abandonment of the Grand Canal (sea shipment had already been partly resumed in 1849), the rationale behind the Yellow River control system collapsed. For a time, the river would have its way.

Notes

Abbreviations

Full publication information may be found in the Bibliography.

DQHDSL	*Qin ding da Qing huidian shili*
"GZD"	"Gongzhong Dang"
HZXZ	*Hunyuan zhou xu zhi*
QDHCZ	*Qingdai hechen zhuan*
"QDWXDA"	"Qingdai Wenxian Dangan"
"SLTB"	"Shuili Tiben"
"SYDFB"	"Shangyu Dang Fangben"
XFXZ	*Xiangfu xian Zhi*
ZXXSJJ	*Zaixu xingshui jinjian*
ZXZ	*Zhongmou xian Zhi*

Introduction

1. Derk Bodde, *Essays on Chinese Civilization,* ed. Charles Le Blanc and Dorothy Borei (Princeton, N.J.: Princeton University Press, 1981), 138.

2. Karl A. Wittfogel, *Oriental Despotism: A Comparative Study of Total Power* (New Haven, Conn.: Yale University Press, 1957), 18. Wittfogel's theory of "oriental despotism" emphasizes the absolute power of the emperor and the pervasive influence of a state bureaucracy, an influence that originates in state control of the hydraulic systems. Wittfogel traced the origins of despotism to a specific variant of "hydro-agriculture," or irrigation farming, that attempts to utilize scarce water resources in a "dry but potentially fertile area." The specific requirements for the emergence of a "hydraulic order of life" in any area are (1) an economy above subsistence level, (2) a location beyond the centers of rainfall agriculture, and (3) a society below the level of property-based, industrial civilization (12–19). That description does not accord well with the large defensive system developed along the Yellow River, and Wittfogel noted that "too little or too much water does not necessarily lead to governmental water control; nor does governmental water control necessarily imply despotic methods of statecraft" (12).

Other theorists of imperial power, such as Etienne Balazs and Joseph Needham, offer variant models of the Chinese state that agree with the image of an all-pervasive bureaucracy with much of its influence founded on the control of public works. For a fuller discussion, see Peter Perdue, *Exhausting the Earth: State and Peasant in Hunan, 1500–1850* (Cambridge, Mass.: Harvard Council on East Asian Studies, 1987), 1–10.

3. Hu Ch'ang-tu, "The Yellow River Administration in the Ch'ing Dynasty," *Far Eastern Quarterly* 14, no. 4 (August 1955): 505, 509. See also Hu Ch'ang-tu, "The Yellow River Administration in the Ch'ing Dynasty" (Ph.D. diss., University of Washington, 1954). There was no such entity as the "Yellow River Conservancy." The interlocking regional engineering bureaucracies were also charged with maintaining the Grand Canal and the other components of the hydraulic system. Moreover, although hydraulic officials did sometimes spend most of their career in river and canal posts, many were shifted in and out of the regular provincial bureaucracy. Additionally, provincial governors and governors-general had significant roles in shaping the agenda of the hydraulic bureaucracy. Hu believed that "excessive bureaucratization" was the primary mechanism of dynastic decline.

4. Susan Mann Jones and Philip A. Kuhn, "Dynastic Decline and the Roots of Rebellion," in *The Cambridge History of China,* vol. 10, pt. 1, *Late Ch'ing,* ed. John K. Fairbank (Cambridge: Cambridge University Press, 1978), 107–162.

5. Cen Zhongmian, *Huang He bianqian shi* [A history of the Yellow River's changes of course] (Beijing: People's Publishing Co., 1957), 563–572; see also *Huang He shuili shi shuyao* [An outline history of Yellow River water conservancy], ed. Shuili Bu, Huang He Shuili Weiyuan Hui (Beijing: Water Conservancy and Electrical Power Publishing Co., 1984), 254–256, 319–321. There are slight discrepancies in the totals given in those two works, with one listing eighteen floods in the Qianlong reign. Nevertheless, the increase in frequency in the Jiaqing reign is clear. Jones and Kuhn, "Dynastic Decline," 127–128. Although Heshen was deposed at the time of the Qianlong emperor's death in 1799, many of the men he managed to get appointed were able to continue to serve in high posts in the Jiaqing bureaucracy.

6. Jane Kate Leonard, *Controlling from Afar: The Daoguang Emperor's Management of the Grand Canal Crisis, 1824–1826* (Ann Arbor, Mich.: Center for Chinese Studies, 1996).

7. For example, the number of defensive sites on both banks of the Yellow River in Henan climbed from none in the early Qing to fewer than five hundred by the late eighteenth century, to more than two thousand in 1840. The accelerating pace of the construction of new sites was a consequence of the river's increased activity within the dikes. Most of the recent research on Chinese water conservancy has been on hydraulic issues arising from irrigation farming, a subject generally associated with the Chinese term *shuili* (water benefits). Water control in this context is viewed as a nexus where local, regional, and imperial interests interacted to shape the agricultural economy. For example, see Pierre-Etienne Will, "State Intervention in the Administration of a Hydraulic Infrastruc-

ture: The Example of Hubei Province in Late Imperial Times," in *The Scope of State Power in China,* ed. Stuart R. Schram (Hong Kong: Chinese University Press, 1985), 295–347; Peter Perdue, "Official Goals and Local Interests: Water Control in the Dongting Lake Region during the Ming and Qing Periods," *Journal of Asian Studies* 41, no. 4 (August 1982): 747–765; Perdue, *Exhausting the Earth;* Prasenjit Duara, *Culture, Power, and the State: Rural North China, 1900–1942* (Stanford, Calif.: Stanford University Press, 1988). For the most part the two realms were separate, but Peter Perdue (in "Official Goals") has shown that there were cases in which decisions involving river engineering were directly influenced by local agricultural practice.

8. Susan Naquin and Evelyn S. Rawski, *Chinese Society in the Eighteenth Century* (New Haven, Conn.: Yale University Press, 1987), 219, point out that the freezing of corvee quotas in 1713 so weakened the state's ability to expand its tax base that by the late eighteenth century, the Qing was able to collect less than 5 percent of the gross national product in taxes. Madeleine Zelin, *The Magistrate's Tael: Rationalizing Fiscal Reform in Eighteenth-Century China* (Berkeley: University of California Press, 1987), 1–2.

9. Yang Lien-sheng, "Economic Aspects of Public Works in Imperial China," in *Excursions in Sinology* (Cambridge, Mass.: Harvard University Press, 1969), hypothesizes that the commercialization of society also produced "greater acquisitiveness" (229). Naquin and Rawski, *Chinese Society,* 221. Thomas A. Metzger, *The Internal Organization of the Ch'ing Bureaucracy: Legal, Normative, and Communicative Aspects* (Cambridge, Mass.: Harvard University Press, 1973), 397, discusses the inhibiting effect of particularistic ties on universalism and uniformity in the Qing bureaucracy.

10. Hu, "Yellow River Administration" (1954), 180.

11. Yang, "Economic Aspects," 235–236, points out that a post in the water conservancy was the least prestigious of all bureaucratic situations. The *libu* (section on civil appointments) within the Board of Personnel was considered the "hottest" post, whereas the *shuibu* (section on water works) of the Board of Works was considered the "coldest," a hierarchy mirrored in the provincial bureaucracy.

12. Jones and Kuhn, "Dynastic Decline," 125.

13. Quotation in Naquin and Rawski, *Chinese Society,* 220–221. Leonard, *Controlling from Afar,* 5.

I   The Evolution of the Yellow River Control System in Late Imperial China, 1495–1835

1. Eberhard Czaya, *Rivers of the World* (New York: Van Nostrand Reinhold, 1981), 52. Its length of five thousand kilometers ranks it seventh among the world's rivers, but in drainage area (745,000 km^2) it ranks only twenty-ninth. The Mekong River, which is comparable to the Yellow River in length and drainage area, has an average annual discharge of 15,900 m^3/s.

2. Erosion alone does not explain how the Yellow River, with a total discharge less than one one-hundredth that of the Amazon and one-tenth that of the Mississippi, manages to rival both in sediment production. What makes the difference is the nature of the loess soil that comprises the silt. Created over many centuries by winds from central Asia, the loess deposits are composed of a "yellowish-brown, fine-grained, compact, friable material . . . [which] carves like cheese [and] is as fine as talcum powder" (Walter Clay Lowdermilk, "A Forester's Search for Forests in China," *American Forests and Forest Life* 31 [July 1925]: 444). Its grain size ranges from 0.02 mm to 0.06 mm in diameter, small enough to be easily transported in water. The almost limitless supply of that easily transported material allows the Yellow River to carry "physically maximum values of both bed and suspended load" (Peter A. Mantz, "Analysis of Sediment Transport Data for the Yellow River," *Renmin Huanghe* 1 [February 1987]: 18). Charles Greer, *Water Management in the Yellow River Basin of China* (Austin: University of Texas Press, 1979), 4. Greer notes that the maximum ever recorded was a 1942 measurement of 575 kilograms per cubic meter. Czaya, *Rivers*, 62–63.

3. Czaya, *Rivers*, 178, says the riverbed is presently some five meters above the surrounding plain in the Kaifeng area of Henan province. That figure appears even more dramatic when we consider that the floods in that area during the last two centuries have also raised the plain several meters. An observer standing on the old city wall on the north side of present-day Kaifeng will notice that the streets within the wall are well below the level of the surrounding countryside; in the other direction one can walk down a gentle slope that reaches right up to the top of the wall. Czaya points out that that raised bed is also responsible for the lack of tributaries to the Yellow River along its lower course (179).

4. Czaya, *Rivers*, 39 (chart), shows that the Yellow River achieves peak discharge in August. The fluctuation in discharge ranges from 500 m^3/s in December and January to 3,000 m^3/s in August. Greer, *Water Management*, 19–21.

5. Lowdermilk, "Forester's Search," 390. Lowdermilk postulates that deforestation may have contributed to the increasing activity of the Yellow River in recent centuries. Marco Polo described vast forests near Xi'an, an area that today is almost totally lacking in tree cover. Lowdermilk cites Polo's observation in order to argue that deforestation in the area is a post-Yuan (1279–1368) phenomenon. He also sees the construction of city walls of burned brick dating from that period as evidence that firewood was available in large quantities, an indication that extensive forests existed nearby. Nicholas K. Menzies, "Forestry," in *Science and Civilization in China*, vol. 6, pt. 3, ed. Joseph Needham (Cambridge: Cambridge University Press, 1996), 444–445, cites recent research indicating that extensive forest cover probably never existed in the region in the period of human habitation. Joseph Needham, Wang Ling, and Lu Gwei-djen, eds., *Science and Civilization in China*, vol. 4, pt. 3 (Cambridge: Cambridge University Press, 1971), 288.

6. Greer, *Water Management,* 24. Quotation in Needham, Wang, and Lu, *Science and Civilization,* 229.

7. Quotation in Guo Tao, "Pan Jixun de zhi-Huang sixiang" [The thought of Pan Jixun on control of the Yellow River], *Kexue yenjiu taolun ji: Shuili* [Collected essays on the study of science: Water conservancy] 12 (December 1982): 32–33, 34. Guo Tao says that by the mid-Ming (1368–1644), the policy of dividing the river to reduce its force had resulted in a profusion of smaller streams that branched off above Xuzhou and flowed south into the Huai; Needham, Wang, and Lu, *Science and Civilization,* 242–243. Cen, *Bianqian shi,* 462–465. *Huang He shuili shi shuyao,* 251–252. Unless otherwise indicated, all translations are my own.

8. Hok-lam Chan, "The Chien-wen, Yung-lo, Hung-hsi, and Hsuan-te Reigns, 1399–1435," in *The Cambridge History of China,* vol. 7, pt. 1, *The Ming Dynasty,* ed. Frederick W. Mote and Denis Twitchett (New York: Cambridge University Press, 1988), 238–247. Although Beijing was designated the national capital in 1420, Nanjing and Beijing would serve as complementary national administrative centers until 1441, after which Nanjing lost much of its former importance.

9. Ibid., 238–247, 252.

10. Harold C. Hinton, *The Grain Tribute System of China (1845–1895)* (Cambridge, Mass.: Harvard University Press, 1956), 68–69. Hinton is citing Ch'ao-ting Chi. That sentiment is echoed in Needham, Wang, and Lu, *Science and Civilization,* who claim it is "the considered judgement of Chinese historians . . . that the governments in all dynasties invariably considered the interests of tax transport above those of irrigation or flood control" (319).

11. The silting of the Yellow River did increase flooding along the Huai; the steady rise of the lake over a period of two centuries made it increasingly difficult for the Huai and its tributaries to empty into the lake.

12. Needham, Wang, and Lu, *Science and Civilization,* 212–214, point out that many of the earlier canals that were eventually combined into the Grand Canal were built for similar purposes. Quotation in Hoshi Ayao, "Transportation in the Ming Dynasty," *Acta Asiatica* 38 (1980): 13. In *Tai Unga* [The Grand Canal], (Tokyo: Kinfu Shuppansha, 1971), 200–203, Hoshi Ayao discusses the continuation of that process in the Qing. He also notes that the Ming government was aware of the commercial role of the canal and made an effort to balance the needs of government and military transport with those of private traders. David Kelley, "Sect and Society: The Evolution of the Luo Sect among Qing Dynasty Tribute Boatmen, 1700–1850" (Ph.D. diss., Harvard University, 1986), 12. Kelley cites a memorial of Kangxi 2 that discusses that subject (359).

13. Chan, "Chien-wen, Yung-lo," 250, 254–255. Leonard, *Controlling from Afar,* 70–71. Kelley, "Sect and Society," 12–13. Jones and Kuhn, "Dynastic Decline," 121, estimate that there were 40,000 to 50,000 boatmen working on the canal in the Daoguang period.

14. Hoshi, "Transportation," 12.

15. Tani Mitsutaka, *Mindai kaikoshi kenkyu* [Studies in the history of river conservation in the Ming], Oriental Research Series, no. 45 (Kyoto: Dohosha, 1991), is a comprehensive account of the work done in that area in the Ming and the early Qing. For specifics of the work of Pan, see Tani Mitsutaka, "Ko-Wai kowai to Han Kijun no kako" [The confluence of the Yellow River and the Huai, and the riverine engineering of Pan Jixun], *Toyo Gakuho* 64, nos. 3–4 (1982): 1–32. For an excellent summary in English, see Edward B. Vermeer, "P'an Chi-Hsun's Solutions for the Yellow River Problems of the Late 16th Century," *T'oung Pao* 73, nos. 1–3 (1987): 33–35.

16. Cen, *Bianqian shi,* 527–530. Zou Yilin, "Wan Gong he *Zhi shui quan ji*" [Wan Gong and (his) comprehensive study of water control], in *Huang He shi luncong* [Essays on the history of the Yellow River], ed. Tan Qixian (Fuzhou, China: Fudan University Press, 1986), 174–176, argues that Pan Jixun's writings and theories were drawn to a large extent from those of his predecessor Wan Gong. Vermeer says that although Pan cited as influences Wang Jing of the Eastern Han and Jia Lu of the Yuan, "there must have been more teachers and lessons from practice than that" ("P'an Chi-Hsun's Solutions," 35).

17. Quotation in Needham, Wang, and Lu, *Science and Civilization,* 237. Needham and his coauthors note that the theory that a constricted channel will cause a stream to dig a deeper thalweg has not been "entirely confirmed" by modern laboratory experiments (237). Czaya, *Rivers,* 66, says that because stream velocity is greatest at the center, erosion of the thalweg can occur, but he does not discuss the factors that influence the process. In *Science and Civilization,* 237, Needham and coauthors refer to Pan as a proponent of the "channel contraction" theory. That can be misleading. Guo, "Pan Jixun de zhi-Huang six-iang," 34, points out that the idea of restricting the flow to attack the silt aimed only to keep the river within its inner dikes during periods of high water, rather than letting it spread out over the banks between widely separated dikes. The increased velocity of the "restricted" water would then scour the channel. There was no attempt to actively narrow the channel in periods of normal flow.

18. For a discussion of the political context in which Pan carried out these reforms, see Ray Huang, *1587, a Year of No Significance* (New Haven, Conn.: Yale University Press, 1981), 106–108 and passim; Ray Huang, "The Lung-ch'ing and Wan-li Reigns," in *Cambridge History of China,* vol. 7, pt. 1, *Ming Dynasty,* 522–528; Wolfgang Franke, "Historical Writing during the Ming," in *Cambridge History of China,* vol. 7, pt. 1, *Ming Dynasty,* 774–777, discusses Pan's technical writings on river control. Guo, "Pan Jixun de zhi-Huang sixiang," 33. Shen Yi, *Huang He wenti taolun ji* [Essays on the problems of the Yellow River] (Taipei: Commercial Press, 1971), 388–390. Shen notes that even Pan's strongest supporter, the powerful minister Zhang Juzheng, had reservations about his river conservancy theories.

19. Cen, *Bianqian shi,* 527–530. Xu Fuling, "Huanghe xiayou Ming-Qing shidai hedao he xianxing hedao yanbian duibi yanjiu" [A comparative study of

changes in the lower course of the Yellow River from the Ming-Qing period to the present], in *Huang He shi luncong* [Essays on the history of the Yellow River], ed. Tan Qixian (Fuzhou, China: Fudan University Press, 1986), 207; see Vermeer, "P'an Chi-hsun's Solutions," 46–47, 58–59, on Pan's construction of reduction dikes. Mechanical dredging was most often carried out by boats that traveled downstream with the current, towing kedges to stir up the silt. It was hoped that the river current would then carry the loosened silt to the sea. Dredging was also carried out from stationary platforms anchored along the edges of the dike, but the same principle was operative. Workers also were sent in to dig out obstructed sections when the river was low or when it was diverted by an upstream flood. Vermeer includes a detailed discussion of Pan's most productive period in office, the two-year term of 1578–1580.

20. Quotation in Needham, Wang, and Lu, *Science and Civilization,* 325. Guo, "Pan Jixun de zhi-Huang sixiang," 33. Shen, *Huang He Wenti,* 383, puts it even more strongly, saying that in one stroke Pan wiped out over a thousand years of erroneous commitment to the "divided stream" theory of river control.

21. Wang Jingyang, "Qingdai Tongwaxiang gaidao qian de hehuan ji qi zhili," in *Huang He shi luncong* [Essays on the history of the Yellow River], ed. Tan Qixian (Fuzhou, China: Fudan University Press, 1986), 197–198. Tani, "Ko-wai kowai to Han Kijun no kako," 26, names several of Pan's critics, including Gu Yanwu and Cen Zhongmian; also see Tani, *Mindai kaikōshi kenkyū,* 390–393.

22. Frederick W. Mote, "The Ch'eng-hua and Hung-chih Reigns, 1465–1505," in *Cambridge History of China,* vol. 7, pt. 1, *Ming Dynasty,* 356–357.

23. Huang, "Lung-ch'ing and Wan-li," 534.

24. Chan, "Chien-wen, Lung-lo," 293. Charles O. Hucker, *A Dictionary of Official Titles in Imperial China* (Stanford, Calif.: Stanford University Press, 1985), 530, says this term is an abbreviation of *hedao* (river and canal) *zongdu;* he translates it "director-general." The term *zongdu* also came to be used to describe officials with jurisdiction over more than a single province and is usually translated "governor-general." For example, see H. S. Brunnert and V. V. Hagelstrom, *Present Day Political Organization of China,* trans. A. Beltchenko and E. E. Moran (Shanghai: Kelly and Walsh, 1912). Because those designations arose from the same source and were created for many of the same reasons—primarily related to the need for both military and transregional authority—I have chosen to retain the designation governor-general. The rank of the two posts in the Qing was different, however, with a governor-general of two provinces ranking 1b and the grain transport and river conservancy governors-general ranking 2a. That placed both above provincial governors at 2b. *Huang He shuili shi shuyao,* 340. Denis Twitchett and Tilemann Grimm, "The Cheng-tung, Ching-t'ai, and T'ien-shun Reigns, 1436–1464," in *Cambridge History of China,* vol. 7, pt. 1, *Ming Dynasty,* 335, cites the case of Xu Yuzhen, who was assigned to deal with the flooding of the Yellow River in 1453 after a vice minister of the Board of Works was

appointed but proved unable to handle the problem. Xu was given the title of assistant censor-in-chief for the duration of the project. Forty years later, a similar ad hoc appointment was used to dispatch Liu Daxia to deal with renewed flooding. See Mote, "Ch'eng-hua and Hung-chih," 356–357. Ray Huang, *Taxation and Government Finance in Sixteenth-Century Ming China* (Cambridge: Cambridge University Press, 1974), 165. Huang says the bulk of the "river work" tax was paid by landowners, which substantially increased Henan's otherwise low per-*mou* tax assessment. Wan Gong, *Zhi shui quanti* [A comprehensive study of water control] (Beijing: Water Conservancy and Electrical Power Publishing Co., 1985), 63.

25. *Huang He shuili shi shuyao,* 340.

26. This accounting is deceptive in one respect, since it records as river officials men whose posts involved work both for the river conservancy and for the county in which they resided. Most importantly, the pay of those lower officials came from the counties, not from the river treasuries. Hu, "Yellow River Administration" (1954), 99. Zheng Chaojing, *Zhongguo shuili shi* [A history of Chinese water conservancy] (Taipei: Commercial Affairs Printing Co., 1986), 335–340, gives slightly higher numbers. The thirteen subprefectures that constituted the river conservancy in Henan were, on the north bank from west to east, Huangbian, Weiliang, Xianghe, Xiabei, and Caokao; on the south bank from west to east, Shangnan, Zhonghe, Xia'nan, Lanyi, Yisui, Suining, Shangyu, and Guihe. The two in Shandong were Caohe and Lianghe.

27. *DQHDSL,* 1818, 903:1.

2   Rising Waters

1. The starting point for understanding the Qing economy is Wang Yeh-chien, *Land Taxation in Imperial China, 1750–1911* (Cambridge, Mass.: Harvard University Press, 1973), 58–60 and passim. For the impact of economic changes on Qing institutions and intellectuals, see Lin Man-houng, "Two Social Theories Revealed: Statecraft Controversies over China's Monetary Crisis, 1808–1854," *Late Imperial China* 12, no. 2 (December 1991): 3–4. For copper-silver exchange rates and their impact on prices, see Hans Ulrich Vogel, "Chinese Central Monetary Policy, 1644–1800," *Late Imperial China* 8, no. 2 (December 1987): 1–52. The classic synthesis of those issues and their relationship to the vitality of the Qing state is Jones and Kuhn, "Dynastic Decline," 128–131.

2. *DQHDSL,* 904: Yongzheng (YZ) 8.

3. Frederic Wakeman, "The Canton Trade and the Opium War," in *Cambridge History of China,* vol. 10, pt. 1, *Late Ch'ing,* 165, notes that 127,500 taels were taken from the Consoo fund to pay for repairs on the Yellow River. The Consoo fund was initially established by the Chinese merchants in Hong Kong, the Cohong, to protect themselves from exactions by officials. When the existence of the fund became known to the government, it became a regular tar-

get of imperial exactions. *DQHDSL,* 904: QL 14, remarks on the opening of land totaling 602 *qing,* 2 *mou* along Anshan Lake in QL 14 (1750), the rent from the land to be earmarked for river works. That land could not be bought or sold. Six hundred two *qing* is a substantial parcel of land, but the rent on it, when compared with the overall budget of the river conservancy, was tiny.

4. After the Yongzheng reign, projects that cost less than five hundred taels, whether *suixiu* or *qiangxiu,* could be carried out without first applying for permission.

5. *DQHDSL,* 904: KX 52, orders the governor-general of the Yellow River and the governors of Henan and Shandong to mutually oversee the auditing of the books of the river conservancy treasuries. At the same time, the former was expected to supervise personally all maintenance and emergency repairs in order to guard against waste and peculation. *DQHDSL,* 904: YZ 2, cites the Yongzheng emperor's order that officials present their repair budgets by the tenth month (November–December) and their final accounts for both maintenance and emergency repairs by the fourth month (May–June) of the following year. Those who failed to meet those deadlines were to be held responsible for the cost of the repairs. "SLTB," Lai Bao, QL 4/5/8, box 494. The maps, called *tushuo,* were commonly submitted with reports of river repairs. Their accuracy in terms of scale is poor, but they are reliable in showing the relationship between the various parts of a conservancy project. "SLTB," Wu Jing, JQ 9/9/28.

6. *DQHDSL,* 904: QL 13; 906: DG 2.

7. Lin, "Two social theories," 1, says that between 1808 and 1854 the value of copper cash depreciated two and one-half times. See also Vogel, "Chinese Central Monetary Policy," 13, 16, table 3.

8. Hu, "Yellow River Administration" (1954), 155–156, points out that already in the Kangxi period, the amounts officially listed as spent on river works were well below the actual expenditures. The Kangxi emperor estimated that expenditures for river work throughout his reign averaged 3 million taels per year.

9. *DQHDSL,* 904: DG 8. Hu, "Yellow River Administration" (1954), 118. Hu points out that there is some confusion concerning the designation of *ling'an.* In the Qianlong edition of the statutes, *ling'an* are defined as projects costing less than five hundred taels. But the definition used in the Jiaqing edition of the *DQHDSL* focuses more on the nature of the work to be done than on the cost. That may be explained by the fact that river officials had blurred the distinction between regular works and supplementary cases to such an extent that the compilers of the statutes found it difficult to clarify the meaning of the latter (159–160 n. 8). *DQHDSL,* 905: JQ 15. The Jiaqing emperor responded by demanding closer reporting to make sure that the supplementary works projects were not the result of inept maintenance or repair.

10. "GZD" (B), Song Yun, JQ 25/10/3, estimates the total cost of one of the repair projects, that resulting from the rupture of the Maying Dike, at 12 million

taels. In Daoguang 5 a debt of 827,240 taels owed by Henan as a result of tax remissions resulting from the floods of Jiaqing 18–25 was forgiven by the emperor so that the people of the region would be able to recoup their previous prosperity; *DQHDSL*, Guangxu ed., *juan* 906, DG 5.

11. *DQHDSL*, 906: DG 2, DG 8, DG 14. An edict of 1833 (*DQHDSL*, 906: DG 15) tried to correct what was viewed as part of the problem—the Board of Works' inability to carry out accurate audits—by ordering new regulations to be drawn up that would include only the categories of yearly repairs *(suixiu)*, miscellaneous works *(ling'an)*, and major works projects *(dagong)*. Those were to be kept track of on a three-year basis, with the most recent year compared to expenditures in the three previous years. The category of emergency repairs *(qiangxiu)* was absorbed into the miscellaneous works account. A separate, smaller emergency account, called *qiangxian*, was retained. That provided for 300,000 taels each to be transferred to the Henan and Jiangsu conservancies at the start of the year for use in emergencies in which a normal funding request would have taken too long. The tracking of yearly totals, obviously intended to put pressure on river officials to reduce expenditures, eventually showed some positive results. "GZD" (B), Zhongxiang, DG 27/10/21, reported that Henan conservancy expenditures for supplementary works in DG 27 totaled 1,686,768 taels, 148,186 taels less than in DG 26 and 251,528 less than in DG 25. But those reductions were achieved in the aftermath of the three major floods of 1841, 1842, and 1843.

12. The term *jintie* has the general meaning of a subsidy or surcharge. I have chosen to translate it as cost assistance in this case because the purpose of those funds was to make up the difference between government-approved prices for materials and the actual cost. *DQHDSL*, 904: QL 49.

13. In the case of sorghum stalks, a major cost of river conservancy, inflation was the primary cause of the rising prices. But greater demand from the river conservancy, along with population growth and the consequent demand for fuel, also encouraged price increases. The cost of earthwork also rose as labor costs went up. *DQHDSL*, 905: JQ 22. An edict of 1830 complained that the cost assistance accounts were designed only to respond to occasional increases in prices but that for all but three years between 1814 and 1828, they had been treated as a regular expense and had risen almost yearly. The names used in the two divisions of the Yellow River conservancy were not always the same. In the Henan conservancy, an account similar to cost assistance funds was called "price assistance funds" *(bangjia yin)*. The increasing use of those funds led, in 1792, to an edict ordering that all future purchases be made with regular funds and that the state-mandated price be paid for materials (*DQHDSL*, 905: QL 57). *DQHDSL*, 906: DG 8.

14. *DQHDSL*, 917: XZ 1, cites an edict that mandated that if a hydraulic structure failed within one year of its completion, the officials in charge were to be lowered in rank and transferred to other posts. If the failure was the result of

unusually heavy flood conditions, the officials were allowed to redeem themselves by repairing the damage. *DQHDSL,* 917: KX 17, mandated that in cases in which the river overflowed the dikes but did not change course, rather than being punished by loss of rank, the officials in charge had to make restitution *(peixiu)* for the repairs. If the river breached again within a year of the completion of those repairs, the officials in charge of the construction (rather than the serving river official) had to pay for the second repair. If failure occurred after the one-year guaranty *(baogu)* period, the officials in charge of river defense had to pay for new construction.

15. *DQHDSL,* 917: YZ 5. The guaranty period for work on the Grand Canal was also extended from one to three years; that on the Yellow River remained one year.

16. *DQHDSL,* 917: QL 39.

17. *DQHDSL,* 917: JQ 7, cites an edict of Jiaqing 2 (1797) that attempted to set limits on the amount of time officials could take to pay restitution. Those owing 300 taels or less had to pay in full within one-half year. Other debts and repayment periods were as follows: 300 to 1,000 taels, one year; 1,000 to 5,000 taels, four years; over 5,000 taels, five years; over 10,000 taels, 70 percent within five years and the remainder according to the above schedule. Those who had not paid could not be promoted or accept a new post.

18. *Qing shi lu* [Veritable records of the Qing dynasty], DG 13/9/25.

19. *DQHDSL,* 917: YZ 4, already refers to that drawback. Some of the emperor's advisers suggested that the only effect of restitution would be that officials would set aside moneys marked for regular repairs, increasing the likelihood of flooding. That opposition prevailed for a time, and restitution was limited to cases involving misappropriation, intentional damage to hydraulic structures in an effort to get repair funds, and the failure of haphazard or shoddy work.

20. Hu, "Yellow River Administration" (1954), appendix, 257–262. An explanation for the large number of officials leaving their posts may be that as the bureaucratic structure of the hydraulic administration bifurcated, more officials served in top posts in the Henan conservancy (Donghe) or the Jiangsu conservancy (Nanhe), so the numbers dismissed would naturally rise. Those figures do not include the third leg of the late-Qing system, the Zhili conservancy (Beihe), or the conservancy in charge of the Yongding River. Some contemporaries charged (and later historians repeated the claims) that officials intentionally let the river flood so that they could get rich off the repairs. The heavy punishments awaiting those held responsible for a flood show that to be unlikely. Hu, "Yellow River Administration" (1954), 201, cites the Jiaqing emperor's concern about that matter. On 210, nn. 69, 70, Hu cites two Daoguang sources that make such charges.

21. James M. Polachek, *The Inner Opium War* (Cambridge, Mass.: Council on East Asian Studies, Harvard University, 1992), 42–43, 229–230 n. 50,

identifies Fei Chun as a protégé of Zhao Yi and the "northern party," a group that came to prominence in the wake of Heshen's demise by helping the Jiaqing emperor find reliable officials. See also Jones and Kuhn, "Dynastic Decline," 116–117, on the removal of officials supposedly part of the "Heshen faction," including the heads of both Yellow River conservancies.

22. "GZD" (B), Fei Chun and Wu Jing, JQ 7/12/2. Thus, a separate official was needed on the opposite bank to take charge during flood season.

23. "GZD" (B), Fei Chun and Wu Jing, JQ 7/12/2. They made similar arguments for a reorganization of the responsibilities of the Huai-Xu and Huai-Yang circuit intendants. To handle the increased workload that went with that growth in the number of *sao* revetments, Wu and Fei recommended the creation of nine new positions. Among them were three second-class subprefects *(tongpan)*, three assistant district magistrates *(xiancheng)*, and three lieutenants *(qianzong)*. "GZD" (B), Fei Chun and Wu Jing, JQ 5/7/13, reveals that already in Jiaqing 5 those same two officials had used the phrase "former and present conditions are not the same" to justify an increase in the number of petty officials in the Jiangsu conservancy. Even before the fall of Heshen, river officials were asking for more administrative help. "SYDFB," edict of Jiaqing 2/2/26, approved the transfer of twenty minor officials to river posts in Jiangsu. Those included two sixth-rank officials, four eighth-rank officials, and fourteen unclassed *(weiruliu)* and lower ninth-rank officials.

Another edict on Jiaqing 4/5/2 reveals that river officials had been forcing civil officials whose posts involved no river responsibilities to nevertheless take part in river repairs. The emperor ordered that practice to stop.

24. Jones and Kuhn, "Dynastic Decline," 114, ascribe the unemployment problem in part to increased competition for posts resulting from expanded opportunities for education. Bureaucratic opportunities were not expanding, so illegitimate or irregular career paths such as dependence on patronage or purchase of posts grew correspondingly important. Benjamin A. Elman, *From Philosophy to Philology: Intellectual and Social Aspects of Change in Late Imperial China* (Cambridge, Mass.: Council on East Asian Studies, Harvard University, 1984), 130–137, points out the changes in literati roles that resulted from the decreased opportunities for employment. Among those, the job of secretary was one of the most common. Pierre-Etienne Will, *Bureaucracy and Famine in Eighteenth-Century China,* trans. Elborg Forster (Stanford, Calif.: Stanford University Press, 1990), comments that the lower stratum of the bureaucratic structure, though necessary, was generally distrusted and held in contempt and "the ranking bureaucracy was forced to conceive every strategy *as a counterweight* to its local agents" (89). Will is discussing the temporary subbureaucracy that emerged in times of famine relief. In the case of the river conservancy, that stratum was permanent. Another important difference lies in the fact that the irregular bureaucracy of the river conservancy included literati and degree holders. Quotation in "GZD" (T), Linqing, DG 17/2/15.

25. "GZD" (B), Wu Jie, JQ 25/10/24.

26. Xu Daling, *Qing dai juanna zhidu* [The system of purchasing offices by contributions during the Qing period, 1644–1911] (Beijing: Harvard Yenching Institute, 1950), 17–18. As shown in case of the corrupt military officials Liu Bu and Zhuang Gang, both of whom had purchased positions in the Henan conservancy for their sons, river conservancy posts could be bought outright. There is little question that those who took advantage of that opportunity did so mainly for the sake of access to government funds.

27. Ibid., 19, 50–53.

28. "GZD" (T), Yan Lang, DG 1/12/1, echoes Wu's charges. Yan's memorial cites an edict claiming that those sent to investigate corruption in the river conservancy are themselves products of the system and so are reluctant to prosecute offenders. The emperor is probably referring to Wu's earlier memorial. "GZD" (B), Wu Jie, JQ 25/10/24. Wu contrasted the contemporary leadership with early Qing engineers like Jin Fu, who rose to positions of prominence on the basis of their native abilities, personally oversaw all aspects of river work, and did not fear sacrificing themselves to see that the job was properly done. Those men were followed by a second generation of river conservancy experts, officials like Yeh Guanchao and Zhang Wenhao, who had risen from the level of magistrate or subprefect to river circuit intendant, then to head of the conservancy. The virtues of that generation, Wu said, were that they were knowledgeable about river engineering, knew the ins and outs of river work, and therefore were able to achieve more with less.

29. Tang Xianglong, "Daoguang chao juanjian zhi tongji" [Statistics on sale of degrees, ranks, and offices in the Daoguang reign], in *Zhongguo jindai shi luncong* [Collected essays on modern Chinese history], ser. 2, 8 vols., ed. Li Dingyi, Bao Zunpeng, Wu Xiangxiang (Taipei, Zhengzhong Bookstore, 1963), 5:47–62. ZXZ, 1870, *juan 5*, reveals that low-ranking degree holders, including some who held degrees by purchase, dominated the local river conservancy bureaucracy. Of the thirty-six Qing river officials who had served in Zhongmou and for whom educational information is available, only five held degrees higher than licentiate; four were *juren*, one a *jinshi* (that calculation includes only officials up to the first appointment made in the Xianfeng reign). A higher number of officials holding the post of Shangnan subprefect are described as *gongsheng, fugongsheng,* or *fusheng,* whereas those holding the posts of second-class subprefect and assistant district magistrate were all *jiansheng* (with the exception of the four *juren* mentioned above). Even the post of district magistrate was filled mainly by officials holding the degree of licentiate *(jiansheng* and *gongsheng),* although two *jinshi* and several *juren* had also held the position.

30. "GZD" (T), Yan Lang, DG 1/12/1.

31. Li Yuerui, *Chunbingshi Yecheng* [Unofficial record from the Spring Ice Studio] (Shanghai: Shijie Chubanshe, 1926), 121–125. Li's collection was compiled much later than the events it purports to describe. For example, the account

of gluttonous feasting is presented as an example of the corruption that led to the river's change of course in 1855. Michael Freeman, "Sung," in *Food in Chinese Culture*, ed. Kwang-chih Chang (New Haven, Conn.: Yale University Press, 1977), 174, points out that the tradition of moral critique that equated gluttony with imperfect character was established at least as early as the Song dynasty. Li's account begins by describing a banquet given by a river official where the main course is a plate of exceptionally tasty pork. After the banquet, a guest on his way to the toilet finds several dozen pig carcasses with a single strip of meat cut from the back. Further inquiry reveals that all of the pigs were needed to produce the single plate of pork served at dinner. The secret to the wonderful taste was the way the pigs were killed. Trapped in a pen, they were driven into a frenzy by being beaten on the back with long sticks. Eventually they died of hysteria. But in their efforts to dodge the blows, they had directed their "essence" *(jing)* to the area on their backs that was being assaulted. The resulting slice of meat was therefore particularly flavorful, but the remainder of the carcass was deemed useless and was thrown away. The account goes on to describe similar exercises of cruelty and excess with camels, monkeys, ducks, and so on.

32. Cited in Hu, "Yellow River Administration" (1954), 200. Bao's comments must be viewed with caution. Arthur Hummel, comp., *Eminent Chinese of the Ch'ing Period (1644–1911)* (Washington, D.C.: U.S. Government Printing Office, 1943), 610–611, notes that Bao was a proponent of sea transport and a critic of statecraft ideas. A strong moralist, Bao dedicated himself to the study of how to reform corrupt administration. Hu, "Yellow River Administration" (1955), 512; Xiao Yishan, *Qing dai tong shi* [History of the Qing period] (Taipei: Commercial Press, 1962–1963), 891.

33. Hu, "Yellow River Administration" (1955), 512. The same statistic appears in Xiao, *Qing dai tong shi,* 890. Hu, "Yellow River Administration" (1954), 181, 206 n. 25, traces the quote to Wei Yuan. Yang, "Economic Aspects," 229, says the statistic originated with Feng Guifen. Hu Ch'ang-tu takes the charges of corruption even further, arguing that river officials did not stop at peculation, but purposely ignored river repairs so that dikes would decay faster, thereby justifying further appropriations. Such corruption was common knowledge, says Hu, but both river officials and gentry ignored it. For many reasons, including the lack of evidence, those claims must be dismissed as specious.

34. Xiao, *Qing dai tong shi,* 890; for Feng's figures, see Yang, "Economic Aspects," 229.

35. "GZD" (B), Wu Jing, Youqi, and Jiaqing (JQ) 5/6/18. Zhuang managed to pilfer twenty to thirty taels for each *duo* of stalks purchased for river conservancy work. He also failed to return eighty *fang* of stone left over from a construction project. The investigators also charged that during the three years Mou was supposedly in mourning for his father, he never once returned to his native place, but stayed near the work site, "helping" from the sidelines.

36. Ibid. According to the confessions of some of those lesser fry, it was envy

evoked by watching Liu Bu grow rich in his post that led them to start extracting funds from the river works under their control. Investigators believed some stolen funds were being hidden but could not prove it. The investigating officials recommended that the sons of primary offenders Liu Bu and Zhuang Gang be stripped of their posts.

37. Ibid.

38. "GZD" (B), Wu Jing and Youqi, JQ 5/6/18. That memorial carries the same date as the one that discusses the details of their investigation but instead concerns itself with measures that should be taken to stop corruption. The military's role in the process may have been based in part on its greater coercive power and the reluctance of stalk producers to dispose of their supplies at government-mandated prices. Wu Jing and Youqi found evidence of serious tensions between stalk producers and officials. Initially, the practice had been for stalk merchants to bring their stocks to official collection centers where they would receive a fixed price (nine *hao*—0.0009 taels—per *jin* at that time). But the abuses of yamen clerks and runners in collecting the materials eventually led to regulations that required officials to take charge of the purchase and transport of stalks collected outside the immediate area. However, those officials could still pay only the fixed price, with no extra funding available to pay for transport. The result was that in order to purchase the required quota of materials, officials had to covertly "borrow" funds from other sources.

When supplies were needed for a major works project, the financial burden on officials grew more severe. Not only did increased demand require that stalks be shipped from greater distances, which raised transport costs, but also, as soon as stalk merchants caught wind of the sudden demand, they began to hike their prices. When officials responded by issuing prohibitions against higher prices, the merchants began hoarding their stalks, so that officials ended up paying two or three times the normal price. The authors noted that with the combined supplemental and regular funds applied to stalk purchases, the price at major works projects in Henan had reached as high as 0.003 to 0.004 taels per *jin*. But in Jiangnan, where supplemental funds were not used, officials were still expected to adhere to the price ceiling of 0.0009 taels per *jin*. Wu Jing and Youqi suggested that supplemental funds *(bangjia)* should be introduced into the Jiangsu conservancy to augment matériel purchases and reduce the need for officials to doctor accounts. The memorial does not mention the use of coercion to extract stalks from would-be hoarders, but that almost certainly played a role in officials' calculations.

39. "GZD" (T), Chu Pengling, DG 2/5/26. Although the governor of Henan was not a river official, his treasury was linked to the river treasuries *(daoku)*, and he participated in a wide range of river conservancy projects. The total amount of silver exchanged during the course of the project was approximately 700,000 taels, leaving Yang with around 60,000 taels in profit from his scheme. Although direct evidence is lacking, the manipulation of the copper-silver exchange rate

when major river repair projects were under way was probably a lucrative source of income for officials and gentry in the region. Yang's plan is remarkable only for its lack of subtlety. In an effort to silence the officials who had actually been in charge of currency exchange, Yang began to press for their promotion. One of those officials was Li Yumei. As it turned out, Li Yumei had not remitted the funds to Yang, and he was eventually found blameless.

40. *Huang He shuili shi shuyao*, 299–321. The table on 319–320 lists thirteen floods for the Jiaqing reign. A flood is also recorded at Taoyuan in 1832, but that was a product of vandalism, not a failure of the dike system, and it was apparently repaired with a minimum of expense.

3   Confucian Engineers

1. *HZXZ*, 1881, 6:24b.

2. *HZXZ*, 6:20b. Li served as a provincial judge in Hubei from 1829 to 1831.

3. The confluence of the Bian and Yellow Rivers is in Wuzhi County. The Bian flows in from the north and is the last tributary to enter the Yellow River. Thus, the duties of the magistrate of Wuzhi County would include organizing and managing river work. *HZXZ*, 6:20a. In 1821 Li's career was temporarily overshadowed when he was implicated in the corruption case involving peculation of river funds by Henan governor Yang Zutong (see chapter 2). The funds peculated by Yang were collected by several lower officials, Li Yumei among them. But Li was fortunate. At the time Yang was found out, Li Yumei had not yet passed the funds on to Yang, and he was eventually found innocent. See "GZD" (T), Chu Pengling, DG 2/5/26.

That was not Li Yumei's first brush with infamy. According to an entry in Li Yuerui, *Chunbingshi yecheng*, 1:48, Li Yumei was temporarily held in a murder case when he was a young man. A talented scholar from a poor family, Li worked as a tutor until a local man named Ming Jing allowed him to board in his home and study with his son. Ming also had a daughter who was taken with Li but was the object of the jealous attentions of a neighbor's son. One night that young man crept into the Ming residence and stabbed to death the person sleeping in Li's bed. But the victim was the younger Ming, who had come home drunk and fallen into the wrong bed. Li was held for the murder, and Ming's daughter married the neighbor's son. But very soon the groom's drunken boasting gave away the secret. His new bride informed on him, and Li was released. The unfortunate young woman committed suicide.

4. *HZXZ*, 6:22a–22b.

5. The term *xun* (commandery) originally designated a military post for river troops but eventually became the designation for the section of the river for which that post was responsible. The *xun* was the lowest administrative unit of the river conservancy. "QDWXDA," *zhuanbao* (ZB) 4, no. 1531 (1–2), draft biography of Li Yumei.

6. Li Yumei, lateral communication to Jingzheng, DG 17/6/2?, *ZXXSJJ*, 2021. (The editor of the *ZXXSJJ* used an empty square to indicate where a date had been obscured by damage to the document. I have indicated that lacuna with a question mark). This account was written two years after the fact, when Li was explaining the origins of his use of brick as a dike construction material.

7. The technique of joining the bricks together has some structural similarity with the traditional use of gabions, wicker baskets in which stones were placed to keep them together. See Needham, Wang, and Lu, *Science and Civilization*, 339–341. Li Yumei, lateral communication to Jingzheng, DG 17/6/2?, *ZXXSJJ*, 2021.

8. DG 17/6/2?, *ZXXSJJ*, 2921. Li also constructed dikes from either bank of the branch stream in order to close it off and redirect its waters. The overall project took twenty days to complete. "QDWXDA," ZB 4, no. 1531 (1–2).

9. DG 17/6/2?, *ZXXSJJ*, 2021–2029. In describing Li Yumei's work style, his biography in the Hunyuan gazetteer claims he took personal charge of much of the construction and that he consulted county and river officials in each area concerning river control efforts. In particular, he focused his efforts on areas where future problems seemed likely. See *HZXZ*, 6:23b–24a. Li Yumei to Jingzheng, DG 17/6/2?, *ZXXSJJ*, 2026, lists the four kinds of structures where Li Yumei felt brick could be used effectively: (1) deflection dikes, (2) rubble revetments to protect the dikes from wind and waves, (3) dikes blocking off branch streams and troughs, and (4) levees to protect the land in front of the main dikes from erosion.

10. Li Yumei to Jingzheng, DG 17/6/2?, *ZXXSJJ*, 2027–2028. In two cases in which Li had ordered shipments of rock for use in river repairs, only partial shipments had made it through before floodwaters blocked further transport. In one case Li had ordered 500 *fang* of rock stored in Zhonghe Subprefecture to be shipped to the Yuanwu and Yangwu work sites, but high water kept all but 270 *fang* from getting through. In another case, a shipment of 1,400 *fang* of rock was dispatched to Shangnan Subprefecture, but only 800 *fang* made it through. Again, rising floodwaters blocked transport.

Those supply problems had an adverse effect on the cost of rock. While the price in Huangbian Subprefecture in the far west was a reasonable 5.5 taels per *fang*, downriver prices ranged between 6.9 taels and 13.2 taels per *fang* (brick prices ranged from 4.6 to 9.2 taels per *fang*).

In spite of those problems, Li continued to make use of rock. In 1836 he requested funds to purchase 2,500 *fang* of broken rock to be kept on hand in subprefectures along the river for emergency repair and construction work. Another 3,700 *fang* were requested the following year.

11. Ibid., 2027. According to *HZXZ*, 6:27a, the rise in the price of bricks stemmed from the fact that brick merchants along the river tripled their prices when the government demand increased. But shrinking supply also played a role. Li Yumei to Jingzheng, DG 17/6/2?, enclosure, *ZXXSJJ*, 2029, notes that many

of the bricks initially purchased by river officials originated in settlements for-merly located between the dikes where houses damaged by earlier floods were dismantled. After two years of construction, that source was exhausted. Li Yumei, DG 17/5/13, *ZXXSJJ*, 2015–2016. The money he requested was to come from the three hundred thousand taels budgeted for yearly stockpiling of matériel for river defense *(beifang ying)*. The bulk of the money would be shifted from the purchase of broken rock to brick. "SYDFB," edict of DG 17/5/20, approved Li Yumei's proposal for the use of brick and the establishment of kilns. The edict cautioned officials in charge of the kilns to keep a close eye on quality and ordered Li Yumei personally to inspect the bricks produced.

12. Li Chun, DG 17/5/29, *ZXXSJJ*, 2016–2019. The successor to the *Xing Shui Jin Jian*, the *Xu Xing Shui Jin Jian*, had been published in 1832 (Hummel, *Eminent Chinese*, 936). Li Chun makes no mention of that newer work, but the former, which covers the period from earliest times to 1721, would have had more of a claim to represent the views of the ancients and so may have had greater appeal for conservatives. The *Zhi He Fang Lue*, which was originally presented to the court in 1689, was not printed until 1767. A second edition was printed in 1799 by Jin Fu's great-grandson, but it contained "serious omissions" (163).

13. Li Chun, DG 17/5/29, *ZXXSJJ*, 2017, 2018. Li Chun argued that if it became necessary to use stalk revetments to protect the dike, the piles of brick would prevent the bundles from settling firmly into the mud of the river bottom, with the result that the revetments would be undercut by the current. If a brick dike began to fail and it was necessary to put stalk revetments in front of it to fend off the current, there would be no place on the dike to drive the stakes needed to anchor the revetments. Information on the failure of the brick dikes could only have come from river officials in Henan. *ZXXSJJ*, 2032–2034, cites reports from two officials in Henan, the Huangbian prefect and the Xia'nan subprefect, crit-ical of Li Yumei's use of brick.

14. That was known as "fighting the water for land" *(yu shui zheng di)*. The building of protective dikes around fields located between the main dikes was prohibited for the same reason.

15. Li Chun, DG 17/5/29, *ZXXSJJ*, 2018–2019. Li Chun implied that exploitation of the common people had already begun, noting that the bricks used in Henan over the past two years were from homes destroyed by floods. The unspoken charge was that river officials were first responsible for the floods that destroyed the houses and now were exploiting the victims for building material.

16. According to Li Chun, a 3.3-meter-long section *(dan)* of deflection dike constructed with stalk bundles and earth would cost 1.7 taels, with the earth used to construct it costing from 100 *wen* to 300 *wen*, whereas a *fang* of bricks would cost twenty-three times as much as that amount of earth. *DQHDSL*, *juan* 916, under "dike construction methods" *(ba gong zuofa)*, says that one *dan* of a deflection dike constructed with stalk bundles requires one-half *fang* of

tamped earth. Though Li Chun's calculations are roughly accurate, he seems to make no distinction between the properties of brick and of earth.

17. Li Chun, DG 17/5/29, *ZXXSJJ*, 2018–2019.

18. Philip A. Kuhn, *Soulstealers: The Chinese Sorcery Scare of 1768* (Cambridge, Mass.: Harvard University Press, 1990), 192. Kuhn notes the strain that put on provincial officials who were charged with the responsibility for checking on their own subordinates. But it also created opportunities for lower officials or for those outsiders with an ax to grind to impeach bureaucratic opponents with a minimum of risk to themselves.

19. *Li Gong Qin Gong Nianpu* [Biography of Li Yumei], cited in *ZXXSJJ*, 2016. Li's biographer also says opposition was aroused by jealousy.

20. *HZXZ*, 6:23b. The charges concerning public works officials are contained in a funerary inscription written by Lin Zexu. The reference to stalk merchants is found in *HZXZ*, 6:17a, a biography of Li Yumei.

21. Yan Lang, letter to Guilang, *ZXXSJJ*, 2019. The editors chose to place that letter right after Li Chun's memorial. Although it is obviously written in support of Li Chun's arguments, it is unclear when it was written; it could have been any time during the subsequent investigation. It is also unclear whether the letter was solicited by government investigators or was volunteered by Yan Lang, perhaps at the request of those opposing Li Yumei. In the letter, Yan Lang recalled that he had worked closely with Li Yumei for six months in 1820 (DG 1), when the latter was the subprefect of Wuzhi County, and again briefly in 1830, when Li Yumei had served a short stint as Kai-Gui circuit intendant.

22. Ibid. Recalling an attempt in 1805 (Jiaqing 10) to use brick on the Gaoyan Dike, Yan noted that the experiment had failed when winter winds and waves cracked the bricks apart. He also recalled brick walls along the Grand Canal that had to be repaired each year because the rise and fall of the water caused the bricks to crack.

23. Ibid. Yan calculated the cost of one *jianfang* (a square measuring one *zhang*—approximately 3.3 meters—per side) of stalks at slightly over 1 tael, then noted that the same volume of brick would cost 13 taels. That is a rather disingenuous comparison. If the two are measured by weight rather than volume, one *jianfang* of brick would weigh around 9,000 *jin* (based on Li Yumei's estimate of 8 *jin* per brick). The same volume of stalks would weigh around 500 *jin*. The cost of 9,000 *jin* of stalks would have been between 15 and 20 taels, considerably more than an equivalent quantity of brick.

Li Yizhi, *Shui gong xue* [Studies in hydraulic engineering] (Taipei: Wenhai Publishing Co.), 183, says the bricks produced in Zhili in the early twentieth century weighed only 4.8 *jin* and that a *fang* contained around fifteen hundred bricks. These were bricks fired for building houses. Li Yumei expected that those fired for the river conservancy would be made to more rigorous specifications.

24. Yan Lang, letter to Guilang, *ZXXSJJ*, 2020. Yan Lang claimed that the bricks then being produced along the river were inferior to the bricks produced

in earlier times. The bricks produced more recently had a higher loess silt content, which made them lighter and more fragile. If permission was given to establish government kilns, Yan said, the bricks produced would be no different from those disparaged by an expression common in the Bianliang market: "Red bricks just look at the water and crack!" That argument seems to be an attempt to counter Li Yumei's claim that as bricks age and absorb moisture, they become heavier and more solid, not fragile and crumbling. Li gave as an example the bricks taken from the walls of old wells. Yan wanted to dismiss those as bricks fired from different materials.

25. *QDHCZ,* "Yan Lang," 3:166. Yan's initial demotion was for failure to maintain adequate stalk supplies. Four years later, his successor in the Henan conservancy, Wu Bangqing, indicted him again for having falsified accounts concerning the use of broken rock in construction projects and for having accepted bribes. As a result of Wu's charges, Yan Lang was further demoted to the rank of assistant salt controller.

26. Jingzheng, DG 17/7/12, *ZXXSJJ,* 2036. "QDWXDA," ZB, no. 5809-1, draft biography of Jingzheng.

27. "QDWXDA," ZB, no. 5809-1, draft biography of Jingzheng. Jingzheng's experience with hydraulic engineering was limited to two cases. In 1832 he accompanied Board of Works president Zhu Shiyan to the Jiangsu conservancy to look into a case in which local peasants had intentionally damaged a dike. And again in 1834, after Jingzheng had been appointed a senior president of the censorate, he undertook an investigation of the construction along the seawall in Zhejiang Province.

28. "GZD" (T), Li Yumei, DG 19/10/17. In parts of Jiangsu, the river traveled through gaps as narrow as 400 meters. Upriver of that bottleneck, and with the exception of two narrow passages 1.3 and 1.9 kilometers wide, the main dikes were anywhere from 3.3 to 20 kilometers apart. Although Li Yumei does not mention it, adherence to Pan Jixun's policy of "restricting the water to attack the silt" also constricted the river and thus contributed to that problem. Quotations in *HZXZ,* 6:11a–11b.

29. Li Yumei, DG 17/5/13, *ZXXSJJ,* 2014.

30. *HZXZ,* 6:11a–11b. The quota of stalks that could be purchased for the Henan conservancy each year had been raised from 2,500 *duo* to 5,000 *duo* in 1806 (Jiaqing 11) but had not been raised since that time. The *Gong Bu Zeli* [Statutes of the Board of Works] (Taipei: Cheng Wen Publishing Co., 1966), 35:6, under "river repairs," gives the standard weight of a *duo* of stalks as fifty thousand *jin,* or roughly fifteen metric tons. The quota established in 1806 was based on the price for stalks set by the state at the time. Although the state-approved price was occasionally raised, it did not keep pace with actual prices.

31. Li Yumei to Jingzheng, DG 17/6/2?, enclosure, *ZXXSJJ,* 2029. Li gave the total length of the existing *sao* sections in the Henan conservancy as 4,850 *zhang,* or approximately sixteen kilometers. Since *sao* came in all shapes and sizes, the

measure of a section, the *duan,* was inexact and affords no reliable way of cal-
culating the length of dike covered by the 931 sections existing in Daoguang 1.
    32. *HZXZ,* 6:11b. Li Yumei to Jingzheng, DG 17/6/2?, enclosure, *ZXXSJJ,*
2029. Regulations also required that the top of the main dikes be kept one *zhang*
(3.3 m) above the high-water mark. Also, "GZD" (T), Li Yumei, DG 19/10/17,
points out that the main dikes in Henan had once been a uniform twelve meters
across the top but had since been eroded to a width of from four to six meters.
In his report to Jingzheng, Li supported his arguments with the following statistics on expenditures for stalk revetment and earthwork for the preceding fifteen
years:

Expenditures (in taels)

Year	Stalk construction	Earthwork
1821	954,177	790,725
1822	1,088,886	570,486
1823	893,351	287,401
1824	938,884	211,888
1825	1,006,351	327,574
1826	955,834	223,455
1827	1,056,974	183,425
1828	1,038,413	132,332
1829	985,536	146,309
1830	1,036,754	144,305
1831	1,140,201	144,134
1832	1,198,842	169,946
1833	1,168,312	254,548*
1834	1,101,926	148,322
1835	1,100,675	177,368

*Li explained this sudden jump as the result of a special project to
rebuild earth embankments in the Xiangfu area.

    33. *HZXZ,* 6:24a. "GZD" (B), Li Yumei, DG 19/3/12. Li claimed to have
saved 110,000 taels in 1836 (DG 16). In *HZXZ,* 6:7b–8a, Li made the point that
the use of brick would also free officials from the demands of stalk merchants
who were able to hoard supplies to drive up prices. In times of high demand,
brick could be substituted for stalk revetments, which would lower the price of
stalks. Moreover, the "itinerant guests, secretaries and friends" *(liuke muyou)* who
looked upon river repair projects as a means of enriching themselves would be
out of work.
    34. *QDHCZ,* 151–152. Linqing, lateral communication to Li Yumei, DG
17/3/26, *ZXXSJJ,* 2011. Li Yumei and Linqing were not strangers to each other.
According to Linqing, *Hongxue yinyuan tuji* [Illustrated traces of a life] (hereafter *HXYYTJ*), 3 vols. (Beijing: Beijing Guji Chubanshe, 1984), vol. 2, pt. 1,

"Dicheng Zhanjin," the two traveled together while on their way to provincial postings in Hebei in 1829.

35. Linqing, lateral communication to Li Yumei, DG 17/3/26, *ZXXSJJ*, 2013.

36. Li Yumei, DG 17/5/13, *ZXXSJJ*, 2015.

37. "Li Gong Qin Gong Zhuanba Chengan" [Collected files on the building of brick dikes by Li Yumei], *ZXXSJJ*, 2032–2033. Yu Qingbao, the Huangbian subprefect, reported that he had arrived on the job in Daoguang 15 (1835) and during the next year was involved with Li Yumei in building a number of brick dikes. He concluded that brick and stalk revetments were two different tools, each with its own uses. Brick could not match stalk revetments for quickly closing a breach in the dikes but could be very effective used in combination with broken rock. The second report was that of Xia'nan subprefect Gao Buyue, who concluded that brick was useful as a protective material but could not stand alone as a dike construction material.

38. During the summer and fall flood seasons, the governor-general of the Henan conservancy moved from his normal residence in Jining to his second home in that temple. From there he directed defense and repair efforts during the periods of high water.

39. Jingzheng, DG 17/7/12, *ZXXSJJ*, 2036. Between 6/21 and 7/6, the trio traveled along the northern dike to the brick works at the Xiabei supply garrison, then examined the Lanhuang Dike in Huangbian Subprefecture. Crossing the river at Rongze, they traveled east along the southern dike to the Henan-Shandong border, recrossed to inspect the construction in progress at Caokao, then returned to the Lanyi Temple.

40. Ibid., 2036–2037. The consensus among lower officials was that brick had been very successful as it was used in Huangbian and along the Lanhuang levee. Using brick topped with broken rock had also proved useful in areas where the current was slow and the water shallow. But most lower officials felt that where the water was deep and fast, neither brick alone nor brick and rock together had been successful in blocking the current. In some cases, officials had been forced to resort to using stalk revetments to control damage to brick dikes.

41. Ibid. Jingzheng sought to ground his conclusions in precedent and physical properties, noting that "formerly, river defense meant nothing more than using earth to control water." Then stalk revetments *(xiangsao)* came into use. A compound of stalks and soil, they could be adapted to almost any location, their yielding *(rou)* quality allowing them to resist that which is forceful *(gang)*. Broken rock, which was heavy and hard, could be used to protect stalk revetments from wind and waves, relying on the unyielding *(gang)* to support the yielding. Bricks, made up of earth as they were, fell midway between the hard and soft *(gang rou zhi jian)*. They could thus be utilized as a supplemental material when supplies of stalks or rock were inadequate. But brick was only a temporary solution, whereas rock offered the advantage of a permanent *(yilao yongyi)* solution. *Yilao yongyi*—the single effort that solves a problem permanently—was the

carrot of many river conservancy schemes. It is significant that those with the greatest practical experience in river conservancy generally dismissed that objective as a pipe dream.

42. Jingzheng and Li Yumei, DG 17/7/11, *ZXXSJJ*, 2034–2035; a joint memorial presented the previous day contained the same recommendations but did not detail Jingzheng's reasoning on the issues at hand. Li Yumei, apparently realizing that his proposal was doomed, chose to submit to the consensus opinion for the time being.

43. Jingzheng, DG 17/7/12, *ZXXSJJ*, 2037. Of course, human labor is also required to quarry stone or grow and harvest stalks. More to the point, the acquisition of both had been troubled by corruption. So Jingzheng's point is somewhat disingenuous. What Jingzheng offered by way of proof was also short on objectivity; he recounted how he compared two bricks found at the Yangchao work site, one a recent product of local kilns and the other an older brick. Although the older brick was smaller, Jingzheng reported, it was heavier. He attributed the lightness of the newer brick to shoddy manufacturing and argued that if quality had already declined to this degree, the passage of time would only increase the number of such poor imitations *(zuowei)*.

44. Ibid.

45. Jingzheng and Li Yumei, DG 17/7/11, *ZXXSJJ*, 2035–2036. A separate memorial coauthored by Jingzheng and Li Yumei proposed that the one hundred thousand taels previously designated for the construction of kilns be redirected to the purchase of broken rock. In their memorial, Li and Jingzheng suggested that the problem of supply of rock be dealt with by estimating the needed quantities of rock earlier in the year, expediting shipment at peak times for transport, and punishing those responsible for delays. "SYDFB," DG 17/7/16, records two edicts approving the suggestions made by Jingzheng and Li Yumei. The edict dealing with the issue of kilns made one last slap at the proposal, noting that building kilns near river defense sites might lead to excavation dangerously close to the main dikes.

46. Leonard, *Controlling from Afar*, 166. Another reason why Jingzheng failed to report Li Yumei's concerns may have been that the emperor was already well versed in many of the fine points of the hydraulic system. As Leonard makes clear, Daoguang had been deeply involved in the engineering deliberations resulting from the 1824 break of the Gaoyan Dike. It might have been assumed that Daoguang already understood the situation in Henan. There is no documentation that this was the case, however. Daoguang's engineering knowledge was focused on the Grand Canal–Yellow River confluence. Moreover, what Daoguang learned in dealing with the 1824–1826 crisis was also a product of the reports of imperial commissioners concerned with countering what Leonard refers to as the "local, short-term interests" of regional administrators (166).

47. "GZD" (B), Li Yumei, DG 18/6/22, is a request for an increase in emergency repair funds. In it, Li once more points to the increase in the numbers of

stalk revetments along the river in Henan. He puts the blame on the increased movement of the river within its bed: "Ever since the river branched at Yuanyang in Daoguang 15 [1835], the main current in every downriver section has undergone changes and shifts, to the point where as the current brings danger to new areas, old revetments *(xiang)* must be repaired and renewed." *HZXZ*, 6:5a–5b, records that again in the fall of 1838, Li memorialized concerning earthwork in the Henan conservancy. Emphasizing that along that section of the river where there were no floodgates or other safety valves, river defense depended entirely on the strength of the main dikes, he asked that funds be taken from the Henan and Shandong provincial treasuries to shore up the dikes. *HZXZ*, 10b. Li also fought with his superiors over the accounting procedures for earthwork. The Board of Works insisted that funds be provided according to a yearly report of work carried out *(an nian bao xiao)*. But Li Yumei wanted funds provided on a pay-as-you-go basis *(fennian daixiao)*. "GZD" (B), Li Yumei, DG 19/3/12.

48. *HZXZ*, 6:8a. One *qing* equals 15.3 acres. That is a substantial amount of land, and those drawing income from it must have represented a powerful lobby. Agriculture between the dikes was once commonplace. Late Ming maps show numerous settlements located on the banks of the river between the dikes (see Pan Jixun, *He Fang Yi Lan* [An overview of river defense] [1590], reprinted in *Zhongguo shixue congshu*, ed. Wu Xiangxiang [Taipei: Taiwan Student Bookstore, 1965], no. 33). Qing maps show far fewer such settlements, but even when they did not live between the dikes, farmers continued to grow crops there. In his struggle to block troughs along the river in western Henan, Li Yumei found that earth and stone dams had previously been built to block off such troughs but that farmers had torn them apart to drain their fields when heavy rains threatened to ruin their crops. The land between the dikes was also used for the cultivation of stalks for use in the river conservancy (Yan Lang, letter to Guilang, *ZXXSJJ*, 2020). Yan Lang noted that early in the Jiaqing reign, the demands of river conservancy repair and maintenance had already outstripped the supply of stalks that could be grown between the dikes. The figure for the amount Li had saved is questionable. "GZD" (B), Li Yumei, DG 19/3/12, gives the following figures for expenditure on stalk revetments:

Year	Taels
DG 15	1,199,400
DG 16	969,000
DG 17	878,900
DG 18	1,082,400

Compared with the statistics for DG 11–DG 14, that represents a savings of only 488,581 taels. *HZXZ*, 6:7b, claims that 360,000 taels were saved in the first three years of Li's tenure. If that is accurate, the lower figure of 488,581 appears more likely than the 1.5 million taels that Li later claims. Xu Ke, *Qing bai lei chao* (Taipei: Commercial Press, 1966), 26:43, accepts the larger figure, saying that Li saved 1.3 to 1.4 million taels during his tenure as head of the river conservancy.

49. "GZD" (B), Li Yumei, DG 19/3/12, points out that the use of brick had slowed to a trickle in 1838, when only 11,800 taels had been spent on new construction. Figures for the preceding years were 93,900 taels in 1836 and 323,200 taels in 1837. *HZXZ*, 6:8a, says that in drawing back from his earlier request for official kilns, Li recognized that there were dozens of private kilns in every district along the river and that those would be able to provide sufficient bricks for the river conservancy.

50. *HZXZ*, 6:8a. Whether Li Yumei actually believed that or was merely mining the emperor's paranoia is impossible to know. But he was no doubt aware of certain phrases and charges that had been used to indict the river conservancy, and they are reflected in the language of his memorial. That Li was utilizing every bit of information he could in order to gain a favorable hearing from the emperor is evident in some of the rather convoluted arguments he indulged in concerning the value of brick. For example, he argued that because of its irregular shape, a *fang* of broken rock had many hollow spaces. Brick, on the other hand, was perfectly regular, so a *fang* of brick contained more material, weighed more, and thus was less expensive than a comparable volume of broken rock. Li Yumei also denigrated the quality of rock quarried in Henan, arguing that because it came from "earth mountains" *(tushan),* it would crumble if repeatedly exposed to rain.

51. *HZXZ*, 6:20a. According to the funerary inscription in the Hunyuan gazetteer, Li owed his eventual success in the brick controversy to the decisive support of the emperor. Edict of DG 19/3/19, *ZXXSJJ*, 2055.

52. "SYDFB," DG 19/10/25. Li Yumei, DG 19/10/??, *ZXXSJJ*, 2064. Edict of DG 19/10/25, *ZXXSJJ*, 2064.

53. It was a case of regulations catching up with reality; river conservancy accounting practices had for some time reflected the acceptance of brick. For example, see "GZD" (T), Li Yumei, DG 19/10/17; and "GZD" (B), Li Yumei, DG 19/10/22. "GZD" (B), Yan Yiyu, DG 29/10/23.

54. *HZXZ*, 6:7a, 6:18a–18b. The other site was in Chenliu district. By specifying Zhangjiawan as the location where Li Yumei planned to build his defensive dike, Li's biographers may be embroidering the facts slightly. Zhangjiawan was the exact site of the 1841 flood, but the documents written by Li himself refer only to the Xiangfu lower commandery.

55. *HZXZ*, 6:18a–18b. "SYDFB," DG 20/2/23. The emperor awarded Li the title of Grand Guardian of the Heir Apparent and granted his eldest son, Li Yao, the *jinshi* degree and the opportunity to take the palace examination for entrance into the Hanlin Academy. There was a touch of irony to these honors; according to *HZXZ*, 6:12a, a mere two months earlier Daoguang had ordered Li punished for failing to maintain adequate stalk supplies at Caohe Prefecture. An inspection by imperial emissaries En Gui and He Rulin found that Li Yumei

had relied upon written reports of stalk purchases at Caohe but had not personally inspected the storage facility. It was discovered that lower officials were peculating funds and stealing supplies. The emperor suggested a lenient punishment *(cong kuan)*, and the board ordered Li Yumei lowered two grades in rank.

56. *QDHCZ*, 183. *HZXZ*, 6:23b–24a.

57. Wang Faxing, "Huang He shen Miao—Jiaqing guan" [Yellow River temples—Jiaqing monastery], *Huang He shi ziliao* [Materials on the history of the Yellow River] 3 (1984): 59, notes that Li was included in the pantheon of the temple of the Fourth Son Golden Dragon Great King *(jin long si da wang)* in Wuzhi County. The term "great king" designated a river god, and temples of various great kings lined the rivers and canals of China. Li was also enshrined in the Bao Gong Si in Jining, a temple housing the tablets of notable river officials *(Jining Zhili zhou zhi* [Gazetteer of Jining County], 1859, 5:24a).

58. Hummel, *Eminent Chinese*, 506–507; "QDWXDA," ZB, no. 1522 (1–2); *QDHCZ*, 178–179.

59. Quotation in Polachek, *Inner Opium War*, 43. Linqing, *HXYYTJ*, vol. 1, "Chai ba xun chun."

60. James Polachek, "Literati Groups and Literati Politics in Nineteenth-Century China," 2 vols. (Ph.D. diss., University of California, Berkeley, 1977), 1:104–105, notes that top statecraft officials encouraged their subordinates to develop specialized skills in such areas as salt administration, flood relief, and waterway repair. Also see 2:559 n. 15. In 1:107 Polachek cites the literary output of Wang Fengsheng, a disciple of the statecraft official Jiang Yuxian, which included works on the course of the Yellow River in Henan as well as other water conservancy systems. Linqing, *Lin Jianting xingshu* [Correspondence of Linqing], c. 1850, 1:9a.

61. Quotation in Linqing, *Hegong qiju tushuo* [An illustrated guide to tools used in river work] (1836; reprint, Taipei: Wenhai Publishing Co., 1969). Linqing, *Lin Jianting xingshu*, 14b, cites such books as Ou-Yang Yuan's *Zheng He Fang Ji*, Pan Jixun's *He Fang I Lan*, Jin Fu's *Zhi He Fang Lue*, and Xu Xinru's *An Lan Ji Yao*, as well as the memorials of other river officials. Linqing, *HXYYTJ*, vol. 2, "Qian yu bian tu."

62. Linqing, *Hegong*, 4.

63. "QDWXDA," ZB, no. 1522 (1–2). That assertion drew praise from the emperor.

64. Quotation in ibid. Linqing, *Huang-Yun hekou gu-jin tushuo* [An illustrated explanation of the Yellow River–Grand Canal confluence from ancient times to the present] (Reprint, Taipei: Wenhai Publishing Co., 1969). The original publication date of this work is not clear, but c. 1840 seems likely.

65. Linqing, *Hekou*, preface, 3–4. The secretaries responded that the transfer lake was not a long-term solution but that there was no other good method.

66. "QDWXDA" ("Yuezhe Dang," Palace Museum Archives, Taipei), Cheng

Guanxuan, DG 16/11/27, refers to the removal of several lower officials in the aftermath of that investigation but gives no names.

67. Hummel, *Eminent Chinese*, 507.

68. Polachek, *Inner Opium War*, 80–83, argues that Daoguang's suspicions of the bureaucracy were heightened by the setbacks of the campaign to suppress the Yao aborigines in 1832–1833 and led him to rely more on the censorate. But Daoguang's distrust of the river conservancy was already evident in his first year on the throne, and his sensitivity to censorial remonstrance had already been clearly demonstrated a decade before this. Quotations in "Yuezhe Dang," Cheng Guanxuan, DG 16/11/27. Jonathan Spence, "Opium Smoking in Ch'ing China," in *Conflict and Control in Late Imperial China*, ed. Frederic Wakeman and Carolyn Grant (Berkeley: University of California Press, 1975), 150, points out that opium smoking had already infiltrated the Qing court in Jiaqing's reign. The habit supposedly originated with corrupt secretaries and merchants. Since the main conduit to the capital in the North was the Grand Canal, it is probable that the habit spread to Jiangsu at least this early. Imperial edicts decrying the use of opium by officials mention cases in both the Jiangsu and the Henan conservancies. For example, an edict of DG 19/2/27 ("SYDFB") relates the cases of two officials in the Henan conservancy, a first-class subprefect named Wang Yangdu and a second-class subprefect named Zhang Han, both of whom were addicted to opium. Wang's face had reportedly turned dark and ashy, but he was still unable to quit. Zhang would smoke during the day and read at night, seldom rising to see to his official duties until well after noon.

69. "Yuezhe Dang," Cheng Guanxuan, DG 16/11/27.

70. Ibid.

71. *Baoying xian zhi* [Gazetteer of Baoying County], 1970, 12:24 (757). Historians have pointed to indictments like Cheng's as evidence of corruption in the river conservancy. What has been conspicuously lacking is any reference to the responding memorials written by river officials. For example, Hu, "Yellow River Administration" (1954), 196, 209 n. 58, refers to Cheng's memorial as the act of one of "a few censors and officials, who made some efforts to bring this situation to the attention of the throne." Hu makes no mention of the memorial refuting the charges.

72. Joseph Needham, *The Grand Titration: Science and Society in East and West* (Toronto: University of Toronto Press, 1969), 30, notes that a great many important technological innovators came from the ranks of minor officials but also "that the greatest group of inventors is represented by commoners, master-craftsmen, artisans who were neither officials, even minor ones, nor of the semi-servile classes" (28). However, Joseph Needham in *Science in Traditional China: A Comparative Perspective* (Cambridge, Mass.: Harvard University Press, 1981), 24–25, points out that because hydraulics was a technology of concern to the imperial state, the study of waterworks was "orthodox" and thus a respectable

pursuit for scholars. Nonetheless, Needham says, it was "exceptional to find an important engineer who attained high office in the Ministry of Works, at any rate before the Ming" (*Titration*, 27). He says that technical innovation was often achieved by craftsmen and engineers working for state-funded enterprises such as kilns, imperial workshops, and public works projects (24).

73. Quotation in "GZD" (T), Linqing, DG 17/4/23. Adam Y. C. Liu, *Corruption in China during the Early Ch'ing Period, 1644–1660*, Center of Asian Studies Occasional Papers and Monographs, no. 39 (Hong Kong: University of Hong Kong, 1979), 40–42, recounts a program initiated in 1653 (Xunzhi 10) that attempted to overcome the tendency of capital officials to pass their entire career without a provincial posting, whereas those who began their careers in the provinces were seldom able to return to capital appointments. Under that program, capital officials slated for promotion were offered the opportunity of first serving in a provincial post. The plan, known as *neisheng waizhuan,* apparently relied on an overt appeal to officials to take the opportunity to get wealthy by holding a provincial office as one of its main enticements. In spite of that, the relative prestige of capital appointments made most capital officials reluctant to participate.

The Yongzheng program was aimed specifically at river conservancy posts and seems to have been motivated more by a desire to broaden technical skill than to moderate the bifurcation of the bureaucracy.

74. "GZD" (T), Linqing, DG 17/4/23. Linqing's purpose in writing the memorial in which this edict is quoted is to report the completion of their two-year stint by two officials, one sent by the Board of Civil Office and one sent by the Board of Punishments. Both officials passed their exams with flying colors and were recommended for posts as first-class subprefects. The timing of Linqing's response, however, suggests that he is also making a plea for the continuation of this program because of Cheng Guanxuan's earlier criticisms.

75. "GZD" (B), Wu Jingzheng and Youqi, JQ 5/6/18. Wu was irritated by the reluctance to supply candidates and chastised such officials for what he believed was their feigned ignorance of river engineering. Polachek, "Literati Groups and Literati Politics," 153, also remarks on the reluctance of "statecraft" officials to accept river conservancy posts. Hu, "Yellow River Administration" (1955), 259–261, lists the officials who headed the two divisions of the Yellow River conservancy in the Qing. According to that list, between 1765—the first year in which a river circuit intendant was promoted directly to the governor-general's office—and 1833, thirteen of the twenty-five officials appointed to head the Jiangsu and Henan conservancies were promoted from the post of river circuit intendant or river treasury intendant. Three of those were from the Yongding River conservancy, the rest from the Grand Canal–Yellow River conservancy. Already in the Jiaqing period, officials were warning of the dangers of that practice. See "GZD" (B), Wu Jingzheng and Youqi, JQ 5/6/18.

76. Edicts of the time contain brief references to both successful and unsuc-

cessful candidates. There was apparently no disgrace associated with being unable to manage the required river conservancy techniques. For example, "SYDFB," DG 20/9/17, orders that an official who has proved a failure at river works *(hegong)* be sent home, but it also recommends him for later selection as a magistrate.

77. "GZD" (B), Tiebao, Dai Junyuan, and Xu Duan, JQ 11/11/8. One of the nine officials mentioned was from Jiangsu Province, so the authors suggested he be dispatched to the Henan conservancy.

As was the case with the problem of too few officials to staff the river bureaucracy, the issue of officials' skill had arisen earlier. An edict of Jiaqing 5/2/25 asked that officials who had shown skill at river engineering but had since been transferred to posts outside the river conservancy be returned to Jiangsu to help on major repairs. One of the officials named was Xu Duan.

78. "GZD" (B), Yan Lang, DG 1/12/18, DG 2/4/16. A limit of thirty probationary officials had been set in Qianlong 18 (1753).

79. "GZD" (T), Linqing, DG 17/2/15. That was based on a proposal apparently made in Jiaqing 2 (1797) but never implemented. Linqing claimed that there were plenty of officials to fill the higher posts in the river conservancy but not enough for the lower positions. That situation probably reflects the reluctance of men with degrees to take the most menial of river conservancy jobs and Linqing's reluctance to employ non-degree-holding men in those positions.

80. "GZD" (T), Tao Zhu and Linqing, DG 17/2/15. Metzger, *Internal Organization,* 25–26, notes that Tao was a proponent of "flexibility and practicality" in dealing with administrative problems. That places Tao among the ranks of those statecraft thinkers Metzger describes as "realist" or "accommodative" (74–80) in orientation. Lin Man-huong, "Two Social Theories," 5, says that school was more inclined toward administrative solutions that recognized the inevitability of human failings and sought to limit their impact. Linqing, in *HXYYTJ,* vol. 1, pt. 2, "Lan guan xie zhao"; vol. 2, pt. 2, "He ting na liang," describes his reliance on his own extensive secretarial staff. For example, in the busy summer and fall of 1836, while undertaking the investigation into the river conservancy's accounting practices, Linqing prepared two documents per day, sending off a total of 266 memorials and reports *(tiben)* in the course of a few months. Handling that volume of work while keeping track of river defense, repair and maintenance of hydraulic structures, grain transport, and military affairs was impossible without a large staff. The former chapter was written during Linqing's stint as Kai-Gui-Chen-Xu circuit intendant, the latter while he was governor-general of the Jiangsu conservancy. Their own dependence on such staff may have made high officials reluctant to criticize the use of secretaries and deputies. Although Linqing appears to have undertaken the on-site inspection of river works personally, it is not difficult to imagine other river officials deputing the arduous and uncomfortable aspects of the job and contenting themselves with managing from the yamen. In fact, it was just such remote-control management that Linqing and Tao Zhu were hoping to eradicate.

81. "GZD" (T), Linqing and Tao Zhu, DG 17/2/15.

82. Ibid. The authors point out that both in Jiaqing 11 (1806) and Daoguang 11 (1831), river officials had promulgated regulations strictly controlling material purchases. In order to make the regulations known to those involved in the purchasing process, "each year, before the time to purchase materials arrives, notices are published and posted near the work sites to warn those who see them. After the purchased materials arrive at the work site, they are reinspected. If shortages are discovered, the officials in charge are punished."

83. Ibid.

84. See Ou-yang Xiu, "The Sound of Autumn," trans. A. C. Graham, in *Anthology of Chinese Literature: From Early Times to the Fourteenth Century,* compiled and edited by Cyril Birch (New York: Grove Press, 1965), 368–369. Linqing's oblique reference to Ou-yang Xiu was laden with meaning. According to *Sung Biographies,* 2 vols., ed. Herbert Franke (Wiesbaden: Franz Steiner Verlag GMBH, 1976), 2:808–815, Ou-yang, like many Qing statecraft officials, rejected administration that relied on complex regulations for a style that emphasized simplicity and the direct involvement of the officials. He also believed in the primary importance of selecting good administrators. Linqing's own writings show strong affinities with those ideas. And the fact that Ou-yang Xiu was repeatedly punished for his principled commitment to them no doubt was viewed by Linqing as a parallel with his own punishment after the Taoyuan flood.

85. Hummel, *Eminent Chinese,* 209–212, records the biographies of Linqing's sons, Chonghou and Chongshi. His elder son, Chongshi (1820–1876), would enjoy a distinguished career as an imperial investigator and bandit suppressor. The younger son, Chonghou (1826–1893), would be China's first envoy to the West, a principal in the events leading up to the Tientsin massacre of 1870, and the signatory for China of the unpopular Treaty of Livadia (1879), for which he, like his father, would be criticized, demoted, and forced to retire into obscurity.

4   The Xiangfu Flood and the Siege of Kaifeng, 1841–1842

1. Kaifeng was at once the provincial capital of Henan, a prefectural city *(fu),* and the seat of Xiangfu County *(xian).* Thus the city was sometimes referred to as Xiangfu. It was also sometimes called by its ancient name, Bian, the designation of the river that ran through the city before the Yellow River shifted south. The flood of 1841 was most commonly referred to as the Xiangfu flood, and I have adopted that usage. But when referring to the city itself I have chosen to use its prefectural and modern name, Kaifeng.

2. Wenchong, DG 21/6/17, *ZXXSJJ,* 2076, claimed that the water had risen as much as 7 meters at one point. But "GZD" (T), Wang Ding, Huicheng, DG 21/8/29, reported that their investigation showed maximum high-water levels of around 4 to 4.5 meters in the period leading up to the flood. *XFXZ,* 1891, 7:85b.

3. In fact, few officials in Henan were experienced in that type of repair. It

had been over two decades since a serious flood had occurred in the Henan conservancy; the last major break had taken place in 1819. Gao Buyue was one of the lower officials who opposed the adoption of brick as an emergency repair material (see chapter 3). Wenchong, DG 21/7/3, *ZXXSJJ*, 2089. Wenchong's biographical record is scanty. With the exception of the few facts noted in the course of this chapter, he does not appear to have made any mark on Qing political life. Ignominy and anonymity were apparently the price of his failure to prevent the Xiangfu flood.

4. Xia'nan Subprefecture was one of the two sites where Li Yumei had stored five thousand *fang* of bricks. But those were undoubtedly used at the large defensive works several kilometers upstream from the thirty-first station. Moving them to the site of the breach would have required a great deal of labor and, more crucially, time.

5. *XFXZ*, 7:85b.

6. That was the same day that Sir Henry Pottinger arrived in Hong Kong.

7. Li Yumei's tenure had been relatively free of charges of corruption, but an edict of DG 19/12/12 ("SYDFB") ordered an investigation into the problem of bribery and gift-giving among officials in Henan. The edict also charged that the Xiangfu magistrate was involved in gambling operations along with his younger brother, his secretaries *(muyou)*, and the local tough guys *(digun)*. Hu, "Yellow River Administration" (1954), 259–260. Between 1810 and 1833, *only* former river intendants were chosen for the top posts. During one period, 1824–1833, two men, Yan Lang and Zhang Jing, took turns at the helms of the two conservancies. Zhang retired in 1833 but continued to play a role in river affairs. In 1843, chastened by Wenchong's failure, Daoguang would promote one last circuit intendant, Pan Xi'en, to head the Jiangsu conservancy.

8. *ZXXSJJ*, DG 20/3/7, 2068.

9. Edict of DG 20/5/25, *ZXXSJJ*, 2069.

10. Ibid. "SYDFB," DG 20/7/1. But from this point on the investigation seems to have lagged. An edict that winter ("SYDFB," DG 20/11/17) complained that Wenchong and Niu Jian had not yet replied to the emperor's demand for a full investigation.

11. "SYDFB," DG 20/11/17. Buttons of rank were worn on the hat to represent rank or honors bestowed in recognition of contributions to the public good. They could also be bought outright. "SYDFB," DG 20/10/22.

12. "SLTB," Mu Zhang'a, DG 22/2/29; Huicheng, DG 22/11/12.

13. Edict of DG 20/11/17, *ZXXSJJ*, 2073. Edict of DG 20/12/10, *ZXXSJJ*, 2074.

14. "SYDFB," DG 20/11/17. No brick was requisitioned for use in the two subprefectures in Shandong Province. Those still relied on stalks and rock.

15. *XFXZ*, 7:86a.

16. *XFXZ*, 6:34b–36a. Niu Jian, DG 21/7/15, *ZXXSJJ*, 2099.

17. "GZD" (B), Niu Jian, DG 21/6/23. According to Zhuang Xiangnan, "A

Record of the 1841 Zhangwan Flood," *XFXZ,* 7:86b, when the floodwaters first entered the city, local officials hid in fear. When Niu Jian arrived, he was greeted by a hysterical and starving populace demanding to know where the prefectural and county officials had gone. Niu Jian, DG 21/7/25, *ZXXSJJ,* 2098; Zhuang, "Zhangwan Flood," 88a–88b. Niu Jian reported that after he took those steps, commerce took place at "fair" prices. But Zhuang's account says that high demand drove the cost of a *dou* (approximately a peck) of rice as high as three thousand cash, and a *jin* of grass cost several hundred cash.

18. Zhuang, "Zhangwan Flood," 86a. According to that account, the soup was made by boiling straw mats.

19. Quotations in Zhuang, "Zhangwan Flood," 86b–87a. According to *Mathews' Chinese-English Dictionary* (Cambridge, Mass.: Harvard University Press, 1956), 1094, the term *yecha* is from the Sanskrit *Yaksha,* "demons that fly like meteors, messengers from hell." In the atmosphere of fear and strain, wild stories found ready listeners. According to Zhuang, "Zhangwan Flood," 88a, when yellow snakes appeared fleeing the floodwaters, the people urged them to crawl onto platters and took them to the Great King Temple where they were worshiped as river spirits. One of the snakes was reluctant to take part in the ceremony and refused to climb onto the platter. It was beseeched in the name of every local river god, but only when someone called to it using the title "Great King Li" *(Li Dawang)* did it respond by climbing onto the tray. This "Great King Li" was none other than the former governor-general of the Donghe, Li Yumei. A short fifteen months after his death, Li Yumei's apotheosis had begun.

20. Nowhere does Wenchong give a clear explanation of what measures he was taking to try to shore up the break. As will be shown, part of the reason for that was his ignorance of the situation there.

21. Wenchong, DG 21/7/3, *ZXXSJJ,* 2089. The dike heads were the two ends of the dike on either side of the break. As the current moved through the break, those would gradually erode, widening the gap. The process could be halted by wrapping the exposed ends in huge *sao* bundles.

22. Ibid.

23. *Zhongguo shuili shigao* [A draft history of Chinese water conservancy], Wuhan Water Conservancy and Electrical Power Institute (Beijing: Water Conservancy and Electrical Power Publishing Co., 1987), 216–220, 286, map 8-8.

24. *Kaifeng Fu Zhi* [Gazetteer of Kaifeng Prefecture], 1863, 6:2a, says that the outer "earth wall" *(tucheng)* was built over what had been the outer wall of the old Song capital. See also the discussion in E. A. Kracke, Jr., "Sung K'ai-feng: Pragmatic Metropolis and Formalistic Capital," in John Withrop Haeger, ed., *Crisis and Prosperity in Sung China* (Tucson: University of Arizona Press, 1975), 50–52; and Randall A. Dodgen, "Salvaging Kaifeng: Natural Calamity and Urban Community in Late Imperial China," *Journal of Urban History* 21, no. 6 (September 1995): 716–740. Zhuang, "Zhangwan Flood," 86a.

25. Niu Jian, DG 21/6/30, *ZXXSJJ*, 2086. Zhuang, "Zhangwan Flood," 87a. Edict of DG 21/7/4, *ZXXSJJ*, 2088.

26. Niu Jian, DG 21/6/30, *ZXXSJJ*, 2086–2087.

27. "SLTB," Wenchong, DG 21/7/12, reported that as of 7/3 only about 70 percent of the current was flowing through the gap in the dikes. Some flow continued in the main course until the floodwaters receded. Zhuang, "Zhangwan Flood," 87a. Niu Jian, DG 21/7/5, *ZXXSJJ*, 2093–2094. Niu Jian, DG 21/8/2, *ZXXSJJ*, 2102, reported that all together some five hundred meters of the city wall had collapsed before the situation could be brought under control.

28. Niu Jian, DG 21/8/2, *ZXXSJJ*, 2102.

29. Ibid.

30. The edict of DG 21/7/25, *ZXXSJJ*, 2101, charged that although there were thousands of *duo* of stalks available along the dikes, only 50 or 60 *duo* made it to Kaifeng in the entire first month of the flood. "GZD," Wang Ding, Huicheng, Niu Jian, DG 21/8/12, says Wenchong's excuse was an alleged shortage of boats. Wang, Huicheng, and Niu noted that in the month from 6/27 to 7/26, only 400,000 *shu* of stalks were shipped to Kaifeng, but that in a nine-day period after the crisis had passed (and after imperial commissioners had arrived from Beijing to investigate matters), from 7/27 to 8/6, 800,000 *shu* of stalks were shipped. How was it, the memorial asked, that in the entire month before, no boats could be found, but in a short ten days boats became available in endless supply?

Wenchong had also claimed that materials were disappearing because officials were docking the boats along the wall at sites near their homes, stealing the cargo, and using the boats to give their families a place to live. Wang Ding and Huicheng investigated those charges and dismissed them. For one thing, they pointed out, the boats in question were grain barges without deck houses and so were not suitable as housing ("GZD," Wang Ding, Huicheng, DG 21/8/11).

31. Zhuang, "Zhangwan Flood," 86a–86b; Niu Jian, DG 21/7/25, *ZXXSJJ*, 2100. Since the weak and helpless were being housed in the Provincial Examination Hall, it is supposed that at least the roof was left on. Niu Jian, DG 21/7/15, *ZXXSJJ*, 2095. Not surprisingly, the price of bricks and other materials rose rapidly.

32. Zhuang, "Zhangwan Flood," 85b. According to Linqing, *HXYYTJ*, vol. 3, "Yin he qiang hong," the labor bosses had enough power over their workers to stage work slowdowns and walkouts in order to pressure officials for higher wages. Niu Jian, DG 21/7/25, *ZXXSJJ*, 2099.

33. Niu Jian, DG 21/7/25, *ZXXSJJ*, 2099. The size of the gangs numbered from one hundred to several hundred men.

34. Zhuang, "Zhangwan Flood," 88b, records that two boats arrived carrying materials.

35. On 7/4 the emperor had appointed two officials, Grand Secretary Wang

Ding and Transmission Office Commissioner Huicheng, to go to Henan and take control of the repair project. "GZD" (T), Wenchong, DG 21/7/12. In support of his argument, Wenchong presented a laundry list of reasons why it would be unwise to try to return the river to its former course immediately. Among them were the difficulty and expense of the project, the shortage of materials, the approach of winter, and so on.

36. Edict of DG 21/7/18, *ZXXSJJ*, 2096.

37. "GZD" (T), Wenchong, DG 21/7/12.

38. Niu Jian, DG 21/8, *ZXXSJJ*, 2103. The two imperial commissioners were actually residing on the main dike at the sixth dike-watcher station. "GZD" (T), Wang Ding, Huicheng, DG 21/8/7. This memorial also rejected Wenchong's use of precedent, pointing out that from the Han (206 B.C. to A.D. 219) and Tang (618–907) dynasties on, closing breaks in the dike, and doing so with all dispatch, had been a fundamental principle of river control. As for the Great Yu's practice of guiding the floodwaters to uninhabited areas, that was no longer practicable in a time when cities stood in sight of each other and the land was everywhere tilled. In contrast to the Great Yu, they cited the policies of such river conservancy luminaries as Jia Lu of the Yuan, Chen Xuan of the Ming, and Jin Fu of the early Qing.

39. "GZD" (T), Wang Ding and Huicheng, DG 21/8/7.

40. They reported that in the fourteen days since they had arrived on the scene, they had made four trips to Kaifeng and two trips to the site of the breach.

41. "GZD" (T), Wang Ding and Huicheng, DG 21/8/11.

42. Ibid.

43. Edict of DG 21/8/17, *ZXXSJJ*, 2133. Edict of DG 21/8/9, *ZXXSJJ*, 2107.

44. For example, *Huang He shuili shi shuyao*, 235, cites the case in Hongwu 22 (1389) of the Yifeng County government's relocation to Bailou village to avoid the constant threat of floods. For a full discussion of the debate about relocation, see Dodgen, "Salvaging Kaifeng." Zou Minghe, *XFXZ*, 75b, listed four necessary tasks for salvaging the city: repairing the city wall, digging a moat around the city, rebuilding the earth dike to protect the city from floods, and dredging the Huiji River (to provide drainage for floodwaters).

45. Niu Jian, "A Request That the Moving of the Provincial City Be Delayed," in *XFXZ*, 75b, in particular noted that families and lineages who had lived in Kaifeng for generations were opposed to the move. Many of those would undoubtedly have been families of influence and wealth. "GZD" (T), Wang Ding, Huicheng, and Niu Jian, DG 21/8/12.

46. "SYDFB," DG 22/2/28.

47. Linqing, DG 21/9/24, *ZXXSJJ*, 2124–2125. Elizabeth Perry, *Rebels and Revolutionaries in North China, 1845–1945* (Stanford, Calif.: Stanford University Press, 1980), 10–47, is the classic study of the relationship between environment and the "endemic peasant violence" of the Huaibei region. "SYDFB," DG 21/9/5.

48. The term *central bureaucracy* is used here to designate the Grand Council and the emperor. The Boards of Works and Revenue also had input into decisions, but their role was secondary.

49. "SYDFB," DG 21/7/23. Officials were also concerned about the problem of draining agricultural land into an elevated lake. "SYDFB," DG 21/7/7.

50. "GZD" (T), Cheng Rocai, DG 21/7/23, vermillion rescript. Edict of DG 21/8/11, *ZXXSJJ*, 2107.

51. Linqing, DG 21/9/24, *ZXXSJJ*, 2124–2125. As with other measures of length and distance, I have used approximate metric equivalents to convey these statistics. In this case I have equated one *li* with one-half kilometer.

52. Ibid., 2125.

53. Ibid.

54. "SYDFB," DG 21/8/27.

55. "SYDFB," DG 21/10/28. The units of measure for villages varied from province to province. In the report on Henan, the terms *she* and *bao* are sometimes used to describe a larger unit containing a number of *cunzhuang,* but the latter is the fundamental unit and is used throughout the report. The situation in Anhui was more complicated, and reports used a number of terms to describe village units. The term *yu* is used to indicate villages or fields located in low-lying areas and protected by a low levee or dike. Village units are also designated by the terms *li* and *ji,* whereas lands belonging to the military fields *(tuntian)* system are described by the term *tunzuo*. It is unlikely that any of those units indicate uniform size or population.

56. "SYDFB," DG 21/11/19.

57. "SYDFB," DG 21/10/28. "GZD" (B), map 939, "Xinagfu manshui jingyou Yu-Wan ge zhou xian ru Huai da Hongze hu qingxing tu."

58. Pierre-Etienne Will, *Bureaucracy and Famine,* translates *yigong daizhen* as "replacing relief by public works" and says it was aimed mainly at providing employment for wage laborers (137 n. 26). He also uses the translation "providing relief in exchange for work" (258). In the case of flood repair projects, where work relief was a mechanism to distribute aid to the general population of rural males, the second translation fits the circumstances more closely. Wang, Huicheng, and Niu Jian, DG 21/8/29, *ZXXSJJ*, 2115, requested that four hundred troops be sent to the area for security purposes. There was no attempt to employ euphemism concerning the job those troops were to perform: as described by Wang, their role was *tanya,* literally "to suppress."

59. Many of the agricultural laborers in the area along the Yellow River almost certainly had experience doing seasonal work on the dikes. Thus, the labor force recruited through work relief was useful and even necessary to the quick completion of the project. Linqing, DG 21/9/24, *ZXXSJJ*, 2126. According to Linqing, grain prices were holding steady, but he feared that as soon as winter came, prices would skyrocket. He argued that rather than have the entire body of refugees and flood victims dependent on state relief, it would be better

to have them work on dredging the bed of the Yellow River in Jiangsu or on similar jobs. Paying these peasants according to the number of *fang* of earth moved,
Linqing argued, was a surer way of getting actual relief money into their hands
than sending money and grain into the countryside to be distributed, and perhaps stolen, by local officials. It was, he said, a way to kill two birds with one
stone *(yiju liang de)*.

60. Edict of DG 21/10/2, *ZXXSJJ*, 2126. "SYDFB," DG 22/1/12.

61. "SYDFB," DG 22/1/9, DG 22/3/24.

62. Wang Ding, Huicheng, and Niu Jian, DG 21/8/17, *ZXXSJJ*, 2110. The
fact that none of the officials on hand were experienced in planning or managing a major flood repair project may also explain their reluctance to undertake
on-site inspection and planning. To men skilled as scholars and administrators
rather than as engineers, the documentary record of past floods was more accessible and more comprehensible than the physical reality of the flood site.

63. The examples were chosen carefully. The Lanyi project was, as officials
admitted, different from the break at Xiangfu (the width of the Lanyi breach was
only 650 meters), and the Maying break was different from both. Dozens of
other projects could have been cited where lack of planning proved disastrous
or led to runaway expenditures, but those go unmentioned. Wang and his coauthors, DG 21/8/17, *ZXXSJJ*, 2110–2111. They wanted to begin work at the start
of the ninth month. The memorial also held forth the possibility that further
requests for funds might have to be made but promised to return any excess funds
to the provincial treasury.

64. Edict of DG 21/8/21, *ZXXSJJ*, 2111.

65. "SYDFB," DG 21/10/7.

66. Edict of DG 21/8/16, *ZXXSJJ*, 2109.

67. "GZD" (T), Wang Ding, Huicheng, and Niu Jian, DG 21/8/29. Prices
paid per *duo* of stalks had ranged from 180 taels on the Yi project to 250 at the
Ma project. Prices per *duo* on the Sui and Heng projects had been 190 taels and
200 taels, respectively.

68. Ibid.

69. Ibid. Although the regulated price paid by the river conservancy for stalks
was 70 taels per *duo*, high demand and scarcity were recognized as legitimate
reasons to ask for higher prices. In view of the prices allowed on previous flood
repair projects, it is not clear how Wang expected to get producers to sell at
those prices. Later problems of extortion by government runners and hoarding
by sellers may have had their roots in this attempt at economy.

70. "GZD" (T), Zhu Xiang and E Xun'an, DG 21/11/19, also complained
about the impact of the stalk shortage on regular river maintenance. While the
Xiangfu project was under way, other normal maintenance works had to be
carried out as well. The prices being paid at Xiangfu were making it difficult to
get stalks for that work. Zhu and E Xun'an asked for *jintie* of from 15 taels to

25 taels per *duo*. The top price being paid would still be only 95 taels per *duo*, however. "GZD" (T), Wang Ding, Huicheng, Niu Jian, DG 21/8/29.

71. Linqing, *HXYYTJ*, vol. 3, pt. 2, "Liao chang wen jie." "SYDFB," DG 22/2/28.

72. "SYDFB," DG 22/2/28.

73. Ibid.

74. Ibid. Wang Ding, Zhu Xiang, and E Xun'an, DG 21/10/20, *ZXXSJJ*, 2128. Punishment for absconding would fall on the lineage members of the officer, who would therefore be likely to discourage that form of theft. What Wang and coauthors do not say is that control of those funds and the common (and obviously accepted) practice of nepotism presented the officer in charge with an unprecedented opportunity to peculate on a more limited scale, benefiting family and friends and at the same time lining his own pocket.

75. Wang Ding, Zhu Xiang, and E Xun'an, DG 21/11/3, *ZXXSJJ*, 2130–2131. There was standing water in some three kilometers of the river course downstream of the breach.

76. *Huang He saogong* [Stalk revetment construction on the Yellow River], ed. Shuili Dianli Weiyuan Hui (Beijing: China Industrial Publishing Co., 1964), 32–33, gives the total number of managerial personnel required to supervise the construction of each dike as 21 to 26. They would be supervising a labor force of from 262 to 291 men. Repair could require that two pairs of dikes be built out into the river, but the Xiangfu site required only one pair. So the number of workers and managerial personnel on both dikes probably totaled around 650. The deflection dike would require another 300 men. Those figures do not include the men involved in dredging operations or other support personnel. "GZD" (T), Wenchong, DG 21/7/12, had claimed that the lack of skilled personnel was one of the reasons the closing of the initial breach was delayed.

77. Wang Ding, Huicheng, and Niu Jian, DG 21/8/17, *ZXXSJJ*, 2111. Wang referred to the situation in the Maying flood, where 400 troops had been sent from the Nanhe to the Donghe, and the Yifeng flood, where 600 troops had been sent. "GZD" (T), Wang Ding et al., DG 21/8/29. Edict of DG 21/10/25, *ZXXSJJ*, 2129.

78. Linqing, DG 21/9/4, *ZXXSJJ*, 2119. Zhu Xiang, the incoming governor-general of the Donghe, had arrived at Qingjiangpu on 9/1, so Linqing had discussed the selection of officials with him. Perhaps being new at the job worked against Zhu Xiang, but he does not appear to have come away with all the expertise Wang had sought. Concerning the replacement lieutenant colonel, Linqing wrote, "Although he has no experience with major projects, he is conscientious in handling daily affairs." The other officials sent included three second captains, one first-class subprefect, one second-class subprefect, and one county magistrate. The three second captains were the only ones experienced in major repair works. "GZD" (T), Zhu Xiang, DG 21/9/25, enclosure, reported that by 9/25 most of the troops from the Nanhe had reached the work site.

79. "SYDFB," DG 21/7/3. Hummel, *Eminent Chinese*, 511. "QDWXDA," draft biography of E Xun'an, no. 1155-4. The portions of this document praising Lin Zexu are marked for deletion, as is the section that admits that E Xun'an, Zhu Xiang, and Wang Ding all lacked experience on this type of project.

80. The house-building prohibition was undoubtedly widely ignored. In chapter 2 it was noted that complaints were heard of houses between the dikes being torn down for their bricks, and maps of the period often show settlements between the dikes. But the destruction of the flood probably left few owners anything to reclaim, and the official proscription, however much honored in the breach, was grounds enough for the government action. "GZD" (T), Wang Ding, Huicheng, and Niu Jian, enclosure of DG 21/8/29.

81. *Huang He saogong*, 31, estimates that for each square meter of *sao* work carried out, some 25 percent of the required 0.3 man hours of labor took the form of handicraft work, whereas the remainder was unskilled labor.

82. One section *(zhan)* was approximately seventeen meters square on top.

83. *Huang He saogong*, 81–121 and passim, contains detailed drawings of different types of *xiangsao* construction, complex rope-work arrangements, types of boats and tools used, and variations on technique that illustrate the sophistication of *xiangsao* and their adaptability to a wide range of conditions.

84. Wang Ding, Huicheng, Zhu Xiang, and E Xun'an, DG 21/9/16, *ZXXSJJ*, 2120. Zhu Xiang, Wenchong's replacement as governor-general of the Donghe, had just arrived at his post. E Xun'an was Niu Jian's replacement as governor of Henan. On 9/5, Niu Jian had been promoted to governor-general of Liangjiang. Obviously, Niu's prompt and successful response to the crisis at Kaifeng had redeemed him in the eyes of the emperor. The dike bases measured 70 meters at the base and close to 4 meters in height. Linqing, DG 21/9/4, *ZXXSJJ*, 2118, reported that on 8/20 Linqing had sent two officials to the work site to measure the breach. Using a silk cord, they measured the gap and found it to be 303 *zhang*, or something over 900 meters across. That turned out to be the exact length of the repair dike when it was completed. The water at the breach was from three to eight meters deep.

85. "QDWXDA," draft biography of E Xun'an, no. 1155-4. Wang Ding et al., DG 21/11/3, 11/18, 12/2, *ZXXSJJ*, 2130–35; DG 21/10/2, *ZXXSJJ*, 2126. "GZD" (T), Zhu Xiang, DG 21/9/25, enclosure.

86. Wang Ding, Zhu Xiang, and E Xun'an, DG 21/11/3, 11/18, 12/2, *ZXXSJJ*, 2130–2135.

87. Ibid.

88. Ibid.

89. Ibid., 2137.

90. "GZD" (B), Wang Ding, Zhu Xiang, and E Xun'an, DG 21/11/3. Wang Ding, Zhu Xiang, and E Xun'an, DG 21/11/18, *ZXXSJJ*, 2133. Pressure of this kind put magistrates in a difficult position, and the temptation to expropriate the needed materials through violence and intimidation must have been great.

91. Wang Ding et al., DG 21/11/18, *ZXXSJJ*, 2133.

92. Wang Ding et al., DG 21/12/26, *ZXXSJJ*, 2139; DG 22/1/6, *ZXXSJJ*, 2144. Edict of DG 22/2/12, *ZXXSJJ*, 2153, orders that the drowned official's family be compensated as though he had died in battle. That accorded with regulations (see chapter 1). Three other officials are listed as having been seriously injured, and the board is asked to comment on whether they should be compensated as having received military injuries.

The information on the drowned workers and troops appears in an excerpt from the biography of Zhang Liangji *(nianpu)*, *ZXXSJJ*, 2154. Reports to the emperor do not mention them.

93. Wang Ding et al., DG 22/1/13, *ZXXSJJ*, 2146.

94. Lin Zexu, *Lin Zexu shujian* [Correspondence of Lin Zexu], ed. Yang Guozhen (Fuzhou, China: Fujian People's Publishing Co., 1985), 180. In one of the few references to the Xiangfu project in Lin's surviving correspondence, he mentions the storm and confirms that it came just as the project was nearing completion. Wang Ding et al., DG 22/1/6, *ZXXSJJ*, 2144–2145. Obviously concerned that they might be held accountable for those losses, Wang and his fellow officials immediately sought precedent in the history of other floods. They reported that both the Maying and Yifeng projects had suffered similar setbacks. They also spoke to officers and dike workers experienced in major repair projects and were told that this was a common problem. They closed the memorial by requesting punishment for their failings.

In the responding edict, the emperor did not deem it necessary to punish Wang and company, but he warned against excessive haste and threatened to hold Wang Ding and the other memorialists responsible for any future collapse.

95. Wang Ding et al., DG 22/1/13, *ZXXSJJ*, 2146–2147.

96. Ibid., 2147.

97. Ibid.

98. Edict of DG 22/1/19, *ZXXSJJ*, 2149. The emperor ordered the Board of Revenue to review the request for funds. The board replied that it had not yet received the account books from the provinces surrounding Henan, and most of the money previously on hand had been paid out, leaving too little to transfer. They therefore suggested that one hundred thousand taels of the spring land tax from Henan be used, along with 1 million taels from the Board of Revenue *(buku)* treasury. The sudden availability of materials as soon as the government raised its price gives some support to the assertions of government officials who complained about hoarding. Wang Ding, Huicheng, Zhu Xiang, and E Xun'an, DG 22/1/19, *ZXXSJJ*, 2149.

99. Edict, undated, *ZXXSJJ*, 2149.

100. Wang Ding, Huicheng, Zhu Xiang, and E Xun'an, DG 22/2/8, *ZXXSJJ*, 2151–2152.

101. Ibid., 2152. In fact, some leakage did continue at the base of the gap, but that was soon sealed with broken rock, stalk bundles, and earth.

102. Wang Ding, Huicheng, Zhu Xiang, and E Xun'an, DG 22/2/16, *ZXXSJJ*, 2155–2156.

103. Board of Revenue, DG 22/2/23, *ZXXSJJ*, 2157. There may be a source missing from that copy, since the memorial concludes by saying that the above amounts total 422,000 taels when in fact they total 402,000 taels.

104. "SYDFB," DG 22/8/27. "GZD" (B), Huicheng and E Xun'an, DG 23/6/2.

105. *XFXZ*, 7:81a–82b.

106. Perry, *Rebels and Revolutionaries*, 43–47. The influx of money for the repair project to some extent redressed the losses suffered by peasants along the river. But it is probable that little of that money reached the inland areas of the province. The fact that much of the dredging was specifically charged to residents of the areas along the river, and that migration to the work site was discouraged, operated to keep river conservancy funds in a narrow belt close to the dikes.

107. Edict of DG 21/9/2, *ZXXSJJ*, 2117.

108. Hummel, *Eminent Chinese*, 763, mentions Zhang as an early supporter of Zou Zongtang. "SYDFB," DG 22/2/17, DG 22/2/20, DG 22/7/16, DG 22/9/12; *ZXXSJJ*, 2158. Many of those rewards promised officials priority in the filling of upcoming vacancies.

5   The Taoyuan Flood and the Zhongmou Debacle, 1842–1845

1. *Huang He shuili shi shuyao* contains examples too numerous to detail.

2. "GZD" (T), Niu Jian, DG 22/6/18. Linqing, DG 22/7/29, *ZXXSJJ*, 2165. As was the case with the Xiangfu flood, the Taoyuan flood occurred at a location where no defensive works had previously been constructed. According to Linqing's account, the local yamen was situated just below the point where the dike broke. Second Captain Zhang Yuanji, who was on the dike working on emergency defense at the time, lost his family to the floodwaters.

3. Linqing, DG 22/7/29, *ZXXSJJ*, 2165.

4. Ibid. Seemingly less concerned about his own career than protecting his subordinates, Linqing rushed to their defense by insisting that the flood was not the product of laxity or incompetence but of unusual weather and unprecedented high water levels. Linqing asked that the officials directly responsible for the area where the flood occurred be removed from their posts but allowed to work on the subsequent repairs to redeem themselves, and that officials who had been working on emergency defense in other areas be allowed to redeem themselves by managing repairs. Such leniency was consistent with earlier cases in which officials under his command were responsible for hydraulic failures. For example, when a section of the towpath dike *(qianti)* on the Central Transport Canal near Taoyuan collapsed in Daoguang 19 (1839), Linqing did not ask that the officials

responsible be removed from their posts but instead recommended that they be punished only by loss of their badges of rank and by being ordered to take charge of repairing the damage ("SYDFB," DG 19/8/21). Whether the emperor and his advisors accepted Linqing's logic or were moved by his long years of successful river control is not clear, but the punishments doled out were generally lenient: although several officials, including Linqing himself, were removed from office, none was exiled or humiliated by wearing the cangue. Edict of DG 22/9/18, *ZXXSJJ*, 2176.

5. The last major dispute over hydraulic policy had taken place in 1824–1826, when a break in the Gaoyan Dike led to a debate over the use of sea transport for tribute grain. See Jones and Kuhn, "Dynastic Decline," 124–125; Leonard, *Controlling from Afar;* Polachek, "Literati Groups and Literati Politics," 1:207–262.

6. Zhang Hanying, *Ming-Qing zhi he gailun* [An outline of Ming-Qing river control] (Beijing: Water Conservancy and Electrical Power Publishing Co., 1986), 105–112. The most often proposed shift was north via the Daqing River, the route the Yellow River would eventually take in 1855.

7. Edict of DG 22/8/26, *ZXXSJJ*, 2169. Jingzheng and Liao Hongquan, DG 22/9/22, *ZXXSJJ*, 2175. Linqing's work included building two deflection dikes and wrapping the dike ends to stop erosion. He had also completed 90 percent of the work needed to prepare a temporary lake or "transfer pond" *(yitang)* that would allow empty grain boats returning from Beijing to cross the Yellow River on their journey south. The preparation of that lake *(tang)* was a primary concern of the central bureaucracy and the monarchy. The engineering involved appears to have been simple, particularly since it was only designed to be a temporary system. Moving the empty grain boats south on schedule was as much a priority as moving the laden grain boats north, since delays in loading would mean the loss of a great deal of tribute grain because of rot and pilfering, as well as a tardy arrival in Beijing the following year. Jingzheng and Liao Hongquan, DG 22/10, *ZXXSJJ*, 2177.

8. Jingzheng and Liao Hongquan, DG 22/10, *ZXXSJJ*, 2178. The actual wording of the memorial is that it would be necessary to build dikes to restrict the current *(bixu zhu ti shu shui)*. The river's new course was too far north to allow the former north dike to be used as part of the control system. Other drawbacks included the fact that the affected areas were used by the government to produce salt and to grow sorghum for use in the river conservancy. Leaving the river in the new course would reduce salt tax revenues and create stalk shortages. Subprefectural offices and housing for river troops would also have to be built at sites along the new course, and the residents, though relatively few in number, would have to be relocated.

The issue of leaving the river in its new course was first raised in a draft memorial appended to Linqing's initial report of the flood (*ZXXSJJ*, 2163–2164). It is not clear who authored that report, but it was probably one of Linqing's subordinates. Linqing's later comment that, without further study, he could neither advocate or oppose the change of course (*ZXXSJJ*, edict of DG 22/7/29, 2167) echoes the neutral tone of the initial report. It is possible that the author of that draft, dissatisfied with Linqing's lukewarm response, passed along the suggestion to the censor who eventually advocated the change. That early proposal estimated that 360 kilometers of dike would have to be built at a cost of 6.8 million taels, with another 800,000 taels required for dredging work.

9. Jingzheng and Liao Hongquan, DG 22/10, *ZXXSJJ*, 2179. The use of a man-made lake that would be flooded twice a year to allow the crossing of grain boats had been suggested earlier. Linqing's *Hekou* had been written partly to illustrate the need for just such a lake. Pan Xi'en was also a proponent of that method.

10. Jingzheng and Liao Hongquan, DG 22/10/?, *ZXXSJJ*, 2177. The commissioners cited two examples of failed attempts to change the river's course. In Kangxi 1 (1662) a breach of the dikes along the north bank led officials to try to change the river's course to follow the bed of the Guan River to the sea. Within two years siltation at the river mouth was blocking egress, and the river had to be returned to its former course. They also mentioned the more recent unsuccessful efforts of the river minister Dai Junyuan (1746–1840) to change the lower course of the river.

Such ideas were typical of those who believed that methods should take advantage of circumstances *(yin shi li dao)*. Zhang, *Ming-Qing Huang He Gailun*, 109, traces the origin of that phrase to Wang Jing, a river expert in the Eastern Han dynasty (29–220). Jingzheng had heard the same phrase from Li Yumei and had rejected it, so it is not surprising to see it unsuccessful here.

11. Jingzheng, Liao Hongquan, and Linqing, DG 22/10/15, *ZXXSJJ*, 2181–2182. The authors recognized that by fall of the coming year, peasants would have reoccupied much of the land previously inundated by the floodwaters. When flood season came around again, those people would have to be warned, evacuated, and fed. They therefore requested that extra civil officials be transferred to the area to help with the inevitable dislocation and needed relief. But only the three counties along the north bank of the Yellow River near the break suffered heavy damage. Moreover, prompt relief measures taken by Linqing in the early days of the flood had minimized the impact of the disaster on those areas (*ZXXSJJ*, 2183). Jingzheng and Liao Hongquan, DG 22/11/?, DG 22/11/2, *ZXXSJJ*, 2186. The cost of closing the breach included the construction of approximately thirteen thousand meters of dikes and levees. Those would require 9,460 *dui* of stalks and 979,970 *fang* of earth. It is not clear whether the unit *dui* is comparable with the *duo*. Edict of DG 22/11/2, *ZXXSJJ*, 2188.

12. DG 22/11/6, *ZXXSJJ*, 2188–2189. Pan's career in river conservancy began in 1824, when he submitted a memorial on hydraulic problems in the

Nanhe (*QDHCZ,* 168–171). His observations were astute enough that he was appointed Huai-Yang circuit intendant the following year and served in the Jiangsu conservancy for the next four years. After a number of capital postings, he was brought back to the river conservancy for the sake of his expertise. Although Linqing's star had faded, Pan was a close associate, and the two officials shared common ideas on river control. Both were supporters of Pan Jixun's methods, and Linqing strongly supported Pan Xi'en's proposal to turn the Central Transport Canal into a closed lake, to be filled twice a year so that the grain boats could cross. Whether appointing Pan from within the river conservancy reflects Daoguang's reassessment of his appointment of Wenchong or simply his faith in Pan is not clear. Pan would be the last river intendant elevated to the post of governor-general in the Qing.

13. Lei Yixian, DG 22/11/2?, *ZXXSJJ*, 2189. That memorial dates between the twentieth and the twenty-fifth, when an edict responding to it was promulgated. Lei claimed that the cost of construction would be 5 to 6 million taels and that dredging would cost another 3 million. Those totals indicate that he was unaware of the budget proposed by Jingzheng and Liao. A *jinshi* of Daoguang 3 (1823), Lei was later to achieve notoriety as the official who invented the *lijin* tax.

14. Ibid., 2191. Much of Lei's proposal harks back to the earlier "divide the streams" school of thinking. That method, dominant prior to Pan Jixun's time, was rejected because dividing the waters of the river also would divide the force of the current, slowing the flow and encouraging more rapid sedimentation. Large-scale dredging, whether by human or mechanical means, had proved prohibitively expensive.

But some of Lei's claims show almost complete ignorance of Pan Jixun's contributions to hydraulic theory. For example, he believed that the narrow valleys through which the river was forced to pass on its way to the sea would not silt up—not because the accelerated current would prevent siltation but because the soil at the base of those mountains was firm and silt would not stick to it. Lei also underestimated the impact of land scarcity on the peasants of the region. He was convinced that the peasants had abandoned the flooded area and would not return because agriculture in the marshy wasteland along the seacoast was untenable; thus, he saw no reason to build dikes to control flooding in the delta.

15. Ibid., 2192. As noted in the earlier chapters, seeking jobs in the river conservancy and utilizing major works projects as employment opportunities were commonplace practices; Lei's complaints were not unfounded. However, his charge that river officials relied only on subordinates is contradicted by a wealth of material showing that even the highest river officials, including Linqing and Li Yumei, regularly undertook personal inspections of the dikes and commanderies under their charge.

16. It is probable that Lei, as a censor in the region, was aware of the central government's special sensitivity in that regard because of the problems that were already being encountered in Taoyuan County and other areas along the north bank of the Yellow River. Late in the summer of 1842, bandits aroused by the incursions of the English had stirred things up. Later in the year, supposedly influenced by a drought in the area along the north bank of the Yellow River, locals in the Taoyuan area banded together, ostensibly for mutual protection, and began raiding nearby villages. After the flood at Taoyuan, bandits began preying on the fleeing flood victims, stealing their food and abducting and raping their women. In the same area, a group of twenty-one men were also known to have taken part in a sworn brotherhood *(jiebai dixiung)* ceremony, a sure sign to many officials that rebellion was brewing ("GZD" [T], Linqing, Li Xiangfen, DG 22/10/15).

17. "SYDFB," DG 22/11/25. Pan Xi'en, DG 22/12/2?, *ZXXSJJ*, 2193.

18. Pan Xi'en, DG 22/12/2?, *ZXXSJJ*, 2193. He also disputed Lei's claim that the narrow valleys through which the Yellow River would have to pass on its new route would not silt up and block the flow. Although it might take years, he said, the eventual result would be blockage downstream and flooding upstream. Pan Xi'en, DG 22/12/2?, *ZXXSJJ*, 2193–2194. Pan found that Lei had also misrepresented the distances involved, claiming it was only about 50 kilometers from the site of the break to the mouth of the Guan River when in fact it was over 180 kilometers.

19. Quotations in ibid., 2195–2196. Edict of DG 23/1/7, *ZXXSJJ*, 2196. The emperor's rejection of Lei's proposal did not signify disapproval of Lei. *Qingshi,* comp. Qingshi Bianzuan Weiyuanhui (Taipei: Guofang Yanjiuyuan, 1961), 4829, notes that Lei's next posting was as a reader of the Grand Secretariat, a rank of 4b, a full grade above the rank of a provincial censor. Not only did Lei suffer no adverse impact for having made that proposal, but the following year, while still serving as the Shandong censor, he felt free to make another suggestion regarding river conservancy practices.

20. *ZXZ*, 1:37b, quotation in 1:7b, 9b.

21. *ZXZ*, 1:37b.

22. The bureaucratic expansion that has been described elsewhere was clearly evident in Zhongmou. Initially, river conservancy in the area had been in the hands of a single official in charge of the Jiangsu conservancy subprefecture. But in Yongzheng 2 (1724), that subprefecture had been split into Shangnanhe and Xiananhe Subprefectures. A further expansion of the bureaucracy took place in Qianlong 46 (1781) with the creation of the posts of Zhongmou upper and lower *xun* assistant district magistrates. The final expansion came in Jiaqing 11 (1806), when Kaifeng's second-class subprefect in charge of grain *(duliang tongpan)* was transferred to head the newly created Zhonghe Subprefecture.

23. *ZXZ*, sec. 4. The river officials who served in the area, their salaries, and supporting funds for their staff were as follows:

Office	Number	Salary/ Appropriation (in taels)	Food Subsidy (in taels)
Shangnanhe subprefect (tongzhih)	1	37.444	9.083
Attendants	2	12.000	0.285
Yamen runners (kuaishou)	7	42.000	10.187
Police runners (zaoli)	5	30.000	7.277
Zhonghe subprefect (tong-pan) (salary not given, probably not paid by Zhongmou County)	1		
Police runner	1	6.000	1.455
Zhongmou upper xun assistant district magistrate (xiancheng)	1	40.000	9.702

The assistant district magistrate's salary was also supplemented by "nourishing goodness" (yanglian) funds totaling 60 taels. All salaries are for one year. The subsidies referred to were called chuhuang (eliminating famine) funds. In leap years a further subsidy was added to the income of certain officials and staff. Although not mentioned here, a Zhongmou lower xun assistant district magistrate was also posted to the area. His salary and staff were in all likelihood the same as his counterpart to the west, but he and his staff may have been paid by the Xiangfu treasury. The Zhonghe subprefect had responsibility for both Zhongmou xun. It is not clear why Zhongmou had to contribute at least a part of the salary of the Shangnanhe subprefect. It may have resulted from the fact that county boundaries and those of the river conservancy subprefectures overlapped, with part of Shangnan Subprefecture extending into Zhongmou County. "QDWXDA," "Liusheng Huanghe Saoba Qingxing Tu" [Map of Yellow River stalk revetment conditions in six provinces along the Yellow River], Palace Museum Archives, Taipei, no. 0773. River troops and workers were also stationed on the north bank in Yangwu and Fengqiu Counties.

24. ZXZ, 1870, sec. 5. Even the post of district magistrate was held mainly by officials holding the degree of licentiate (jiansheng and gongsheng), although two jinshi and several juren had also held the position. Low-ranking degree holders dominated the local river conservancy bureaucracy as well. Of the thirty-six Qing river officials who had served in Zhongmou and for whom educational information is available, only five held degrees higher than licentiate; four were juren, one a jinshi (this calculation only includes officials up to the first appointment made in the Xianfeng reign). A higher number of officials holding the post of Shangnan subprefect are described as gongsheng, fugongsheng, or fusheng, whereas those holding the posts of second-class subprefect and assistant district magistrate were all jiansheng (with the exception of the four juren mentioned above).

25. According to ZXZ, 1870, 5:35b, of the forty-five officials whose place of origin is listed, fourteen came from Jiangsu, five from Zhejiang, three from Anhui, two from Shandong, and two from Zhili; two were bannermen. In an apparent attempt to circumvent the exam quotas of the various native areas, a further eight officials were registered as natives of Xuntianfu, the prefecture in which Beijing is located. A parenthetical note in the gazetteer gives evidence of such subterfuge, reporting that an official listed as coming from Xuntianfu was in fact a native of Zhejiang.

26. Local civil officials occasionally took over positions in the river conservancy, often on an acting or short-term basis. ZXZ, 5:35b.

27. Ibid. That practice seems to have been confined to the Daoguang reign. There were also times when more than one official was appointed to a single post, but it is unclear whether special circumstances such as illness or the demands of an emergency produced that condition.

28. ZXZ, 8:32b, 8:34b. Edict of DG 23/7/7, ZXXSJJ, 2201.

29. ZXZ, 8:34b.

30. ZXZ, 2:41a.

31. "GZD," Dushuisi, packet 34.

32. Huicheng, DG 23/7/1, ZXXSJJ, 2199–2200. According to a report from the Zhonghe Subprefect, the area near the breach had previously been a major defensive site composed of twenty-one sections *(duan)* of stalk revetments. But those had been covered by silt in Daoguang 2 (1822) and since that time had been left to decay until nothing of the old defensive works remained. Once more Li Yumei's warning about "old works born anew" proved prescient.

33. QDHCZ, 183–184, records that Huicheng, a Manchu of the bordered yellow banner, was a *jinshi* of 1836. In his brief public career, Huicheng had been appointed to the Hanlin Academy and served as imperial superintendent of instruction to the heir apparent and as imperial diarist. In the fall of 1841 he accompanied Wang Ding to the site of the Xiangfu flood. In the following months he was made a junior vice president of the Board of War and served briefly as governor-general of the Henan conservancy until the new acting head, Zhongxiang, arrived. In the spring of 1842, Huicheng was punished because of the setbacks at the dike repair site at Xiangfu, but when the breach was closed, his ranks and titles were restored and he received praise from the emperor. In the latter part of that year, he was made governor-general of the Henan conservancy. Huicheng, DG 23/7/1, ZXXSJJ, 2199, 2200.

34. Here Huicheng's report diverges once more from the gazetteer account (ZXZ, 1:40a), which claims that the number of people drowned was incalculable *(wusuan)*. Perhaps that reflects a difference in the perspectives of the local gentry and the bureaucrat held responsible for the disaster. The former were likely to exaggerate local suffering to gain tax remissions; the latter would naturally minimize the figure to reduce his culpability. Huicheng, DG 23/7/1, ZXXSJJ, 2200.

35. Ibid., 2200–2201.

36. "SYDFB," DG 23/3/27. That edict carries an imperial emendation that alters one passage reading "If each of these offices continues to disburse funds as they have in the past, we fear there will be shortages [of funds]" to read "The use of funds by each of these offices was already great; if they continue to waste funds as they have in the past . . . "

37. "SYDFB," DG 23/4/9.

38. Tang, "Daoguang chao juanjian zhi tongji," 46–62.

39. Huicheng also displayed a seasoned bureaucrat's nose for funding opportunities. Reasoning that the Zhongmou flood would make repairs at Taoyuan easier, he asked that funds already collected for the Taoyuan flood be diverted to Zhongmou. That attempt to carve into the resources of the Jiangsu conservancy was unjustified—some of the work at Taoyuan would be simplified, but extensive repairs would still be necessary—and met with reluctant compliance by officials in Jiangsu. Quotation in "GZD," Huicheng, DG 23/7/7.

40. Edict of DG 23/7/4, *ZXXSJJ*, 2202. Jingzheng's rank at that time was assistant grand secretary and president of the Board of Revenue; He Rulin was a junior vice president of the Board of Revenue. Quotation in Jingzheng, He Rulin, DG 23/7/20, *ZXXSJJ*, 2208.

41. Jinzheng and He Rulin, DG 23/*run*7/1, ZXXSJJ, 2213 (hereafter, the Chinese word *run* will be used to indicate an intercalary month). The distribution of food by name *(anming)* required some form of registration, but how that was carried out is not made clear. The food being distributed is described as "sweet cakes" *(tangbing)*. Pierre-Etienne Will, *Bureaucratie et Famine en Chine au 18e Siècle* (Paris: Mouton, 1980), 123–133, discusses the use of tickets or receipts given to famine victims and the problem of determining who was truly a victim and who was just trying to get a free handout.

42. ZXZ, 2:8a. Ironically, it was Kaifeng that once more was endangered. As the flood turned east, the current partly destroyed the dike protecting the city, which had to be repaired with stalk revetments. But the Kaifeng city wall suffered only minor damage, and the city escaped with minimal flooding (edict of DG 23/7/21, *ZXXSJJ*, 2209).

43. Edict of DG 23/7/20, *ZXXSJJ*, 2209. "GZD," Cheng Maocai, DG 23/*run*7/20.

44. "GZD," Cheng Maocai, DG 23/*run*7/20. For that reason, prices of sorghum stalks had remained low.

45. "GZD," Zhongxiang, DG 23/9/3. Concurrently, the Yellow River underwent another surge, so that in a single day the floodwaters in Taihe County rose two-thirds of a meter.

46. Huicheng, DG 23/7/9, *ZXXSJJ*, 2203. Most of the efforts to wrap dike heads had focused on the western side of the break: the eastern end was still too unstable to work on. Jingzheng, He Rulin, DG 23/7/20, *ZXXSJJ*, 2208; DG 23/*run*7/1, *ZXXSJJ*, 2212. At the center of the gap, the water was ten meters deep.

47. Jingzheng and He Rulin, DG 23/*run*7/1, *ZXXSJJ*, 2114. Those sums did not include the cost of relief or tax remissions.

48. Jingzheng and He Rulin, DG 22/7/1, *ZXXSJJ*, 2213.

49. Ibid., 2214–2215, 2217. The Zhongmou officials had already written Pan Xi'en, ordering him to hand over 1.7 million taels that were sent to the Jiangsu conservancy in the fifth month for repairs at Taoyuan. In addition, they requested that 194,000 strings of cash collected in Jiangxi through the sale of degrees and ranks and sent to the Jiangsu conservancy for use in river repairs be commuted to silver and forwarded to Henan. The rationale for changing the cash into silver was to avoid the difficulty of shipping bulky copper. But their insistence on the unrealistic (albeit official) exchange rate of one thousand cash to the tael was an obvious attempt to shift some of the fiscal burden of the repair to the Jiangsu conservancy. The figure in the *ZXXSJJ* is 1.3 million taels rather than 2.3 million, but the responding edict and later documents indicate that that is a misprint. Edicts of DG 23/*run*7/5, *ZXXSJJ*, 2215; DG 23/*run*7/16, *ZXXSJJ*, 2218.

50. Pan Xi'en, DG 23/*run*7/?, *ZXXSJJ*, 2220, 2221. The total cash on hand in Jiangsu was 190,000 strings. Pan reported that a total of 3.7 million taels had been ordered transferred to the project in two installments. Of that amount, approximately 1.2 million taels had already been spent and another 1.2 million was needed for work that could not be delayed. Of the remaining 1.3 million taels, over 900,000 taels had not yet arrived in the Jiangsu conservancy. Pan had already written to the various treasuries responsible for those funds and ordered that they be rerouted to the Henan conservancy for use on the Zhongmou project. In addition, nearly 400,000 taels was still on hand at the work site, and Pan found almost 200,000 taels in the river conservancy treasury. He offered to send the Henan conservancy the funds from those two sources, which, combined with the funds being rerouted, totaled 1.5 million taels. Edict of DG 23/*run*7/30, *ZXXSJJ*, 2221.

51. Jingzheng and He Rulin, E Xun'an, DG 23/8/8, *ZXXSJJ*, 2223–2225. On DG 23/8/23, Zhongxiang memorialized concerning funds to be transferred from the Canton customs to the Donghe. The total amount of the contribution was supposed to be 924,000 taels, but the amount actually on hand was only 717,000 taels. Officials in Canton promised to send the remaining 200,000-plus taels as it became available ("GZD," Zhongxiang, DG 23/8/23). In the end, 550,000 taels of that allotment was not sent directly to the Zhongmou site but was routed through Anhui to supplement relief funds there until the fall harvest came in. The total amount was then to be sent on to the flood site. But because of the need for relief funds in Anhui, the officials at Zhongmou despaired of ever getting the money. They pointed out that 360,000 taels that was previously supposed to be sent from Anhui had yet to arrive. "It is even more difficult to believe that ordering them once more to transfer [funds] will lead to [the money's] timely arrival," Liao wrote ("GZD," Liao Hongquan, Zhongxiang, and E Xun'an, DG

23/9/25). That type of leakage and delay in the transfer of funds was one of the most serious problems officials faced in responding to a flood emergency.

52. Pan Xi'en, Cheng Gang, and Li Hui, DG 23/8/25, *ZXXSJJ*, 2230–2233; edict of DG 23/8/28, 2233. Cheng and Li were capital officials sent by the emperor to double-check Pan's estimates.

53. "GZD," Jingzheng, He Rulin, and E Xun'an, DG 23/*run*7/22; DG 23/*run*7/28. Edict of DG 23/*run*7/27, *ZXXSJJ*, 2219.

54. Liao Hongquan, Zhongxiang, and E Xun'an, DG 23/9/9, *ZXXSJJ*, 2237–2238. A total of 5.8 million taels had been approved for the project. As of 9/6 only 2,380,440 taels had been received by the Henan treasurer, and a further 1,251,000 taels was reported to be in transit. The remaining 2,168,560 taels was due from various provinces and customs treasuries. Edict of DG 23/9/29, *ZXXSJJ*, 2238.

55. Liao Hongquan, Zhongxiang, and E Xun'an, DG 23/9/20, *ZXXSJJ*, 2241. The term used for that treasury, *neiku*, indicates that the funds came from one of the treasuries of the Imperial Household Department. That is borne out by the fact that in the original memorial, the characters for *neiku* are raised one space above the body of the memorial. Later references to the source of that loan, however, use the term *buku*, indicating a board treasury, probably the Board of Revenue. I suspect the anomaly reflects the likelihood that, rather than count on the unreliable funding sources indebted to the Zhongmou project, the Imperial Household Department treasury insisted on being repaid from the Board of Revenue treasury, with the Zhongmou debt then transferred to the board. Edict of DG 23/9/24, *ZXXSJJ*, 2242.

56. "SYDFB," DG 23/*run*7/12.

57. "GZD," Jingzheng, He Rulin, and E Xun'an, DG 23/*run*7/28. Eventually, grain was accepted only at Kaifeng and was used to feed the refugees or the workers on the dikes.

A second censor, Li Enqing, also offered a suggestion on how to deal with fiscal shortages and the need for materials. He pointed out that almost all the money being transferred to the Henan work site was in the form of silver, but copper cash was needed to pay for labor and materials. Since flood conditions made cash difficult to transport, shortages near the work site would often drop the price of silver to less than 1,000 cash per tael, leading to inflation in the price of materials. Li suggested that materials be paid for with paper certificates, redeemable at a rate of 1,050 cash per tael, either in Beijing or at the provincial treasury in Kaifeng. In reply, Jingzheng et al. recalled the problems of paper currency in the Song, Yuan, and Ming periods, including counterfeiting and hoarding. But their main objections were the difficulty of putting such currency into use on short notice and the fear that stalk merchants would be unwilling to accept paper currency for their goods, which would only worsen the problem of matériel shortages. The suggestion was eventually rejected ("GZD," Jingzheng, Liao Hongquan, He Rulin, and E Xun'an, DG 23/8/19).

Hu, "Yellow River Administration" (1954), 223, points out that 70 percent of the river conservancy budget during the Taiping Rebellion was paid in paper currency.

58. The edict of DG 23/8/13, *ZXXSJJ*, 2226, ordered Liao Hongquan and Zhongxiang to investigate the abuses reported by Chen Tan. Liao Hongquan and Zhongxiang, DG 23/8/21, *ZXXSJJ*, 2228, reported that the pair toured nearby collection centers, reiterating the emperor's injunctions on paying for materials and sourcing through merchants. They ordered the opening of new collection centers *(liaochang)* near the work site. Collection officials were to pay merchants as soon as the stalks were delivered. The price being offered for stalks was the same as that paid during the Xiangfu project, 180 taels per *duo*. An effort was also made to inform stalk merchants of that policy, probably by posting placards near the collection centers. The collection centers were set to open on October 2. "SYDFB," DG 23/*run*7/22. Chen estimated that markets within a one-hundred-kilometer radius would be able to supply enough stalks for the repairs.

59. "SYDFB," DG 23/*run*7/22. The emperor also expressed the concern that Nian bandits *(nianfei)*, indigenous to the area, might be attracted by the concentration of merchants and attempt to rob them. He ordered officials to eradicate any sign of bandit activity (a task more easily ordered than done).

Fears that the flood would provoke bandit activity were widespread. In a memorial on flood conditions in Anhui ("GZD," DG 23/*run*7/20), Governor Cheng Maocai noted that bandit *(gunfei)* activity had flared up in Anhui in the wake of English military campaigns the year before. Although the bandits had been dispersed, many had escaped capture, and Cheng feared that the disaster would bring them out again. Efforts had therefore been made to round up the ringleaders, but, Cheng wrote, it was difficult to pluck out the offenders without harassing the law-abiding.

60. "SYDFB," DG 23/8/27; edict of DG 23/8/27, *ZXXSJJ*, 2229. Those two versions of the edict differ slightly. The former, sent to the emperor in draft, was emended by him in two places. In describing the abuses Linqing was to watch for, the initial document mentioned only the coercion of stalk producers *(liaohu)* and underpayment. In the margin the emperor added "or [acceptance of] materials unfit for use." Several lines later, the emperor wrote in the margin, "I consider Linqing capable of self-renewal *(zi xin zhi ren)*; how better to show his good conscience than by reporting early success." Those lines both appear in the final document printed in the *ZXXSJJ*.

61. Liao Hongquan, Zhongxiang, and E Xun'an, DG 23/9/9, *ZXXSJJ*, 2236–2237; DG 23/9/16, *ZXXSJJ*, 2238–2240. Since Linqing had been placed in charge of the collection process, it is probable that he conducted that investigation. Linqing's autobiography *(HXYYTJ)*, vol. 3, "Liao chang wen jie," echoes the conclusions of the memorial. Linqing's comments *(wen)* are included in the memorial. The local toughs are referred to as *jin'gun*, a term the *Zhongwen Da Cidian* [Encyclopedic dictionary of the Chinese language], 10 vols., ed. Lin Yin

and Gao Min (Yangmingshan, Taiwan: Chinese Culture University, 1985), defines as "bad elements associated with the literati."

62. Liao Hongquan, Zhongxiang, and E Xun'an, DG 23/9/16, *ZXXSJJ*, 2238–2240. Linqing also discussed efforts to guarantee supplies of other materials, including hemp, grasses, palings, rock, and brick. But all of those were lower priority, and efforts to broaden their base of supply were still in the early stages. The one expedient that was almost certain to increase the supply of materials, that is, raising the price paid for them, was not entertained.

63. Linqing, *HXYYTJ*, vol. 3, "Liao chang wen jie." Linqing does not make clear what quantities were on hand at the collection centers but merely refers to them as "complete" *(wan)* or "finished" *(juan)*. It is unlikely, given the pace of collection described in other memorials, that the entire amount of stalks required for the project was on hand by those dates.

The title of this section of Linqing's autobiography refers to the fact that while carrying out his duties at the flood site, he received word that his eldest son, Chongshi, had passed the *juren* exam. Thus he is punning on the word *jie,* success, as applicable to both his son's test results and his own efforts at operating the matériel collection centers.

64. "SYDFB," DG 23/11/4, DG 23/11/23.

65. "GZD," Han Chun, DG 23/*run*7/7. Long before repairs began, Han, a senior metropolitan censor, warned that after matériel purchases, wages *(jiaojia)* were the greatest expense on a repair project.

66. "GZD," Liao Hongquan and Zhong Xiang, DG 23/9/1.

67. "GZD," Liao Hongquan, Zhong Xiang, and E Xun'an, DG 23/9/20. Since the daily salary of 1.2 taels also had to pay for the services of the two or three runners they generally employed, even the upright might find peculation a temptation.

68. Ibid. For workers carrying earth, a standardized measure was used to check carrying baskets. Workers hauling materials were expected to carry ten *shu* per trip, with each *shu* weighing six *jin*. Linqing, *HXYYTJ*, vol. 3, "Mou gong helong," depicts workers carrying those bundles over their shoulders. Most are shown carrying only one bundle, but several men are shown carrying two.

69. Edict of DG 23/9/24, *ZXXSJJ*, 2242. Linkui and Liao Hongquan, DG 23/10/28, *ZXXSJJ*, 2253–2255. Most of the abuses that did come to light were related to dredging projects and usually involved lower civil and military officials trying to pass off substandard work or falsifying the amount of work done. Those men were summarily punished, often by wearing the cangue.

70. Zou Minghe, *ZXXSJJ*, 2299. Pan Xi'en, DG 23/9/5, *ZXXSJJ*, 2235. For the victims in Anhui, however, every effort was to be made to keep them from leaving their native areas and wandering across the countryside.

71. Linkui and Liao Hongquan, DG 23/11/16, *ZXXSJJ*, 2256.

72. Linqing, *HXYYTJ*, vol. 3, "Yinhe chiang hong." Those rewards were offered when the work was 50 percent to 60 percent complete. Linqing's elaborate

preemptive strategy indicates that such labor tactics were commonplace. The instigators were probably experienced laborers, not country bumpkins fleeing the flood.

73. Ibid. Dredging the last 130 meters of the diversion canal and finishing the work would provide the income needed to keep the workers alive until spring. Edict of DG 23/12/6, *ZXXSJJ*, 2265.

74. Linkui and Liao Hongquan, DG 23/12/17, *ZXXSJJ*, 2265; quotation in DG 24/1/2, 2271–2272. "SYDFB," DG 24/2/4, cites a memorial charging that the workers had been so badly underpaid that many had fled the work site.

75. Liao Hongquan and Zhongxiang, E Xun'an, DG 23/10/1, *ZXXSJJ*, 2245–2246. Linqing was also in attendance in a supervisory capacity, as was Niu Jian. Engineering expertise was not in short supply. Linkui and Liao Hongquan, DG 23/11/16, *ZXXSJJ*, 2255–2256. But Linkui cautioned that it was too soon to predict a day for the closing of the breach *(helong)*. Among the problems he claimed were slowing repairs were the large size of the breach and the fact that the loose soil in the area made construction more difficult.

76. Linkui and Liao Hongquan, DG 23/12/1, *ZXXSJJ*, 2263–2264. Edict of DG 23/12/6, *ZXXSJJ*, 2264.

77. Linkui and Liao Hongquan, DG 24/1/2, *ZXXSJJ*, 2271–2273.

78. Ibid. The soft silt did not provide a firm base for the stalk sections, allowing them to be undercut by erosion.

79. Linkui and Liao Hongquan, DG 24/1/17, *ZXXSJJ*, 2274.

80. Ibid., 2275.

81. Linkui and Liao Hongquan, DG 24/2/2, *ZXXSJJ*, 2277.

82. Linkui and Liao Hongquan, DG 24/2/7, *ZXXSJJ*, 2278–2279.

83. Linkui and Liao Hongquan, DG 24/2/9, *ZXXSJJ*, 2281. In his subsequent memorial on 2/15 (April 2) (*ZXXSJJ*, 2282), Linkui blamed the failure partly on the fact that "Your ministers originally had no knowledge of river control," adding that that was why he had requested the help of officials familiar with river affairs.

84. Edict of DG 24/2/13, *ZXXSJJ*, 2281–2282. However unforgivable that was, it did not match the failure of Wenchong. Linkui and Liao were demoted to the seventh rank and removed from their posts but were to remain at the site to help with repairs. The emperor added that if they were able to somehow reverse the situation, they might receive more lenient treatment. Zhongxiang, because he had been on the job only a short time, was also demoted to the seventh rank and lost his title, but he was allowed to remain in his post for the time being. E Xun'an was demoted to the third rank and also allowed to remain in his post temporarily.

85. Linkui and Liao Hongquan, DG 24/2/15, *ZXXSJJ*, 2282–2283. That memorial was written three days before the Qingming festival. The summer flood season began approximately twenty days after Qingming day. Linkui estimated that four thousand *duo* of stalks and 5 million *jin* of hemp would be required to

complete repairs. With the increased depth of the water at the center of the breach, each section required six or seven days to complete. Perhaps seeking solace (and leniency) in precedent, Linkui cited the Yifeng flood in the Qianlong reign and the Shaojiaba (Ma) project in the Jiaqing reign as cases where similar problems had led to the suspension of repairs until the fall. Although he stopped short of requesting a similar delay, he did request that the official sent by the emperor to replace him consider those factors and make recommendations.

86. Edict of DG 24/2/15, *ZXXSJJ*, 2284.

87. Edict of DG 24/1/8, *ZXXSJJ*, 2272. That edict repeated charges contained in a secret memorial that the Jiangsu conservancy was riddled with corruption. According to the indictment, river officials were allowing their secretaries *(muyou)* to take charge of river conservancy repairs, and the secretaries were using funds skimmed from those projects to pay for lavish banquets. Pan Xi'en was ordered to investigate the charges. The edict also claimed that officials still in Beijing awaiting appointment were seeking letters that would recommend them to river officials.

88. "SYDFB," DG 24/2/4.

89. "GZD," Linkui, Liao Hongquan, Zhongxiang, and E Xun'an, DG 24/2/5. Some of the charges against Zou were absurd. One story supposedly making the rounds in Beijing held that the actual depth of the water at the breach was only three meters and repairs should have been made easily. But Zou had dawdled. When the first freeze came (and pressure to finish the project increased), in an effort to "cover up his crime of delaying work," Zou suddenly claimed the water flowing through the gap was twenty-five meters to thirty meters deep.

90. Ibid. Other charges were that material storage centers had been set up four kilometers from the construction site, too far to provide the workers on the dikes with timely supplies of materials; that officials in charge of paying the workers had pocketed so much of the money that half of the workers had fled; that those in charge of matériel purchasing had fabricated purchases and pocketed the difference; that those same officials had refused to pay full value for hemp, making merchants reluctant to come forward and thus contributing to shortages of matériel.

91. *Qing shi gao* [Draft history of the Qing Dynasty], 48 vols., ed. Zhao Erxun (Beijing: New China Books, 1991), in a biography of Linkui, records that he was ranked first among the second rank of successful *jinshi* exam candidates in 1826. In addition to his position as board president, he was in charge of the Court of Sacrificial Worship and the Court of State Ceremonial. He may have been reluctant to accept the assignment; it took him three months after his appointment to show up at the repair site (38:2721). Two of the other officials at the work site—Zhongxiang and Liao Hongquan—were also board presidents. One clue to Linkui's apparently higher status may be the edict ordering him to Zhongmou (DG 23/*run*7/19, *ZXXSJJ*, 2219), which refers to him as *neige*, indicating some link with the Grand Secretariat, perhaps even provisional rank as a grand

secretary. But Linqing's autobiography also notes his arrival and refers to him only as a board president (*HXYYTJ*, vol. 3, "Huang Miao Yang Ke").

92. Edict of DG 23/10/20, *ZXXSJJ*, 2252. Linqing's description of Linkui's role is likewise brief and vague, saying only that he was ordered to come to "help manage" *(huiban)* the construction (*HXYYTJ*, vol. 3, "Huang Miao Yang Ke").

93. He was appointed on *run* 7/19 and arrived around 10/23 (*ZXXSJJ*, 2152.)

94. "GZD" (B), Linkui, Liao Hongquan, Zhongxiang, and E Xun'an, DG 24/2/15. I suspect, although I have found no evidence to support the suspicion, that that defense harks back to Linkui's reluctance to take the job and to excuses he probably made when first assigned.

95. Ibid. Linkui also pointed out that, in addition to Zou, Treasurer Zhang Rizhen, Kai-Gui circuit intendant Wang Chouchang, and Prefect Zhang Cheng'en also played a part in the planning of the repairs. Among the arguments Linkui put forward, some were disingenuous. For instance, he claimed that workers were not fleeing the work site because of mistreatment. His proof was that when workers were needed, men still crowded around seeking employment. All that proved was that the number of desperate refugees was still substantial. To the charge that officials charged with purchase of materials had pocketed money, he responded that they had in fact returned over twenty thousand taels to the treasury. The return of this money, of course, did not mean that even greater amounts had not been peculated. In defending the location of the collection centers, he was on more solid ground. Although some centers were located as much as two kilometers from the dikes, establishing relatively remote sites was a security measure necessary to prevent the refugees and laborers housed along the dikes from filching sorghum stalks for firewood. The Xiangfu flood took place on August 2 (6/16), whereas the Zhongmou flood happened on August 23 (6/26). Construction on the former got under way on October 29 (9/15); on the latter on November 13 (10/1).

96. The stalks being received each month probably were those shipped from remote locations. Linkui and Liao Hongquan, DG 24/2/18, *ZXXSJJ*, 2284–2285. Looking for a positive side to the situation, Linkui argued that postponement of the project would allow more workers to return to the fields, increasing the fall harvest and therefore the availability of stalks when the repairs began again.

97. Edict of DG 23/2/22, *ZXXSJJ*, 2286.

98. Edict of DG 24/2/22, *ZXXSJJ*, 2285. The emperor's anger is evident in the widespread—if not particularly severe—punishments he inflicted on the lower officials in charge of the repairs at Zhongmou. The two officials directly responsible for the sections of the dike that collapsed were removed from their posts and forced to wear the cangue for a month; six other lower officials were stripped of their posts. But all eight were to be allowed to redeem themselves by continuing to work on the repair project.

99. Polachek, *Inner Opium War,* 196, 356 n. 17, points out that Jiang was

a friend of Huang Entong, sent to Guangdong in 1842 to take charge of demobilizing the "Canton irregulars." Huang's critical comments concerning the southern militias apparently provoked opposition from Wei Yuan, who believed them to be of great value. But Wei Yuan was also an ardent critic of the Yellow River conservancy. At least on that issue, Jiang and Wei were on the same side.

100. Edict of DG 24/2/25, *ZXXSJJ*, 2286. In an exercise that had perhaps grown stale with repetition, Zhongxiang and Pan Xi'en were ordered to investigate and eliminate such abuses. Pan responded to Jiang's charges the following month ("GZD," Pan Xi'en, DG 24/3/19). He repudiated Jiang's generalities by examining specifics. For example, he pointed out that expenditures for earthwork had not increased significantly since DG 12 (1832). In contrast, he described the middle years of the Jiaqing reign when, in the space of twelve years, annual overruns for earthwork totaled 9.7 million taels. Moreover, the budget of 869,700 taels for earthwork in 1843 had been established under the watchful eye of an imperial emissary.

As to the quality of officials in the river conservancy, Pan profiled those appointed as subprefects during his tenure. Many held *juren* degrees, and one was a *jinshi*. Only the Gaoyan second-class subprefect held a purchased *jiansheng* degree. The remainder of the subprefects in the Nanhe, he said, were former *xun* officials of proven reliability, none of whom were luxury-loving types. Although one could not always tell whether a man was honest by his appearance, Pan admitted, the assertion that there were only two or three honest officials in the river conservancy was inaccurate.

Finally, Pan pointed out that the first thing he did on his rounds of the various subprefectures was to inventory matériel stores to verify that no peculation was taking place. Anyone caught cheating on matériel purchases or dredging work was immediately punished, as was the case with an official caught falsifying the dimensions of a dredging job that winter. Pan's overall point was clear; Jiang did not know what he was talking about.

101. "Junji Chu Laiwen," First Historical Archives, Beijing, Linkui, DG 24/2/26. The actual total that Linkui gives is rounded off to exclude 60 taels. A further 460,000 *wen* not included in the above chart was also contributed to the project through the sale of degrees and titles.

102. Ibid.

103. Edict of DG 24/3/17, *ZXXSJJ*, 2290–2291. For reasons not made clear in the memorial, the board determined that of the 40 percent compensation owed, only 90 percent was to be paid by officials in Henan. It appears that the remaining 10 percent was to be paid by officials from the Jiangsu conservancy who had helped on the project.

104. Ibid.

105. Ibid. Edict of DG 24/3/7, *ZXXSJJ*, 2289.

106. "GZD" (B), Zhongxiang and E Xun'an, DG 24/3/10. Most of the work required only the hauling of earth and the digging of ditches, so a minimum of

skilled labor would be required. The total cost was estimated at 283,790 taels (less than the cost of yearly repairs [*suixiu*] for the previous year). In his edict of DG 24/3/25 (*ZXXSJJ*, 2290), the emperor stressed the necessity of keeping control of the refugees so that they would not "wander off to become bandits and thieves," and he approved the use of work relief "so that none will be displaced *(shisuo)*."

107. "GZD" (B), Zhongxiang, E Xun'an, DG 24/3/10.

108. Zhongxiang and E Xun'an, DG 24/5/?, *ZXXSJJ*, 2293–2294. Among the measures taken were the raising and strengthening of the deflection dike, reinforcing the levee that closed off the mouth of the diversion canal by building a second levee a few yards farther into the canal, and constructing a deflection dike over five thousand meters long on the north bank to force the current away from the mouth of the diversion canal.

6   A Change of Course, 1844–1855

1. Zhongxiang and E Xun'an, DG 24/7/3, *ZXXSJJ*, 2295. Those recommendations were based on estimates prepared by the Kai-Gui and Hebei circuit intendants, who had toured the site in the company of several lower officials and officers known for their expertise in river repairs. The report also called for rebuilding sections of the deflection dike that were lost during flood season and adding another three hundred meters in order to push the current more forcefully toward the diversion canal. A second deflection dike was also to be built to back up the first. In order to get the full impact of the deflected waters, the mouth of the diversion canal would be shifted thirty meters to the north.

2. Ibid. If this is not implicit criticism of the emperor, it is at least an indictment of the parsimony that resulted from his insistence on fiscal restraint.

3. Ibid., 2296.

4. Ibid. See also 2297–2301, which contains the reports of Zou Minghe, who actually made the estimates (which were apparently found among the private papers of Linqing). Zou gave four reasons why the project should not be delayed. First, agriculture had to be restored in the areas that had been flooded. Zou noted that the frequency of city markets in the flooded areas was low, indicating a continued decline of agricultural vitality.

Second, several million people had been displaced by the flood, and many continued to wander about in search of food and refuge. Further delays would weaken their spirit, and they would begin to scheme for their own survival. The strong would prey on the weak, and large groups would begin to engage in plunder.

Third, the continued pressure on Lake Hongze was endangering the dikes along its eastern edge. If they gave way, both salt and grain transport routes would be flooded, with serious economic consequences.

Finally, Zou once again came to the defense of Kaifeng, pointing out that the residents of the city had exhausted themselves in their efforts to restore the city after the 1841 flood. They had just begun to see results when the new catastrophe struck. Although the city had so far withstood the waters, the people were in a constant state of anxiety about their fate and could not continue in uncertainty.

5. Edict of DG 24/7/12, *ZXXSJJ*, 2297; edict of DG 24/7/16, *ZXXSJJ*, 2301. The source of part of those funds was the *guangchusi*, the office in charge of the various treasuries of the Imperial Household Department *(neiwufu)*.

6. Ibid., 2301–2302.

7. Zhongxiang and E Xun'an, DG 24/7/20, *ZXXSJJ*, 2302.

8. Ibid., 2302–2303. They also cautioned that although the current year's stalk harvest was adequate for the needed repairs, it was impossible to know what next year's harvest would be like.

9. Ibid. Zhongxiang and E Xun'an's arguments were almost certainly based on Zou Minghe's report (see note 4). Since Zou was not technically a river official (in spite of his earlier river conservancy posting), having him prepare the response did not violate the emperor's order not to involve river officials in the decision-making process. Zou's loyalty was perhaps less to the river conservancy than to the Kaifeng gentry.

Certain differences do exist between the two documents. Zou's figures on relief expenditures and tax remissions are more specific. He claimed that a three-month extension of relief granted in the spring had cost around 800,000 taels, whereas the total cost of relief for the year in Jiangsu and Anhui had come to around 1 million taels. Zou calculated that tax remissions had so far totaled 1.2 to 1.3 million taels.

10. Edict of DG 24/7/29, *ZXXSJJ*, 2304.

11. "GZD" (B), Bao Xing, DG 24/11/26, cites the recommendation of a censor named Yu Shan that the solicitation of funds for the Zhongmou project be broadened to allow gentry and officials from all the provinces to contribute. That idea had already been put forward by Zou Minghe in his report written in the seventh month (*ZXXSJJ*, 2299). It is not clear whether that later suggestion was a result of Zou's initial prodding.

The response to the campaign was enthusiastic. On 11/26 Sichuan governor Bao Xing reported that 117,000 taels had already been collected. Other areas followed suit in rapid order. The sources and amounts received include Zhejiang, 268,760 taels ("GZD" [B], Liang Baochang, DG 24/12/2); Hunan and Hubei, 44,074 taels ("GZD" [B], Yutai and Zhao Bingyan, DG 24/12/13); Shanxi, 17,890 taels ("GZD" [B], Liang Ehan, DG 24/12/14); Minzhe, 18,708 taels ("GZD" [B], Liu Yunke and Liu Hong'ao, DG 24/12/18); Anhui, 35,419 taels ("GZD" [B], Wang Zhi, DG 24/12/26). Most of those contributions originally included large amounts of copper cash, which the provincial chiefs were instructed to exchange at a rate of 1,500 cash per tael. The exception was Minzhe, where the market rate of one tael for 1,769 cash was used.

Those sums represent only the ones reflected in the surviving documents. There are indications that other provinces also contributed to the fund. For example, a memorial from Yunnan governor Wu Qijun thanked the emperor for awarding him and another official promotion to the fifth rank for their contributions to the project ("GZD" [B], Wu Qijun, DG 24/12/19).

12. Zhongxiang and E Xun'an, DG 24/11, *ZXXSJJ*, 2312–2314. Linqing, *HXYYTJ*, vol. 3, "Mou gong helong," notes that Huicheng was in charge of provisioning and materials on the dikes and later helped with "entering by sections."

13. Zhongxiang and E Xun'an, DG 24/11/25, *ZXXSJJ*, 2314–2316.

14. Zhongxiang and E Xun'an, DG 24/12/21, *ZXXSJJ*, 2318–2319.

15. Based on Linqing's experience digging the diversion canal the year before, that was almost certainly what the workers and the work bosses had in mind. *HXYYTJ*, vol. 3, "Yin he qiang hong."

16. Zhongxiang and E Xun'an, DG 24/12/30, *ZXXSJJ*, 2319–2320. Linqing, *HXYYTJ*, vol. 3, "Mou gong helong." Linqing says that the target of the exorcism was a certain "moss goose." According to his account, each time that creature had been sighted the previous year, sections of the dike had subsequently collapsed.

17. Linqing, *HXYYTJ*, vol. 3, "Mou gong helong." That would keep them from hanging around the work site creating trouble.

18. Zhongxiang and E Xun'an, DG 24/12/30, *XZZSJJ*, 2319–2320.

19. Edict of DG 25/1/3, *ZXXSJJ*, 2321. Niu Jian was ordered to finish what work he had on hand before returning. Linqing was to stay and help with the finishing work.

20. Zhongxiang and E Xun'an, DG 25/1, *ZXXSJJ*, 2325. The remaining 400 taels were to be kept in the subscription office *(juanshu ju)* to be used for river works. Compensation totaling 51,686 taels was assessed against the officials deemed responsible for the five sections lost in the initial attempt to close the breach ("GZD" [T], Zhongxiang and E Xun'an, DG 26/3/10, enclosure).

21. Although the breach was closed after eighteen months, relief could not be discontinued until some crops were harvested and the land that had been under water had a chance to dry out.

22. "SYDFB," edict of DG 25/5/22.

23. "GZD" (T), Zhongxiang, E Xun'an, and Chongen, DG 25/5/15. Edict of DG 25/5/22, *ZXXSJJ*, 2328–2329.

24. "Junji Chu Laiwen," Board of Revenue lateral communication, DG 27/8/2. That fear was well founded. Zhihozhi, the market town that served at the center of the Nian movement for a time, had been situated directly in the path of the flood. See Perry, *Rebels and Revolutionaries*, map 2, 114.

25. "Junji Chu Laiwen," Board of Revenue lateral communication, DG 27/8/2.

26. "GZD" (B), Yan Yiyu, DG 30/6/11. Yan Yiyu can hardly be considered a career river official or a mouthpiece of the river conservancy, since he had almost no experience in hydraulic engineering.

27. Those amounts exclude Grand Canal expenditures, which remained relatively stable at around one hundred thousand taels per year. "SLTB," Zhong Xiang, DG 24/12/7; Yan Yiyu, DG 30/11/2; "GZD" (T), Zhongxiang, DG 25/11/29, enclosure. The precipitous decline in 1844 is explained by the fact that fiscal shortages and the need for funds on the Zhongmou repair project forced officials to call a temporary halt to supplementary works construction.

28. The Daoguang emperor's impatience with river officials reached a point where he became uncharacteristically sarcastic in his response to some funding requests. In a memorial of 1846, Zhongxiang and Chongen had requested 49,990 taels for Grand Canal dredging. In the margin Daoguang wrote "These figures are laughable" *(ci shumu kexiao)* and urged them to verify that such costs were truly necessary before submitting their requests ("GZD" [B], Zhongxiang and Chongen, DG 27/11/19).

29. *DQHDSL*, 906: DG 29.

30. *Qing shi gao* [Draft history of the Qing dynasty], 48 vols., ed. Zhao Erxun (Beijing: China Books, 1991), 13:3741. Even at this late date, the fiction of the state's intention to return the river to its course had to be maintained.

31. Ibid., 2741. The long-term impact of the Yellow River's change of course and of subsequent Qing policy in North China is detailed in Ken Pomeranz's remarkable work *The Making of a Hinterland: State, Society, and Economy in Inland North China, 1853–1937* (Berkeley: University of California Press, 1993).

Conclusion

1. Needham, Wang, and Lu, *Science and Civilization*, plate 362, caption.

2. Thomas A. Metzger, "The Organizational Capabilities of the Ch'ing State in the Field of Commerce: The Liang-huai Salt Monopoly, 1740–1840," in *Economic Organization in Chinese Society*, ed. William E. Willmott (Stanford, Calif.: Stanford University Press, 1972), 11, 30. Metzger comments that imperial power in the Qing "to a large extent turned on scattering power among many offices with executive authority and capital offices with 'staff' authority" (30).

3. Etienne Balazs, *Chinese Civilization and Bureaucracy*, trans. H. M. Wright, ed. Arthur F. Wright (New Haven, Conn.: Yale University Press, 1964), 11. Metzger, *Internal Organization*, 57.

4. Metzger, *Internal Organization*, 79, 42.

5. Jones and Kuhn, "Dynastic Decline," 125. See Hu, "Yellow River Administration" (1954), 260, on Wu's appointment as a Hanlin compiler.

6. Derk Bodde, *Chinese Thought, Society, and Science: The Intellectual and Social Background of Science and Technology in Pre-modern China* (Honolulu: University of Hawai'i Press, 1991), 365–367.

7. Metzger, *Internal Organization*. Metzger comments that the impact of the statecraft movement was to "lift practical concerns out of the mundane sphere of ordinary administration into that of intellectually prominent writing, thereby

increasing interest in reform" (26–27). I would argue that a by-product of that was that technical knowledge gained a new level of respectability.

8. Lin, "Two Social Theories," 21–25; Metzger, *Internal Organization,* 74–80.

9. Metzger, *Internal Organization,* 397–408.

10. Jane Kate Leonard, "'Controlling from Afar,' Open Communications and the Tao-kuang Emperor's Control of Grand Canal–Grain Transport Management, 1824–26," *Modern Asian Studies* 22, no. 4 (1988), ascribes the practice of appointing capital officials to take charge of major repair projects to the emperor's need for "open communications and reliable data." Since the "ability and willingness of provincial officials to provide reliable reports could not be taken for granted," the emperor appointed trusted emissaries (666). See also Leonard, *Controlling from Afar,* 121. The prestige wielded by a direct imperial appointee could be useful in overcoming a provincial official's unwillingness to cooperate or share resources. But in the case of river repair projects, if the official dispatched did not have a strong grasp of the hydraulic situation, his reports could be ill-informed and misleading. Moreover, the basic data for those reports would still be coming from the very provincial officials he was sent to oversee. Dispatching a "reliable" but inexperienced official could therefore be self-defeating.

11. Metzger, *Internal Organization,* 58. That phrase comes from Tao Zhu, but it was echoed many times in other cases by river officials.

12. Kuang-Ching Liu, "The Ch'ing Restoration," in *Cambridge History of China,* vol. 10, pt. 1, *Late Ch'ing,* notes similar developments in the period of the Taiping Rebellion, including Zeng Guofan's use of *muyou* as personal advisers and occasionally as deputies *(weiyuan).* The same practice was commonplace in the river conservancy in the 1840s and earlier. Liu notes that although Zeng sought to employ only "men of rectitude" in those posts, "he found to his sorrow that his standards of conduct had to be relaxed" if the fighting capability of his army was to be maintained (413). Officials who served in the Yellow River conservancy in the decades prior to the Taiping Rebellion would no doubt have appreciated Zeng's dilemma.

13. Kuhn, *Soulstealers,* points out that in the system of patronage that was at the heart of Qing bureaucratic life, a patron's personal image was "sullied every time he had to throw the book at a subordinate. . . . The dignity of a superior was hurt along with the career of the subordinate" (197–198).

14. Quotation in Jones and Kuhn, "Dynastic Decline," 114. Wider educational opportunities and the flourishing of provincial academies "fostered ambitions for upward mobility among a broader spectrum of the population" (114), but the failure of the bureaucracy to increase in size led more of those men to seek employment in other careers. Min Tu-ki, *National Polity and Local Power: The Transformation of Late Imperial China,* ed. Philip A. Kuhn and Timothy Brook (Cambridge, Mass.: Harvard University Press, 1989), 43–44, discusses some of the other alternative careers pursued by the lower literati strata, including pandering, gambling, management of pawnshops, and working as clerks and secretaries.

15. Zelin, *Magistrate's Tael,* notes that the loss of legitimate sources of funds encouraged officials to "resort to illegal surcharges, forced contributions, customary fees (lou-gui), manipulation of silver-copper ratios, and other devices for raising funds." She adds that Jiaqing even went so far as to admit that customary fees were necessary and proposed that they be standardized. Zelin remarks, "From that point on, any effort by the government to improve official discipline was doomed to failure" (301).

16. Wang, *Land Taxation,* 58–60.

17. Metzger, "Organizational Capabilities," 44, says the Qing use of remunerative sanctions reflects the state's flexibility in punishments. Certainly they were intended as alternatives to loss of rank and other, harsher measures. In the case of the river conservancy in the nineteenth century, however, they were often combined with other punishments as an additional burden on disgraced officials. Metzger, *Internal Organization,* 399, points out that the harsh punishments that resulted from a lack of trust between the emperor and his officials and the desire to maintain imperial authority were mediated by the desire to elicit performance. At times, however, punishments grew so severe that they had the opposite effect.

18. Naquin and Rawski, *Chinese Society,* 235, note that the emperor was probably unaware of the relationship between the silver drain and opium imports until 1836, when the connection was first pointed out. Prior to that, proposed solutions to the state's fiscal problems were bound to fail because they were based on erroneous assumptions. A similar analysis could be applied to the river conservancy.

19. Hu, "Yellow River Administration" (1955), cites Wei Yuan's claim that "with all decisions being made by the emperor, the hundreds of functionaries simply follow without exerting any efforts of their own. . . . Consequently, the officials are averse to responsibility, averse to change, and averse to giving a name to reality" (509). Beatrice Bartlett, *Monarchs and Ministers: The Grand Council in Mid-Ch'ing China, 1723–1820* (Berkeley: University of California Press, 1991), disputes the despotism thesis, noting that "the rise of the Grand Council created a government that could run effectively whether or not a strong monarch prevailed in Peking" (278).

20. Kuhn, *Soulstealers,* 190, 210, quoted phrase on 210. Kuhn points out that both emperor and bureaucrat were ambivalent toward regulations. The former needed them to control the latter but resented the restriction on his ability to exercise his greatest weapon, arbitrary power. The bureaucrat was "bedeviled" by red tape but understood that regulations protected him from unreasonable demands (190). Kuhn also notes that, in addition to using the standard system of administrative discipline to elicit performance from high provincial officials, the emperor "used the personal relationship . . . to goad, to blame, and to frighten" (210).

21. Quotation in Jones and Kuhn, "Dynastic Decline," 125. Hummel, *Eminent Chinese,* 574, describes a very different young man, one who boldly defended

the imperial palace against sectarian rebels by opening fire on them with a fowling piece.

22. Khun, *Soulstealers*, 220–225, discusses the nature and role of "events" in a bureaucrat's career. Events, whether floods, battles, or more mundane crises, were opportunities to advance a career or attack an opponent. I would argue that shifts in imperial attitude could similarly be called events. Such shifts were not linked with any specific official but were available as free-floating opportunities for the pursuit of ideological, factional, or other goals. The emperor's growing frustration with the river conservancy was such an opportunity.

23. Hu, "Yellow River Administration" (1954), 259–261. Several of those appointees had river conservancy experience or had earlier served in the river conservancy in Henan or Jiangsu but in the interim had been appointed to other provincial posts.

24. Metzger, *Internal Organization*, 45–48, discusses the concepts of linear development and cyclical change and argues that Chinese officials had a clear understanding of both.

25. Ibid. Metzger points out that bureaucrats understood that a "seamless joint report by high provincial officials" was more effective in deflecting imperial anger than the report of a lone official. Likewise, unity against a lone innovating official could prevent unwanted change (218).

26. Metzger, "Organizational Capabilities," 60–61, points to a similar situation in the Board of Revenue, when the board did not share the same objectives as line officials and did not understand the minutiae of regulations. In the case of the river conservancy, the misunderstanding was over the details of construction and hydraulic engineering.

27. Metzger, *Internal Organization*, 405.

28. Ibid. Metzger points out that moderate, gradual reforms were seen as "hypocritically following fashionable moral trends of the day" (406–407). The quotation in the text is in Polachek, *Inner Opium War,* 52. The problems cited—"over-population, economic stagnation, ecological decline, and exhaustion of the labor-absorbing potential of the traditional rural economy" (52)—were no doubt real. The charge that Qing officials avoided those issues because contemplating them would have driven them to despair is open to question. More convincing is Polachek's assertion that the inability to think in terms of those larger issues constituted a conceptual problem for Qing reformers. For example, that conceptual barrier made impossible the discussion of the need for more rather than less bureaucracy. Even the most ardent critics of Qing administration, men like Wei Yuan and Bao Shichen, were not prepared to cross that conceptual divide.

29. Kuhn, *Soulstealers,* 232.

Character Glossary _____

anlian	諳練	*baofu zhuangsao shou*	堡夫椿埽手
anming	按名	*baogu*	保固
an nian bao xiao	按年報銷	*ba tou*	壩頭
ba	壩工作法	*bawei*	壩尾
bage zi	八個子	*beifang yin*	備防銀
bagong	拔貢	*bishui ba*	逼水壩
ba gong zuofa	壩工作法	*bixu zhu ti shu shui*	必須築堤束水
baifu	白夫	*buchengzai*	不成災
baji	壩基	*buku*	部庫
bangjia yin	幫價銀	*buzhengsi*	布政司
bao	堡	*buzu*	不足
bao (village)	保	*caineng*	才能
baofu	堡夫		

caishu	菜蔬		*dagong*	大工
cao	草		*dagong zongju*	大工總局
chaiwei	差委		*dan*	擔
chi	尺		*daoku*	道庫
chongti	重隄		*daotai*	道台
chouxie	酬謝		*dayi*	大役
chuangxing	創行		*diding*	地丁
chuanhu	船戶		*digun*	地棍
chuhuang	除荒		*dingdai*	頂戴
chunxun	春汛		Donghe	東河
chu yu guan	出於官		*dou*	斗
chu yu ren	出於人		*duan*	段
cipin	次貧		*duanliu*	斷溜
ci shumu kexiao	此數目可笑		*duhuo*	黷貨
cizhi	次支		*dui*	堆
cizhong	次重		*duliang tongpan*	督糧通判
cong kuan	從寬		*duo*	垛
cun	寸		*erba*	二壩
cunzhuang	村莊		*fang*	方
daba	大壩		*fangxun*	防汛
da bing chuan	打冰船			

fei	費	*guotou*	裹頭
fennian daixiao	分年代銷	*hao*	毫
fu	府	*hao wu er zhi*	毫無二之
fugongsheng	附貢生	*hebing*	河兵
fusheng	附生	*hedao zongdu*	河道總督
futou	夫頭	*hefang*	河防
fuxun	伏汛	*hegong*	河工
fu zonghe	副總河	*hegong jingfei*	河工經費
gang	剛	*hegun*	河棍
gang rou zhi jian	剛柔之間	*heiling*	黑凌
genyi	跟役	*helong*	合龍
gongsheng	貢生	*heshen*	河神
gongyuan	工員	*houbu*	候補
goucao	溝槽	*Huanghe Zonghe*	黃河總河
guan	關	*huchengti*	護城堤
guandi nei kuangjian	官地內	*huiban*	會辦
guangchusi	廣儲司	*huifu*	洄復
guanliu	官柳	*huimintou*	回民頭
guan tang	灌塘	*ji*	集
gunfei	棍匪	*jianfan*	奸販
		jianfang	見方

jiansheng	監生	*juan*	卷
jiaojia	腳價	*juanjian*	捐監
jiaoqing	較輕	*juanna*	捐納
jie	潔	*juanshu*	捐輸
jie	楷	*juanshu ju*	捐輸局
jiebai dixiong	結拜弟兄	*juanxiang*	卷廂
jin	精	*jun*	竣
jin	斤	*juren*	舉人
jing	精	*kaoyu*	考語
jingfei	經費	*kecheng*	課程
jin'gun	衿棍	*ketou*	磕頭
jingshi	經世	*kouliang*	口糧
jingzhuang ganlian	精壯幹練	*kuaishou*	快手
		lanhuang ba	攔黃壩
jin long si da wang	金龍四大王	*laoren*	老人
jinmen	金門	*leling xiuzhi*	勒令休職
jinshi	進士	*li*	里
jintie	津貼	*liangmo*	良模
jinzhan	進占	*liaochang*	料廠
jipin	極貧	*liaohu*	料戶
jiu gong xin sheng	舊工新生	*libu*	禮部
		Li Dawang	栗大王

liemu	劣幕	*neiwufu*	內務府
lifu	里夫	*nianfei*	捻匪
lijia	里家;例價	*nianpu*	年譜
lijin	釐金	*paitong*	牌桶
ling'an	另案	*paizhuo*	牌桌
liuke muyou	流客幕友	*peixiu*	賠修
liumin	流民	*piaohan*	剽悍
lougui	陋規	*qian*	錢
luti	摟堤	*qian*	縴堤
ma	麻	*qiangxian*	搶險
mantou	饅頭	*qiangxian fuche*	搶險夫車
menzhan	門占	*qiangxiu*	搶修
mou	畝	*qianti*	縴堤
mufu	幕夫	*qianzong*	千總
muke	幕客	*qing*	頃
muyou	幕友	*qinqi*	侵欺
najie	那借	*qiuxun*	秋汛
Nanhe	南河	*qi yao quan zai yong ren*	其要全在用人
neige	內閣	*rou*	柔
neiku	內庫	*san xun*	三汛
neisheng waizhuan	內升外轉		

sao	埽	*shu shui gong sha*	束水攻沙
saoshou	埽手	*songfu*	鬆浮
shangshu	尚書	*suixiu*	歲修
shanhou	善後	*tang*	塘
shao	梢	*tangbing*	糖餅
she	社	*tanya*	彈壓
shilang	侍郎	*taosan*	逃散
shisuo	失所	*ti*	堤
shiyong	試用	*tianliang*	天良
shiyong renyuan	試用人員	*tiaoshuiba*	挑水壩
shouxian	守險	*tiben*	提本
shu	束	*tigu*	提估
shuangjiang	霜降	*ting*	廳
shu an he wu	熟諳河務	*tingchai shuyi*	廳差書役
shubaiwan	數百萬	*tixiao*	提銷
shui bu	水部	*tiyuan*	堤園
shuili	水利	*tongpan*	通判
shu jiu he	疏九河	*tongzhi*	通知
shunliu shudao	順流疏導	*tucheng*	土城
shunshui zhi xing	順水之行	*tugun*	土棍
		tuhuo	土貨

tuntian	屯田	*xuanfangju*	宣防局
tunzuo	屯坐	*xun*	汛
tuoqian	拖欠	*xu qing shua huang*	蓄清刷黃
tuotai	脫胎	*yanglian*	養廉
tushan	土山	*yanxiao*	鹽梟
tushuo	圖說	*yaofu*	徭夫
waigong	外工	*yaogong*	要工
wan	完	*yaoti*	遙隄
weiguan	委官	*yecha*	夜叉
weiruliu	未入流	*yeshi*	野史
weiyuan	委員	*yigong daizhen*	以工代賑
wen	文	*yiju liang de*	一舉兩得
wusuan	無算	*yilao yongyi*	一勞永逸
xian	縣	*ying*	營
xiancheng	縣丞	*yin'gou*	陰溝
xiang	廂	*ying zheng diding*	應徵地丁
xiangkun	廂梱	*yinhe*	引河
xian'gong	險工	*yinjian*	引見
xiangsao	廂埽	*yinliu*	引溜
xiangyu	鄉愚	*yin shi li dao*	因勢利導
xiao liu pei si	銷六賠四		
xiucai	秀才		

yitang	移塘	*zhibi*	指臂
youji	遊擊	*zhiqian*	制錢
youke muyou	游客幕友	*zhong yun he*	中運河
you lizhe	有力者	*zhoupan*	州判
youmin	游民	*zhoutong*	州同
you tianchan	由天產	*zhuanbao*	傳包
yu	圩	*zhuangsao*	椿埽
yuezheng guanshui	約徵關稅	*zhubu*	主簿
		zi xin zhi ren	自新之人
yu shui zheng di	與水爭地	*zongdu*	總督
zaoli	早隸	*zongju*	總局
zhan	占	*zongzi*	粽子
zhang	丈	*zuizhong*	最重
zhangcheng	章程	*zuowan*	坐彎
zhengxiang	正項	*zuowei*	作偽

Bibliography

Archival Sources

"Gongzhong Dang" ("GZD") 公中檔. First Historical Archives, Beijing (B); Palace Museum Archives, Taipei (T).

"Junji Chu Laiwen" 軍機處來文. First Historical Archives, Beijing.

"Liusheng Huang He Saoba Qingxing Tu" [A map of revetment conditions in six provinces along the Yellow River] 六省黃河埽情形圖. Palace Museum Archives, Taipei.

"Neige Dangan" 內閣檔案. First Historical Archives, Beijing.

"Qingdai Wenxian Dangan" ("QDWXDA") 清代文獻檔案. Palace Museum Archives, Taipei.

"Shangyu Dang Fangben" ("SYDFB") 上諭檔方本 [Square-form record books]. First Historical Archives, Beijing.

"Shuili Tiben" ("SLTB") 水利題本. First Historical Archives, Beijing.

"Yuezhe Dang" 月摺檔. Palace Museum Archives, Taipei.

Published Sources

Balazs, Etienne. *Chinese Civilization and Bureaucracy.* Trans. H. M. Wright. Ed. Arthur F. Wright. New Haven, Conn.: Yale University Press, 1964.

Baoying xian zhi 寶應線志 [Gazetteer of Baoying County]. 1970.

Bartlett, Beatrice. *Monarchs and Ministers. The Grand Council in Mid-Ch'ing China*, 1723–1820. Berkeley: University of California Press, 1991.

Bennett, Adrian Arthur. *John Fryer: The Introduction of Western Science and Technology into Nineteenth-Century China*. Cambridge, Mass.: East Asian Research Center, Harvard University, 1967.

Bodde, Derk. *Essays on Chinese Civilization*. Ed. Charles Le Blanc and Dorothy Borei. Princeton, N.J.: Princeton University Press, 1981.

———. *Chinese Thought, Society, and Science: The Intellectual and Social Background of Science and Technology in Pre-modern China*. Honolulu: University of Hawai'i Press, 1991.

Brunnert, H. S., and V. V. Hagelstrom. *Present Day Political Organization of China*. Trans. A. Beltchenko and E. E. Moran. Shanghai: Kelly and Walsh, 1912.

Cen Zhongmian. *Huang He Bianqian Shi* 黃河變遷史 [A history of the Yellow River's changes of course]. Beijing: People's Publishing Co., 1957.

Chan, Hok-lam. "The Chien-wen, Yung-lo, Hung-hsi, and Hsuan-te Reigns, 1399–1435." In *The Cambridge History of China,* vol. 7, pt. 1, *The Ming Dynasty.* Ed. Frederick W. Mote and Denis Twitchett, 182–304. New York: Cambridge University Press, 1988.

Cheng Ch'ao-ching. *Zhongguo Shuili Shi* 中國水利史 [A history of Chinese water conservancy]. Taipei: Taiwan Commercial Affairs Printing Office, 1986.

Ching-tai Ho-ch'en Chuan 清代河臣傳 [Biographies of Qing river officials]. Taipei: Wenhai Publishing Co., 1967.

Ch'ü T'ung-tsu. *Local Government in China under the Ch'ing.* Stanford, Calif.: Stanford University Press, 1969.

Cosgrove, Denis. "An Elemental Division: Water Control and Engineered Landscape." In *Water, Engineering, and Landscape: Water Control and Landscape Transformation in the Modern Period,* ed. Denis Cosgrove and Geoff Petts, 1–53. London: Belhaven Press, 1990.

———. "Platonism and practicality: Hydrology, Engineering and Landscape in Sixteenth-Century Venice." In *Water, Engineering, and Landscape: Water Control and Landscape Transformation in the Modern Period,* ed. Denis Cosgrove and Geoff Petts, 35–53. London: Belhaven Press, 1990.

Czaya, Eberhard. *Rivers of the World.* New York: Van Nostrand Reinhold, 1981.

Debus, Allen G. *Man and Nature in the Renaissance.* Cambridge: Cambridge University Press, 1978.

Dodgen, Randall A. "Hydraulic Evolution and Dynastic Decline: The Yellow River Conservancy, 1796–1855." *Late Imperial China* 12, no. 2 (December 1991): 36–63.

———. "Salvaging Kaifeng: Natural Calamity and Urban Community in Late Imperial China." *Journal of Urban History* 21, no. 6 (September 1995): 716–740.

Duara, Prasenjit. *Culture, Power and the State: Rural North China, 1900–1942.* Stanford, Calif.: Stanford University Press, 1988.

Elman, Benjamin A. *From Philosophy to Philology: Intellectual and Social Aspects of Change in Late Imperial China.* Cambridge, Mass.: Council on East Asian Studies, Harvard University, 1984.

Elvin, Mark. *The Pattern of the Chinese Past.* Stanford, Calif.: Stanford University Press, 1973.

———. "The Inner World of 1830." *Daedalus* 120, no. 2 (spring 1991): 33–61.

Elvin, Mark, et al. *Japanese Studies on the History of Water Control in China: A Selected Bibliography.* Canberra: Institute of Advanced Studies, Australian National University; Tokyo: Centre for East Asian Cultural Studies for UNESCO, Toyo Bunko, 1994.

Esherick, Joseph M. *Origins of the Boxer Uprising.* Berkeley: University of California Press, 1987.

Fang Chaoying and Carrington L. Goodrich. *Dictionary of Ming Biography,* 1368–1644. New York: Columbia University Press, 1976.

Franke, Wolfgang. "Historical Writing during the Ming." In *The Cambridge History of China,* vol. 7, pt. 1, *The Ming Dynasty, 1368–1644,* 726–782. Cambridge: Cambridge University Press, 1988.

Freeman, Michael. "Sung." In *Food in Chinese Culture,* ed. Kwang-chih Chang, 141–176. New Haven, Conn.: Yale University Press, 1977.

Gamble, Sidney D. *North China Villages.* Berkeley: University of California Press, 1963.

Greer, Charles. *Water Management in the Yellow River Basin of China.* Austin: University of Texas Press, 1979.

Guo Shu. "Hongze Hu Liangbai nian de Shuiwei" 洪澤湖兩百年的水位 [The water level of lake Hongze over a two-hundred-year period]. *Kexue Yenjiu Taolun Ji: Shuili* 科學研究討論集：水利 [Collected essays on the study of science: Water conservancy] 12 (December 1982): 47–60.

Guo Tao. "Pan Jixun de zhi-Huang sixiang" 潘季馴的治河思想 [The Thought of Pan Jixun on Control of the Yellow River]. *Kexue Yenjiu Taolun Ji: Shuili* [collected essays on the study of science: Water conservancy] 12 (December 1982): 32–45.

Hinton, Harold C. *The Grain Tribute System of China (1845–1895).* Cambridge, Mass.: Harvard University Press, 1956.

Hoshi Ayao. *Tai Unga* [The Grand Canal]. Tokyo: Kinfu Shuppansha, 1971.

———. "Transportation in the Ming Dynasty." *Acta Asiatica* 38 (1980).

Hsiao Kung-ch'uan. *Rural China: Imperial Control in the Nineteenth Century.* Seattle: University of Washington Press, 1960.

Huang, Philip C. C. *The Peasant Economy and Social Change in North China.* Stanford, Calif.: Stanford University Press, 1985.

Huang, Ray. *Taxation and Government Finance in Sixteenth-Century Ming China.* Cambridge: Cambridge University Press, 1974.

———. 1587, a *Year of No Significance: The Ming Dynasty in Decline.* New Haven, Conn.: Yale University Press, 1981.

———. "The Lung-ch'ing and Wan-li Reigns, 1567–1620." In *The Cambridge History of China,* vol. 7, pt. 1. *The Ming Dynasty,* 1368–1644, ed. Frederick W. Mote and Denis Twitchett, 511–584. Cambridge: Cambridge University Press, 1988.

Huang He Saogong 黃河埽工 [Stalk revetment construction on the Yellow River]. Ed. Shuili Dianli Weiyuan Hui. Beijing: China Industrial Publishing Co., 1964.

Huang He Shuili Shi Shuyao 黃河水力史述要 [An outline history of Yellow River water conservancy]. Ed. Shuili Bu, Huang He Shuili Weiyuan Hui. Beijing: Water Conservancy and Electrical Power Publishing Co., 1984.

Hu Ch'ang-tu. "The Yellow River Administration in the Ch'ing Dynasty." Ph.D. diss., University of Washington, 1954.

———, "The Yellow River Administration in the Ch'ing Dynasty." *Far Eastern Quarterly* 14, no. 4 (August 1955): 505–513.

Hucker, Charles O. *A Dictionary of Official Titles in Imperial China.* Stanford, Calif.: Stanford University Press, 1985.

Hummel, Arthur, comp. *Eminent Chinese of the Ch'ing Period (1644–1911).* Washington, D.C.: U.S. Government Printing Office, 1943.

Hunyuan Zhou Xu Zhi 渾源州續志 [A Continuation of the Gazetteer of Hunyuan County] *(HZXZ).* 1881.

Jining Zhili Zhou Zhi 濟寧直隸州志 [Gazetteer of Jining County]. 1859.

Johnson, David, Andrew J. Nathan, and Evelyn S. Rawski. *Popular Culture in Late Imperial China.* Berkeley: University of California Press, 1985.

Jones, Susan Mann, and Philip A. Kuhn. "Dynastic Decline and the Roots of Rebellion." In *The Cambridge History of China,* vol. 10, pt. 1, *Late Ch'ing,* ed. John K. Fairbank, 107–162. Cambridge: Cambridge University Press, 1978.

Kaifeng Fu Zhi 開封府志 [Gazetteer of Kaifeng Prefecture]. 1863.

Kelley, David. "Sect and Society: The Evolution of the Luo Sect among Qing Dynasty Tribute Boatmen, 1700–1850." Ph.D. diss., Harvard University, 1986.

Kuhn, Philip A. *Rebellion and Its Enemies in Late Imperial China.* Cambridge, Mass.: Harvard University Press, 1970.

———. *Soulstealers: The Chinese Sorcery Scare of 1768.* Cambridge, Mass.: Harvard University Press, 1990.

Kuo, Ting-yee, and Kwang-ching Liu. "Self-Strengthening: The Pursuit of Western Technology." In *The Cambridge History of China,* vol. 10, pt. 1, *Late Ching,* ed. John K. Fairbank, 491–542. Cambridge: Cambridge University Press, 1978.

Kwong, Luke S. K. "The T'i-Yung Dichotomy and the Search for Talent in Late-Ch'ing China." *Modern Asian Studies* 27, no. 2 (1993): 253–79.

Leonard, Jane Kate. "'Controlling from Afar': Open Communications and the Tao-Kuang Emperor's Control of Grand Canal-Grain Transport Management, 1824–26." *Modern Asian Studies* 22, no. 4 (1988): 665–699.

———. *Controlling from Afar: The Daoguang Emperor's Management of the Grand Canal Crisis,* 1824–1826. Ann Arbor, Mich.: Center for Chinese Studies, 1996.

Lin Man-houng. "Two Social Theories Revealed: Statecraft Controversies over China's Monetary Crisis, 1808–1854." *Late Imperial China* 12, no. 2 (December 1991): 1–35.

Linqing. *Lin Jianting Xingshu* 麟見亭行疏 [Correspondence of Linqing]. Ca. 1850.

———. *Hegong Qiju Tushuo* 河工器具圖説 [An illustrated guide to tools used in river work]. 1836. Reprint, Taipei: Wenhai Publishing Co., 1969. Unpaginated.

———. *Huang-Yun Hekou Gu-Jin Tushuo* 黃運河口古今圖説 [An illustrated explanation of the Yellow River–Grand Canal confluence from ancient times to the present]. c. 1840? Reprint, Taipei: Wenhai Publishing Co., 1969.

————, *A Wild Swan's Trail: The Travels of a Mandarin.* Ed. T. C. Lai. Hong Kong: Hong Kong Book Center, 1978.

————. *Hongxue yinyuan tuji* 鴻雪因緣圖記 [Illustrated traces of a life] *(HXYYTJ).* 3 vols. Beijing: Beijing Guji Chubanshe, 1984. Unpaginated.

Lin Zexu. *Lin Zexu Shujian* 林則徐書簡 [Correspondence of Lin Zexu]. Ed. Yang Guozhen. Fuzhou, China: Fujian People's Publishing Co., 1985.

Liu, Adam Y. C. *Corruption in China during the Early Ch'ing Period, 1644–1660.* Center of Asian Studies Occasional Papers and Monographs, no. 39. Hong Kong: University of Hong Kong, 1979.

Liu, Kuang-ching. "The Ch'ing Restoration." In *The Cambridge History of China,* vol. 10, pt. 1, *Late Ch'ing,* ed. John K. Fairbank. Cambridge: Cambridge University Press, 1978.

Li Yizhih. *Shui Gong Xue* 水工學 [Studies in Hydraulic Engineering]. Taipei: Wenhai Publishing Co., 1969.

Li Yuerui. *Chunbingshi yecheng* 春冰室野乘 [Unofficial record from the Spring Ice Studio]. Shanghai: World Publishing Co., 1926.

Lowdermilk, Walter Clay. "A Forester's Search for Forests in China." *American Forests and Forest Life* 31 (July 1925).

Mantz, Peter A. "Analysis of Sediment Transport Data for the Yellow River." *Renmin Huanghe* 1 (February 1987).

Martin, William Alexander Parsons. *A Cycle of Cathay.* New York: Fleming H. Revell, 1896.

Matsuda, Yoshirō. "Shin-dai no Kō-ga chisui kikō" [The organizaton of flood control on the Yellow River during the Qing dynasty]. *Chūgoku suirishi kenkyū* 16 (1986): 31–56.

Menzies, Nicholas K. "Forestry." In *Science and Civilization in China,* vol. 6, pt. 3, ed. Joseph Needham, 539–667. Cambridge: Cambridge University Press, 1996.

Metzger, Thomas A. "The Organizational Capabilities of the Ch'ing State in the Field of Commerce: The Liang-huai Salt Monopoly, 1740–1840." In *Economic Organization in Chinese Society,* ed. William E. Willmott. Stanford, Calif.: Stanford University Press, 1972.

————, *The Internal Organization of the Ch'ing Bureaucracy: Legal, Normative, and Communicative Aspects.* Cambridge, Mass.: Harvard University Press, 1973.

Min Tu-ki. *National Polity and Local Power: The Transformation of Late Imperial China.* Ed. Philip A. Kuhn and Timothy Brook. Cambridge, Mass.: Harvard University Press, 1989.

Morita Akira. *Chugoku suirishi no kenkyū* [Studies in the history of Chinese water conservancy]. Tokyo: Kokusho Kankōkai. 1995.

Mote, Frederick W. "The Cheng-hua and Hung-chih Reigns, 1465–1505." In *The*

Cambridge History of China. vol. 7, pt. 1; *The Ming Dynasty, 1368–1644,* ed. Frederick W. Mote and Denis Twitchett. Cambridge: Cambridge University Press, 1988.

———. *Intellectual Foundations of China.* New York: McGraw-Hill, 1989.

Naquin, Susan, and Evelyn S. Rawski. *Chinese Society in the Eighteenth Century.* New Haven, Conn.: Yale University Press, 1987.

Needham, Joseph. *The Grand Titration: Science and Society in East and West.* London: Allen and Unwin, 1967.

———. *Science in Traditional China: A Comparative Perspective.* Cambridge, Mass.: Harvard University Press, 1981.

Needham, Joseph, Wang Ling, and Lu Gwei-djen, eds. *Science and Civilization in China.* Vol. 4, pt. 3. Cambridge: Cambridge University Press, 1971.

Ou-yang Xiu, "The Sound of Autumn." Trans. A. C. Graham. In *Anthology of Chinese Literature: From Early Times to the Fourteenth Century.* Comp. and ed. Cyril Birch, 366–369. New York: Grove Press, 1965.

Pan Jixun. *He fang yi lan* 河防一覽 [An overview of river defense] [1590]. Reprinted in *Zhongguo shixue congshu* 中國史學叢書, ed. Wu Xiangxiang, no. 33. Taipei: Taiwan Student Bookstore, 1965.

Perdue, Peter C. "Official Goals and Local Interests: Water Control in the Dongting Lake Region during the Ming and Qing Periods." *Journal of Asian Studies* 41, no. 4 (August 1982): 747–765.

———. *Exhausting the Earth: State and Peasant in Hunan, 1500–1850.* Cambridge, Mass.: Council on East Asian Studies, Harvard University, 1987.

Perry, Elizabeth. *Rebels and Revolutionaries in North China, 1845–1945.* Stanford, Calif.: Stanford University Press, 1980.

Polachek, James M. "Literati Groups and Literati Politics in Nineteenth-Century China." Ph.D. diss., 2 vols. University of California, Berkeley, 1977.

———. "Gentry Hegemony in Soochow." In *Conflict and Control in Late Imperial China,* ed. Carolyn Grant and Fredrick Wakeman, 211–256. Berkeley: University of California Press, 1985.

———. *The Inner Opium War.* Cambridge, Mass.: Council on East Asian Studies, Harvard University, 1992.

Pomeranz, Kenneth. *The Making of a Hinterland: State, Society, and Economy in Inland North China, 1853–1937.* Berkeley: University of California Press, 1993.

Qin ding da Qing huidian shili 欽定大清會典事理 [Collected statutes of the Qing dynasty] (DQHDSL). Beijing, 1899.

Qin ding gong bu zeli 欽定工部則利 [Statutes of the Board of Works] Taipei: Cheng Wen Publishing Co., 1966.

Qing Bai Lei Chao 清稗類鈔. Ed. Xu Ke. Taipei: Commercial Press, 1966.

Qinding Hubu Zeli 欽定戶部則例 [Administrative precedents of the Board of Works]. Taipei: Cheng Wen Publishing Co., 1968.

Qingdai Hechen Zhuan 清代河臣傳 [Biographies of river officials of the Qing period] *(QDHCZ)*. Comp. Wang Huzhen and Wu Weizu. Nanking: Chinese Engineer Society, 1937. Reprint, Taipei: Wenhai Publishing Co., 1969 (page citations are to the reprint edition).

Qing Shi Gao 清史稿 [Draft history of the Qing dynasty]. 48 vols. Ed. Zhao Erxun. Beijing: China Books, 1991.

Qing Shi Lu 清實錄 [Veritable records of the Qing dynasty]. N.p., n.d.

Shen Yi. *Huang He Wenti Taolun Ji* 黃河問題討論集 [Essays on the problems of the Yellow River]. Taipei: Commercial Press, 1971.

Spence, Jonathan. "Opium Smoking in Ch'ing China." In *Conflict and Control in Late Imperial China,* ed. Frederic Wakeman Jr., and Carolyn Grant, 143–173. Berkeley: University of California Press, 1975.

Sun, E-tu Zen. "Wu Ch'i-chun: Profile of a Chinese Scholar-Technologist." *Technology and Culture* 6, no. 3 (summer 1965).

Sung Biographies. 2 vols. Ed. Herbert Franke. Wiesbaden: Franz Steiner Verlag GMBH, 1976.

Tang Xianglong. "Daoguang chao juanjian zhi tongji" 道光朝捐堅之統計 [Statistics on the system of sale of degrees, ranks, and offices during the Daoguang reign]. In *Zhongguo Jindai Shi Luncong* 中國近代史論叢 [Collected essays on modern Chinese history], ser. 2, 8 vols., ed. Li Dingyi, Bao Zunpeng, Wu Xiangxiang, 5: 47–62. Taipei: Zhengzhong Bookstore, 1963.

Tani Mitsutaka. "Ko-wai kowai to Han kijun no kako" [The confluence of the Yellow and Huai Rivers and the river engineering of Pan Jixun]. *Toyo Gakuho* 64, nos. 3–4 (1983): 1–32.

———. *Mindai kaikoshi kenkyu* [Studies in the history of river conservation in the Ming]. Oriental Research Series, no. 45. Kyoto: Dohosha, 1991.

Tao Hanyuan. *Zhongguo shuili shi gangyao* 中國水利史綱要 [An outline of Chinese river conservancy]. Beijing: Water Conservancy and Electrical Power Publishing Co., 1987.

Todd, Oliver Julian. *Two Decades in China.* Peking: Association of Chinese and American Engineers, 1938.

Twitchett, Denis, and Tilemann Grimm. "The Cheng-tung, Ching-t'ai, and T'ien-shun Reigns, 1436–1464." In *The Cambridge History of China,* vol. 7, pt. 1, *The Ming Dynasty, 1368–1644.* Cambridge: Cambridge University Press, 1988.

Tyler, William Ferdinand. *Pulling Strings in China.* London: Constable and Co., 1929.

Van Slyke, Lyman P. *Yangtze: Nature, History, and the River.* Menlo Park, Calif.: Addison-Wesley, 1988.

Vermeer, Eduard B. "P'an Chi-Hsun's Solutions for the Yellow River Problems of the Late 16th Century." *T'oung Pao* 73, nos. 1–3 (1987): 33–67.

Vogel, Hans Ulrich. "Chinese Central Monetary Policy, 1644–1800." *Late Imperial China* 8, no. 2 (December 1987): 1–52.

Volti, Rudi. *Technology, Politics, and Society in China*. Boulder, Colo.: Praeger, 1982.

Wakeman, Frederic. "The Canton Trade and the Opium War." In *The Cambridge History of China*, vol. 10, pt. 1, *Late Ch'ing*, ed. John K. Fairbank. Cambridge: Cambridge University Press, 1978.

Wang Faxing, "Huang He Shen Miao—Jiaqing Guan" 黄河神廟—嘉慶館 [Yellow River temples—Jiaqing monastery]. *Huang He Shi Ziliao* 黄河史資料 [Materials on the history of the Yellow River] 3 (1984).

Wang Jingyang. "Qingdai Tongwaxiang gaidao qian de hehuan ji qi zhili" 清代銅瓦廂改道前的河患及其治理 [River disasters and their control in the Qing period prior to the change of course at Tongwaxiang]. In *Huang He Shi Luncong* 黄河史論叢 [Essays on the history of the Yellow River], 186–203. Fuzhou, China: Fudan University Press, 1986.

Wan Gong. *Zhi Shui Quanti* 治水全題 [A comprehensive study of water control]. Beijing: Water Conservancy and Electrical Power Publishing Co., 1985.

Wang Yeh-chien. *Land Taxation in Imperial China, 1750–1911*. Cambridge, Mass.: Harvard University Press, 1973.

Wang Yuquan. "Some Salient Features of the Ming Labor Service System." *Ming Studies* 21 (spring 1986): 1–44.

Weber, Max. *Economy and Society*. Ed. Guenther Roth and Claus Wittich. Berkeley: University of California Press, 1977.

Will, Pierre-Etienne. *Bureaucratie et famine en Chine au 18e siècle*. Paris: Mouton, 1980.

———. "Un cycle hydraulique en Chine: La province du Hubei du XVIe au XIXe siècles." *Bulletin de l'Ecole Française d'Extreme-Orient* 68 (1980): 187–261.

———. "State Intervention in the Administration of a Hydraulic Infrastructure: The Example of Hubei Province in Late Imperial Times." In *The Scope of State Power in China*, ed. Stuart R. Schram, 295–347. Hong Kong: Chinese University Press, 1985.

———. *Bureaucracy and Famine in Eighteenth-Century China*. Trans. Elborg Forster. Stanford, Calif.: Stanford University Press, 1990.

Wittfogel, Karl A. *Oriental Despotism: A Comparative Study of Total Power*. New Haven, Conn.: Yale University Press, 1957.

Wu Lo. *Zhongguo Du Liang Heng Shih* 中國度量衡史 [A history of weights and measures in China]. Taipei: Commercial Press, 1981.

Xiangfu Xian Zhi 祥符縣志 [Gazetteer of Xiangfu County] *(XFXZ)*. 1891.

Xiao Yishan. *Qing Dai Tong Shi* 清代通史 [History of the Qing period]. Taipei: Commercial Press, 1962–1963.

Xu Daling. *Qing Dai Juanna Zhidu* 清代捐納制度 [The system of purchasing offices by contributions during the Qing period, 1644–1911]. Peking: Harvard Yenching Institute, 1950.

Xu Fuling. "Huanghe xiayou Ming-Qing shidai hedao he xianxing hedao yanbian duibi yanjiu" 黄河下游明清時代河道和現行河道演變對比研究 [A comparative study of changes in the lower course of the Yellow River from the Ming-Qing period to the present]. In *Huang He shi luncong* 黃河水利史論叢 [Essays on the history of Yellow River conservancy], ed. Tan Qixian. Fuzhou, China: Fudan University Press, 1986.

Yang Lien-sheng. "Economic Aspects of Public Works in Imperial China." In *Excursions in Sinology,* 191–248. Cambridge, Mass.: Harvard University Press, 1969.

Zaixu Xingshui Jinjian 再續行水金鑑 [A further continuation of the golden mirror of the waterways] *(ZXXSJJ).* Ed. Wu Tongju. Taipei: Wenhai Publishing Co., 1966.

Zelin, Madeleine. *The Magistrate's Tael: Rationalizing Fiscal Reform in Eighteenth-Century China.* Berkeley: University of California Press, 1987.

Zhang Hanying. *Ming-Qing Zhi He Gailun* 明清治河概論 [An outline of Ming-Qing river control]. Beijing: Water Conservancy and Electrical Power Publishing Co., 1986.

Zheng Chaojing. Zhongguo Shuili Shi 中國水利史 [A history of Chinese water conservancy]. Taipei: Commercial Affairs Printing Co., 1986.

Zhongguo Shuili Shigao 中國水利史稿 [A draft history of Chinese water conservancy]. Wuhan Water Conservancy and Electrical Power Institute. Beijing: Water Conservancy and Electrical Power Publishing Co., 1987.

Zhongmou Xian Zhi 中牟縣志 [Gazetteer of Zhongmou County] *(ZXZ).* 1870.

Zhongwen Da Cidian 中文大辭典 [The encyclopedic dictionary of the Chinese language]. 10 vols. Ed. Lin Yin and Gao Min. Yangmingshan, Taiwan: Chinese Culture University, 1985.

Zou Yilin. "Wan Gong he *Zhi Shui Quan Ji*" 萬恭和治水全題 [Wan Gong and (his) comprehensive study of Water Control]. In *Huang He Shi Luncong.* [Essays on the history of the Yellow River], ed. Tan Qixian. Fuzhou, China: Fudan University Press, 1986.

Index

About the Author ⎯⎯⎯⎯⎯⎯⎯⎯⎯⎯⎯⎯

RANDALL A. DODGEN holds a doctorate in Chinese history from Yale University. He has published on various aspects of the history of the Yellow River, including god cults, the impact of floods on urban community, and the role of hydraulic engineering in the development of the late imperial state. He is currently associate professor of history at Sonoma State University.